PLANNING FOR DIVERSITY

POLICY AND PLANNING IN A WORLD OF DIFFERENCE

The practical importance of diversity and equality for spatial planning and sustainable development is still not widely understood. Using international examples, this book shows planners and educationalists the benefits of building in a consideration of diversity and equality at each stage and level of planning.

Despite being one of the most diverse and gender-balanced of the built environment professions, complacency has been widespread in planning. This book shows why a diverse profession is important and, drawing on a wide range of good practice, shows how those involved in planning can develop their sensitivity to and expertise in diversity and equality.

Dory Reeves is an independent adviser on planning for equality and diversity. Her work involves facilitating, creative problem-solving, writing and teaching. She was Maude Clarke Visiting Professor at Queens University, Belfast (2000–2003) and chaired the steering group that produced the RTPI Gender Audit Toolkit.

THE RTPI Library Series

Editors: Cliff Hague, Heriot Watt University, Edinburgh, Scotland
Tim Richardson, Sheffield University, UK
Robert Upton, RTPI, London, UK

Published in conjunction with The Royal Town Planning Institute, this series of leading-edge texts looks at all aspects of spatial planning theory and practice from a comparative and international perspective.

Planning in Postmodern Times
Philip Allmendinger, University of Aberdeen, Scotland

The Making of the European Spatial Development Perspective
No Masterplan
Andreas Faludi and Bas Waterhout, University of Nijmegen, The Netherlands

Planning for Crime Prevention
Richard Schneider, University of Florida, USA and Ted Kitchen, Sheffield Hallam University, UK

The Planning Polity
Mark Tewdwr-Jones, The Bartlett, University College London

Shadows of Power
An Allegory of Prudence in Land-Use Planning
Jean Hillier, Curtin University of Technology, Australia

Urban Planning and Cultural Identity
William J. V. Neill, Queen's University, Belfast

Place Identity, Participation and Planning
Edited by Cliff Hague and Paul Jenkins

Planning for Diversity
Policy and Planning in a World of Difference
Dory Reeves

Forthcoming:
Indicators for Urban and Regional Planning
Cecilia Wong, University of Liverpool

Public Values & Private Interest
Heather Campbell and Robert Marshall

PLANNING FOR DIVERSITY

POLICY AND PLANNING IN A WORLD OF DIFFERENCE

DORY REEVES

Routledge
Taylor & Francis Group

LONDON AND NEW YORK

First published 2005
by Routledge
2 Park Square, Milton Park, Abingdon, Oxon OX14 4RN

Simultaneously published in the USA and Canada
by Routledge
711 Third Ave, New York, NY 10017

Routledge is an imprint of the Taylor & Francis Group

Typeset in Akzidenz Grotesk by
Integra Software Services Pvt. Ltd, Pondicherry, India

British Library Cataloguing in Publication Data
A catalogue record for this book is available from the British Library

Library of Congress Cataloging in Publication Data
Reeves, Dory, 1957–
  Planning for diversity / Dory Reeves.
    p. cm. — (The RTPI library series ; 8)
  Includes bibliographical references and index.
  ISBN 0–415–28656–5 (hardcover : alk. paper) — ISBN 0–415–28657–3 (pbk. : alk. paper)
  1. City planning—Social aspects. 2. Sustainable development. 3. Social justice.
  4. Multiculturalism. 5. Pluralism (Social sciences) I. Title. II. Series.
  HT166.R3369 2005
  307.1′216—dc22

                                                                    2004016588

ISBN 978–0–415–28749–4 (hbk)
ISBN 978–0–415–28657–2 (pbk)

CONTENTS

PREFACE

When I reflect on this project, I think it probably started about 20 years ago when I was working on my PhD at Sheffield University and wondering why it was that women were having more difficulty entering the housing market than men. Since the early 1980s, I have been concerned like many others about inequalities and discrimination. About five years ago, Robert Upton asked if I would consider writing a book for this series and I think I replied at the time that I would think about it. Appreciating the commitment, resources and time involved, I did not say 'yes' lightly. When I got going I contacted Leonie Sandercock and she emailed to wish me luck. I still have the email! Well a few years later, now the book is complete and the area has become even more central to our need to create sustainable environments which work for everyone.

ACKNOWLEDGEMENTS

I thank Yunus Ahmed, Christine Booth, Paul Barnard, Sue Bryant, Ken Burley, Margaret Catran, Wendy Davies, Lisette Dekker, Pam Dobby, Margaret Dunn, Judith Eversley, The Fawcett Society, Jean Forbes, Sandra Fredman, Anne Goring, Ali Grant, Clara Greed, Patsy Healey, Hilary Howatt, Julia Long, Anne-Marie McGauran, Mhairie Mackie, Beth Milroy, Jacky Nieuboer, Graham Ogilvie, Pattsi Petrie, Judith Petts, Linda Radcliffe, Laura Rheiter, Franklin Riley, Teresa Rees, Tim Richardson, David Rose, Leonie Sandercock, Henry Sannof, Anne Simpson, Rowena Swinbourne, Huw Thomas, TCPAS, Robert Upton, Derick Wilson, Chan Wun, Eileen Yeo for helping me at various stages of the project. Special thanks to Stewart Devitt.

Cartoons: Creative Visioning Artwork by Graham Ogilvie <graham@ogilviedesign.co.uk> and reproduced with permission from the National Development Plan Gender Equality Unit in Ireland.

The Weave of Diversity (1999) by Helen Averley commissioned by the Cultural Diversity Group of the Community Relations Council and now hanging in the Ulster Museum, Belfast.

LIST OF FIGURES

LIST OF TABLES

LIST OF ABBREVIATIONS

EC	European Commission
EOC	Equal Opportunities Commission
EU	European Union
NDP	National Development Plan, Ireland
ODPM	Office of the Deputy Prime Minister, UK
EIA	Equality Impact Assessment
RTPI	Royal Town Planning Institute

INTRODUCTION

This book focuses on spatial planning and town planning, probably one of the most misunderstood professions today, not to be confused with project planning, financial planning or human resource planning.

Spatial planning has an important role to play in shaping the future of the places and spaces in which we live and in helping create sustainable communities. A sustainable community functions at an economic, environmental and social level, and yet many reports, articles and debates on sustainability make no explicit reference to diversity and equality. This book illustrates the importance for spatial planning of the relationship between space and place; sustainability, difference and diversity; equity and equality. Sustainable development is more than inter-generational equity. To work, it must not reproduce inequality or create the potential for discrimination. Given the diversity of our communities as reflected in Helen Averley's piece of art in Figure I.1, a workable approach to sustainability recognizes the important role everyone can play as individuals, as members of a community and as part of the productive economy.

We live in evermore complex and diverse societies. Planners are being drawn into the challenges of building cities for multi-cultural societies (Milroy and Wallace, 2002: 1). Legal systems are often ill-equipped. In the West, planning's legal framework is embedded in a particular conception of democracy as majority rule and a corresponding belief that the right to difference in effect disappears once the majority has spoken. The norms and values of the dominant culture are not only embedded in the legislative framework of planning but also embodied in the attitudes, behaviour and practices of professionals.

The chosen title of this book, like that of Kirton and Greene's (2000) *Managing Diversity*, reflects changes in thinking on equality issues and a shift towards conceptualizing communities as diverse social groups which may need to be treated differentially. As with Kirton and Greene, I have chosen to appropriate a term which is used and misused in management and employment literature. Many equality advocates are sceptical of diversity. Not only has it deflected the focus away from the needs of specific sectoral groups, it has made some needs appear invisible. I have purposefully chosen to use the term in order to promote an approach to diversity which embraces equality issues head-on and which recognizes the importance of power.

In 1996 when I ran a workshop on equality, I called it the ABCD of equality (A for attitudes, B for behaviour, C for codes and D for diversity) (Reeves, 1996a). Looking back at my notes for the session, I can see how long change takes. I can also appreciate even more the importance of working on professional attitudes to

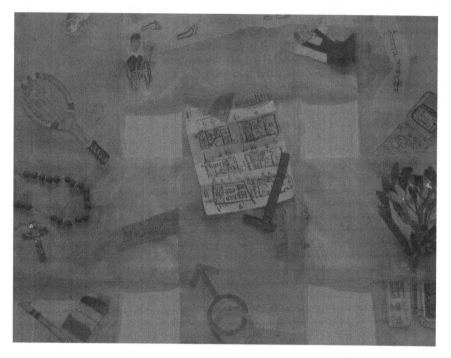

Figure I.1 Weave of Diversity by Helen Averley

difference and diversity in order to effect long-term change. Professional codes of practice tell members and the public and communities that planners and built-environment professionals should be constantly aware of the impact of diversity and equality issues.

A – Attitudes are about the way we perceive and the way we think about issues. Attitudes to equality vary but at heart no one wants to see or experience unfairness and that is what inequality creates. It is often easier to change people's behaviour and this is where energies tend to go.

B – Behaviour tells you something about someone's attitude. Although it is possible to work on behaviour, there is no guarantee that this will change attitudes. To effect deep and lasting change, it is important to work on people's attitudes.

C – Codes of practice and legislation have proved essential to changing people's attitudes. They set down responsibilities and duties.

D – Diversity. Equality has tended to be associated with race, sex and disability. Diversity is now a common term in the management field and is being used by many who feel that it is more inclusive and more likely to get people on board and take on these issues. Equal Opportunities legislation has increased awareness of the discriminatory effects of some current practices; the whole issue of managing diversity has highlighted the need for service directors to look closely at the range of people working in and involved in planning decisions. Customer care has focused attention on who benefits from the planning service.

We have reached the point in the education and training of planners and related professionals when we need to have confidence; in addition to everyone having an awareness and understanding of diversity and equality issues, they also need to have an ability to confidently and competently build the issues into their day-to-day work. As David Harvey pointed out, planning for difference is not just about respecting difference but doing something about the process which leads to home-lessness and racial and sexual oppression (Harvey, 1996: 363).

Although most professional accrediting bodies explicitly look for and expect equality and diversity in planning courses, the subject matter is often not handled consistently. Equality and diversity are still seen by many as specialisms and options within planning education rather than themes running through entire courses. Within practice, equality and diversity are even seen by some to sit outside the practice of spatial planning rather than integral to it. Many professionals feel confused and exasperated at the potential scope of the learning ahead, the responsibilities they face and the repercussions if they get it wrong. This is not peculiar to planning. In the future we need professionals who can engage with the issues of diversity and equality in their everyday work. There is no doubt that we will need specialists to provide expert advice and support in relation to access, race, gender and mainstreaming. Separate legislation for different sectoral groups has led to the development of specialists and advocates for different sectoral groups. Throughout the world, the historic development of separate equality bodies for sex, race and disability has reinforced this. Often one group of people has been played off against another in the disadvantaged stakes.

THE BOOK'S CONTRIBUTION

As recently as 2002, Beth Milroy, working in Toronto, found that the planning literature still offered little to professionals wrestling with issues of equality. Although Sandercock (1998) felt, when writing the ground-breaking book *Towards Cosmopolis*, that difference had been inscribed onto the planning map over the last ten years, she also found a dearth of material for planning professionals. There is an extensive literature on race, disability, gender and age and a growing literature on sexuality. However, there is little addressing the specific needs of the planning and related professional.

This book illustrates, in practical ways, the value of using a mainstreaming approach to embed equality and diversity into all aspects of planning. It shows that we need a conception of diversity which in effect embraces equality.

The book draws on academic material from sociology, environmental psychology and sustainability, and in the process of researching the book I have sought out new work by PhD students. Use is made of important non-academic sources; the news media and contemporary literature as well as my personal experience working, researching and teaching planning for the last 20 years. In addition to being valuable resources in themselves, books provide gateways to Internet sources. The World Wide Web means that professionals can draw on a network of experience and expertise as never before. I have designed this book for students of planning and practitioners. Those engaged in planning such as politicians and community representatives will also find it useful. It is written for those who want to explore new directions in planning practice. The field of diversity and sustainability is continuously evolving and this book can raise questions about current theory and practice.

STRUCTURE OF THE BOOK

Chapter 1, which has three parts, introduces the concepts of space and place which form the building blocks of spatial planning and sustainable regeneration. It introduces the facets of difference which those engaged with planning and the regeneration of sustainable communities needs to be aware of. Part 1 looks at the concept of difference and diversity, equity and equality. What impact do they have on planning for sustainability? What models of understanding do we have of difference and diversity? How does one difference become more important or significant than another? Part 2 introduces the concept of sustainability and, in particular, examines what it means for people as individuals. It examines the nature of difference, how difference and diversity are constructed and understood. Part 3 looks at the nature of space and place and how this relates to sustainability.

Building on the first chapter, Chapter 2 examines developments in planning and shows how approaches to planning conceptualize people and what it means for these approaches to become more people-centred. This chapter outlines the main strands of thought which have influenced the development of spatial planning. It shows where people fit in, what social divisions and sectoral groups the different approaches use and how they consider difference and diversity. Situated in a particular space and time, each approach influences and is influenced by its socio-political context. The issues planners identify, how problems are defined, what planners understand as their legitimate knowledge base all relate to these contexts. Using examples from the UK, Germany and Australia, the chapter shows how the approaches to planning provide a common language across time and space.

Chapter 3 looks at how countries have responded to equality and diversity through legislation, positive action and more recently a strategy of mainstreaming. What does this mean for planning and sustainable regeneration? It explains the conceptual frameworks and how they apply to all aspects of planning. It shows that strategies such as mainstreaming can help ensure that equality and diversity are built into planning practice. Part 1 starts by looking at the broad legislative frameworks. Part 2 looks at the evidence of planning in the UK and Part 3 introduces mainstreaming as a strategy and shows how it developed, particularly in the European context.

Chapter 4 uses examples to show how agencies mainstream equality and diversity issues into their planning processes. The first case study looks at London's strategic plan; Plymouth provides the basis for the second case study involving a local plan. The work commissioned by the Irish Department of Justice Equality and Law Reform for the National Development Plan is particularly relevant to national spatial development frameworks.

Chapter 5 considers the key issues for involving diverse publics in planning. The chapter presents examples from the Netherlands, Finland, the UK and South Africa.

Drawing on interdisciplinary work, the chapter concludes with a consideration of how participation techniques are likely to develop. What impact will technology have on people's involvement in planning? Who could be included and, more importantly, excluded by innovative developments? In planning, what is public involvement trying to achieve? How do we intertwine the voices of technical and local knowledge? What techniques have been used and who has been engaged? What approaches work best for different sectoral groups – those protected by legislation and those not protected by legislation?

Internationally, diverse professions demonstrate, promote and value equality of opportunity. Chapter 6 examines the importance of diverse professions and, drawing on a range of surveys, highlights the issues and barriers facing under-represented groups and the strategies which professions need to pursue in order to become more diverse. It looks at the important ways in which professions can change as they become more diverse and how the mainstreaming approach can be applied to professional institutes.

Chapter 7 shows how those involved in creating sustainable and livable communities can develop, test and reflect on their awareness of and competence in dealing with difference, diversity and equality. This chapter presents two approaches. The first approach is the 'Five Habits' developed by teachers in the medical legal field and adapted for planning by the author. The 'Five Habits' helps develop an awareness of how individuals perceive and stereotype, and it helps professionals reassess their approach to their professional work. Delivering diversity's added value is achieved when, habitually and creatively, individuals learn how to look at differences as social and organizational strengths. Significantly, the 'Five Habits' approach teaches us to look for similarities as well as differences so that we are in a better position to empathize with clients whoever they might be. The second approach is useful when addressing organizational change and was developed in Northern Ireland. The Equity, Diversity and Interdependence Approach (EDI) demonstrates the interrelatedness of equality and diversity and how a conception of diversity must embrace equality if sustainable communities can be achieved.

A feature of the book is the use of case examples to illustrate good practice. The author has researched many. Others have been adapted from published sources and acknowledged accordingly. A list is provided in the contents section.

How to use the book

New students to planning will probably want to browse the book initially, get a feel of it and then start with the two introductory chapters. The practitioner who wants to get up to speed on approaches to equality and diversity including mainstreaming may want to start with Chapter 3 and then look at Chapter 7 which presents ways of helping you to look at what you do differently. Chapter 6 on the diverse professions will be of interest to all those concerned with understanding and thinking about how to ensure our professions are inclusive and representative. Chapter 8 contributes to the discussion about the future of planning.

No book is produced in a vacuum. When I started the book, in 2000, Holy Cross School in North Belfast had become known around the world for the sectarianism children experienced on their way to school, as they walked through 'other's space'. Four years later, the violence has ceased and there is talk of reconfiguring some of the space. The year 2002 saw London's Gay Pride festival being held for the first time in one of the city's royal parks. Ken Livingstone, Mayor of London, said how pleased he was to support the annual Pride Parade symbolizing as it does the diversity, tenacity and strength of a community that has struggled to achieve equal rights and legal recognition for many years. The year 2003 saw the fortieth anniversary of Martin Luther King's famous speech to civil rights protesters. Although remembered for its 'I have a dream', the speech also reminds us of the litany of broken promises to all groups striving for equal rights. The year 2003 was the 10th anniversary of the UK McPherson Inquiry into the handling of the police inquiry into the death of Stephen Lawrence, made more poignant by the fact that he was an aspiring architect. The year 2003 was also the European Year of the Disabled. May 2003 saw Election Results for the newly devolved Welsh Assembly where women are now in the majority. On the downside, the British National Party gained seats in Burnley. The summer of 2003 was dominated by The Hutton Inquiry into the background to the apparent suicide of David Kelly, the UK's expert on Iraq's weapons. When it reported in January 2004, it was the media which bore most of the criticism; distrust of government, however, runs at an all-time high. On a cultural note, 2003 saw Allison Pearson's book about women's current work contract, 'I Don't Know How She Does It', become a best-seller on both sides of the Atlantic. Captivating moviegoers later in the summer was the film of Witi Ihimaera's book *The Whale Rider* about cultural traditions and the gendered cross-cultural issues in traditional Maori, New Zealand. In November 2003, the UK announced the setting up of the single equality and human rights body. As I finish the book, the European Union (EU) has enlarged to encompass ten new states, highlighting once again the importance of considering difference and diversity.

Planners operate at a range of different spatial scales. For those working at the supranational European and the national spatial planning levels, issues of equality and diversity are often not seen as relevant. These planners see diversity and equality as something to do with the local community level of planning. Yet, not to integrate diversity and equality issues into the big picture often means that policies fail to take account of the huge inequalities which exist between women and men and other sectoral groups, and governments fail to allocate much needed projects.

Issues of diversity and equality have become much more of a consideration to professionals. However, it is by no means central. The service delivery and added value case still has to be made. This book should help professionals understand better how to build the consideration of diversity and equality into planning for sustainable development. Young people are acutely aware of diversity and equality issues. When asked what key issues face Scotland in the future, students highlighted the social differences within society, the inequality between women and men, as well as racism, domestic abuse and sectarianism, which in the Scottish context is reflected in the support for one or other of the two main football clubs.

CHAPTER 1

DIVERSITY, SUSTAINABILITY, SPACE AND PLACE

Planning for Diversity means constructing approaches to spatial planning, which address difference and equality of opportunity. Diversity needs to address difference as well as discrimination, social exclusion and environmental injustice. Since difference by itself cannot capture all inequalities, diversity becomes benign without a strong link to equality.

To progress we all have a huge amount of learning to do. We need to continuously update our understanding of what planning for diversity means for our communities and us; as citizens, politicians and professionals. Spatial planning needs to reflect the relationship between sustainable development, space and place, diversity and equality.

This chapter has three parts. Drawing on contemporary psychological and sociological literature, Part 1 introduces the interrelated concepts of diversity and equality as they relate to sustainability and the planning of spaces and places. It looks at the nature and politics of diversity and how we understand difference. It introduces some of the facets of difference which anyone engaged in planning and regeneration needs to be aware of. It considers how one difference becomes more important or significant than another. Part 2 introduces sustainability and, in particular, examines what the concept means for people as individuals. A sustainable community functions at an economic, environmental and social level and yet many reports, articles and debates on sustainability make no explicit reference to diversity and equality. Sustainable development is more than inter-generational equity in that, to work, it must not reproduce inequality or create the potential for discrimination. Part 3 looks at the nature of space and place, the building blocks of spatial planning and how these relate to sustainability.

PART 1   INTEGRATING EQUALITY AND DIVERSITY

Three examples from the USA, Ireland and the UK illustrate how agencies apply the concept of diversity in practice.

1.   The Director of the New York planning department mapped out her vision for planning when she said that it works for an 'inclusive city, with economic opportunities for everyone, a healthy environment and an improved quality of life in revitalized neighbourhoods' (Burden, 2003).
2.   The Equality Authority of Ireland has as its mission 'Equality in a diverse Ireland' (Equality Authority, 2003).

3.   The UK disability group Royal Association for Disability and Rehabilitation (RADAR) launched a campaign in 2003 'for a world where human difference is anticipated, accommodated and celebrated' RADAR (2003a) Mission. Online. Available HTTP: http://www.radar.Org.uk/RANE/Templates/frontpage.asp?1HeaderID=227 (accessed 30 Nov 2004).

The above statements all recognize the ways in which diversity and equality are intertwined. Equal opportunities and diversity are not mutually exclusive. Equality should be the normative value underpinning diversity, giving it teeth and meaning. Equality means ensuring that people with different needs have equality of opportunity and outcome. Diversity without equality addresses only difference. Diversity with equality also addresses power.

There is legislation in place in many countries to protect people from the worst excesses of discrimination although we live in societies where discrimination on racial, sexual, disability and age grounds still persists. Commentators on the EU have found that, although law is in place to ensure equality, full equality cannot be achieved until the traditional social stereotypes which are a feature of everyday life are broken down (Rosof, 1998).

Diversity is 'a state or quality of being different or varied, a point of difference'. Across a large part of the world, people tend to use the term 'difference' to refer to the state of being unlike the majority and diversity as the quality of being different. Difference tends to need a reference point to make sense. So, for example, A is different from B, meaning that B is the reference point. Diversity does not imply a reference point. Wendy Davies, along with many equality experts, has explored the problems in taking a narrow view of diversity. She sees diversity dealing with and involving the management of differences. The confusion arises because some differences give rise to discrimination and disadvantage and some do not. Gender, race, disability and age are key issues at the root of much discrimination in UK society (Reeves, 2003b: 24). Legislation provides some protection in the UK and by 2006 it will cover sexual orientation, religion and age, so organizations need to move towards examining issues and policies from a number of perspectives (EU, 2000a,b). Chapter 3 looks at this in more detail.

In the summer of 2002 Wendy Davies spent some time in South Africa where she met a number of black community leaders. After the elections, many white community leaders felt that the black and the white communities needed to get to know each other better. Needless to say many black leaders were wary. They felt they knew a lot about the white community; after all they had oppressed them for decades (Davies and Ohri, undated).

One of the characteristics of the relationship between a powerful and a less powerful group is that the norms and values of the powerful are well known to the less powerful. Their survival may even be dependant on that knowledge. However the powerful group do not have the same need to know a great deal about the less powerful. The idea of getting to know one another better and learning to appreciate and value differences needs to take account of, both the impact of the power imbalance, and the need to undo some of the damaging stereotypes and misconceptions that may have served to reinforce the power imbalance (Davies in Reeves, 2003b: 24).

The values we as individuals attach to characteristics reflect power relationships. Far from being neutral, our value base including our professional value base can be gendered or racialized. Our institutions and structures often reflect this. It is not that we simply ascribe different qualities and characteristics to different groups; we attach values to the differences. At the heart of inequality lies an ideology of superiority – an ideology that has traditionally served to maintain the interests of the powerful. Power is at the heart of the distinction between diversity and equality. Equality addresses power; diversity addresses difference. Both need to be addressed. So we need a conception of diversity which embraces equality and discrimination. According to Gramsci's (1971) doctrine of hegemony or power, the ascendancy of a group rests on their ability to translate their worldview into a pervasive and dominant ethos. It helps, although it is not critical, if the group is in the majority. The subordinate group then becomes quiescent, having come to believe that the dominant ethos is somehow pre-ordained or natural (Drake, 1999: 16). Put another way, the ascendancy of a particular view of the world depends on the ability of a group or class to impose its views on everyone else. Drake used this concept to show how, when those in the disability movement developed a social understanding of disability, very different to the established medical model, more disabled people felt empowered to advocate their real desires.

The normative nature of equality is best reflected in Sweden where equality between women and men is a crucial part of the country's welfare state model. This has as its starting point the view that society can progress in a democratic direction and become effective and open only when both women and men, de facto, influence the development of all spheres in society. The overall assumption (and the national goal agreed by the Parliament) is that women and men have the same rights, obligations and opportunities in all areas of life: to pursue work which provides economic independence; to care for children and the home; to participate in politics, unions and other societal activities; to share power and influence; to live a life free from gender-related violence (Astrom, 2003).

Equality between men and women was stressed in the Social Justice Report of 1994, the report which formed the basis of the British Labour Government's political agenda following their 1997 election victory (The Commission on Social Justice,

1994). In contrast to Sweden, where equality became more enshrined in practice, in the UK, social inclusion became the more accepted political goal within which the equality dimension was subsumed. In 1997, the Labour Government in the UK set up the Social Exclusion Unit with a view to tackling people and areas experiencing linked problems such as unemployment, educational performance, poor skills, family breakdown, high crime rates, housing and health. Studies show poverty as highly gendered, racialized with a disability dimension (Lister, 1997, 2003; May, 1997; Bronstein, 1999; Brundtland, 2000). However, attempts to address the way in which these social problems also reflect discrimination have been patchy. The framing of social inclusion in terms of poverty and unemployment can make the underlying differences between groups of people invisible. Further studies show that issues are understood and experienced very differently by different groups as illustrated by Pain's (2001) work on fear and crime in the city and Ruddick's (1996) work on the construction of difference. Nonetheless, there are government programmes in the UK such as the Diversity Challenge which recognize that diversity and equal opportunities should be used together to make the idea of equality real (Equality Direct, 2002).

The concept of diversity originated in the USA in the 1970s in the field of management (Kanter, 1977) and during the1990s it was adopted by many European organizations. There are still fundamental differences resulting from important cultural and historical roots which affect the way it plays out in practice. Simons (2002) observes that the USA has a more multi-cultural tradition whereas Europe is more mono-cultural and noted for putting pressure on incomers to assimilate and learn the language. In a series of speeches in 2002 and 2003, David Blunkett, Britain's Home Secretary, stressed the importance of immigrants learning English and understanding what it means to be British. The USA/Canadian and New Zealand citizenship ceremonies which every new citizen takes have always marked an important and symbolic belonging to a country but there has never been such a formal requirement in Britain.

Problems occur when organizations think they are moving to diversity from an equal opportunity approach in the belief that discrimination no longer exists. What must be central to an integrated model of diversity which encompasses inequality is the concept of change and transformation of existing power relationships (Kirton and Greene, 2000). It is important that professionals value diversity, promote equality and become more conscious of the power relationships that exist within any group or community and take account of the ideological basis of that power difference. Diversity needs to address difference and inequality. One of the key problems is that within the arena of politics, academics such as Philips (1999) have argued that difference has actually displaced equality as the dominant concern of progressive politics and it has become a self-fulfilling prophesy. The responsiveness of liberal democracy, she argues, exerts pressures for political rather than economic equalization which means that it is proving easier to persuade people to act against a demonstrated political inequity than against an economic one.

Commentators such as Jackson (2003) believe that the equality agenda in the USA has been shaped by a felt need to right the wrongs of the past, to redistribute power and opportunity, and to develop unused potential particularly between black and white communities. The theme of Martin Luther King's famous speech in 1963 which is remembered for the phrase 'I have a dream' contained a very strong message that governments had consistently broken their promises in delivering equality (Jackson, 2003). In the USA individuals and groups are more likely to work out diversity issues in court since the legislation provides a much sharper tool which can be accessed by groups rather than individuals. In Britain, the equality agenda has been shaped more by a commercial imperative brought about by the need to increase the effective labour force. Over the past 20 years, the USA and Europe have converged on diversity partly as a result of globalization and the need for corporations to understand cross-cultural issues fully if they are to succeed in the global marketplace. Britain has possibly more similarities with the USA than other European countries.

The public sector case for equality and diversity is not only analogous to but also different from the business case outlined by Rutherford and Ollerearnshaw (2002). The business case encompasses issues of fairness in employment practices, having a good reputation, access to wider client and customer base and avoiding litigation as a consequence of discrimination. Unique to the public sector are issues of equality of access and representation. Although both the USA and the UK have much to learn from each other, experts in the corporate and business fields warn against the indiscriminate import and export of models and approaches (Simons, 2002: 25). Governments at the national and local levels are bound by mutually agreed United Nations declarations such as The Convention on the Elimination of all Forms of Discrimination Against Women (CEDAW).

UNDERSTANDING DIVERSITY THROUGH PSYCHOLOGY – RACE AND SEX

As professionals and members of a community, it is important that we are as explicit as we can be about the identities we impose on others or assume for ourselves (Heikkila, 2001). In this way we should be able to identify potential sources of stereotyping, bias or discrimination using the tools outlined in Chapter 7. Differences between people reveal themselves in a variety of ways: physical, language or dialect, faith, beliefs and values. Once stereotyping sets in, it can be difficult to change (Figure 1.1).

Figure 1.1 I'm not changing

Perceptions can be as important as reality. Often valued judgements result from ignorance or stereotyping (Milroy, 1999). We may perceive ourselves different to those around us and yet others may see us as very similar to them. We may see no difference between ourselves and those around us yet others may see us differently. Our sense of people around us is based on our personal and social identity. According to the theory of identity developed by Tajfel (1981) and Turner (1987, 1991) we categorize or put labels on people, we identify or associate ourselves with certain groups and we compare 'our' groups with other groups (Hogg, 1996). This tendency to categorize can be seen throughout the social and physical sciences.

Contemporary psychology shows that most people use ethnicity and sex rather than age or disability as the most significant ways of categorizing people and so these are the two principle ways by which we distinguish individuals (Myers, 2001). When asked to comment on who made a particular statement in a video-recorded interview, people (and they were sighted people in these experiments) often forgot who said what, but remembered the race of the person who made each statement (Hewstone, Hantzi and Johnston, 1991). When we talk about cities we say we live in diverse communities or more specifically we might say we live in culturally diverse cities. For instance, Toronto has the highest level of foreign-born population in Canada at 40 per cent, exceeding Miami, New York, Chicago and Los Angeles (Bourne, 2000). The Borough of Newham, London (UK), has the highest proportion of non-white ethnic groups in the UK at 61 per cent (Burbage, 2003). For all this, children do not seem to have the same awareness of racial difference. An anecdote helps illustrate this. On a BBC radio current affairs programme in 2001, the following story was told to illustrate how adults influence the way children start to see themselves. A parent tells of their young child coming home from school talking excitedly about their day; whom they played and talked with and what they did. The child mentions the name of their new friend and the mother pausing, asks if the child is black. 'What's black mum? I'll need to ask him', says the child.

Although sex and race are the most common identifiers, for sociologists and economists, paid work plays a key role in defining an individual's position in society. Access to and the nature of employment helps determine an individual's socio-economic status or class, and a person's ability to access employment is first and foremost determined by their access to education. Lack of paid work then leads to poverty and social exclusion. Comparing different sectoral groups, the majority of disabled people are without paid work and are seen by many as the most vulnerable to poverty. In Canada 70 per cent of disabled women of working age are unemployed, compared with the national average of just over 9 per cent (Chouinard, 1999: 150). The class position held by the majority of disabled people is largely determined by working status and affects their ability to influence the creation of policy (Drake, 1999). If society values people in paid work it also tends to exclude those who cannot work and those excluded from work because of disabling environments.

In other arenas, such as health and marketing, 'life stages' are key identifiers of the ageing population and the impact of global recession. We have MOBYs (mommy older, baby younger), DOBYs (their daddies), PUPPIES (Poor urban professionals), WOOFs (Well-off older folk), SANWICHERS (adults caught between caring for their children and older parents), PIEs (school kids with income and purchasing power), GLOBAL KIDS (kids with strong feelings about the environment plus strong influence over family purchase choices) (Popcorn, 1991). These groups have eclipsed the YUPPIES (young urban professionals), DINKS (double income and no kids) and SINKS (single and no kids) of the 1980s. Reflecting our diverse and multi-cultural societies, trendspotters have started to see new identity groups based on the copycat phenomenon; WIGGERS describes young whites copying blacks and METROSEXUALITY describes heterosexual men doing things that are decidedly gay (Salzman, 2003).

Two theories have been put forward to help explain why we tend to categorize people more readily in terms of race or sex. Essentialists such as Fuss (1989) argue that social differences are mapped on to sexual difference; Constructionists argue that what we understand by essence is in itself a social construction. Malik (1996) goes much further and questions the way in which terminology and meaning become effused. Based on a historical study of the development of ideas about race, racism and racial science, Malik links the language and meaning of race to developments in working-class democracy. He shows how, by 1860 in England, the social elite equated non-white races with lower social orders. Although the political use of racial science was discredited as a result of Nazism, he contends that the conceptual framework simply became re-invented through culturalism and multi-culturalism. Significantly, Malik warns that 'contemporary visions of cultural difference seek to learn about other cultural forms, not to create a richer and more universal culture but to imprison us more effectively in a human zoo of differences' (Malik, 1996: 150). If multi-cultural education or diversity studies simply preserve differences as they present themselves in society, we must look again at the way we define problems and policy responses.

FAITH AND RELIGION

Faith and religion have always been important identifiers in society, and today planners and urban regenerators cannot ignore the importance of faith, religion and secularism to people's sense and their understanding of place. Some religious commentators have said that until recently religion was not considered relevant to equality of opportunity; that the dominance of humanist ideology led people to define their cultural identity by their first language, ethnicity or nationhood (Brierley, 2003). The 2001 census for the UK revealed that four out of five people align themselves with one of the major faiths, despite other surveys showing that only a small percentage of the population engage in 'active worship' (ONS, 2003). There are 37.3 million people in England and Wales who state their religion as Christian. In England, 3.1 per cent of the population state their religion as Muslim (0.7 per cent in Wales), making this the most common religion after Christianity. A total of 7.7 million people state they have no religion. Religion has re-emerged as a key concern of social policy, particularly in the areas of education, employment and social exclusion. At an international interfaith workshop on 'religious identity in public places' (hoping to learn about European initiatives for greater public respect for different faiths), Indarjit Singh (2003) found that the French and German delegates spoke with concern and passion about the danger, to national identity, of allowing religious symbols like the Muslim headscarf in public places. The general consensus seemed to be that all would be well if religion was kept safely locked up in the home. When Singh explained that Britain is encouraging people of different faiths to engage with government and local government in initiatives such as urban regeneration, health and welfare, he said there was an air of incredulity. The Sikh view requires people to look beyond external and superficial differences to our common identity. Singh believes that the UK is ahead of continental Europe in looking to promote interfaith relations. While public attention has focused on Muslims, the notion of religious identity generally is relevant (Voas, Olson and Crockett, 2002). Evangelists have worked hard to lobby governments (Faithworks, 2003) and within the UK government, a new high-powered ministerial grouping has been set up by the Home Office to 'consider the most effective means of achieving greater involvement of the faith communities in policy making and delivery across Whitehall and to identify specific policy areas such as regeneration where this input would be most valuable' (Ahmed, 2003).

THE EFFECTS OF DIFFERENCE: STEREOTYPING, BIAS, PREJUDICE AND DISCRIMINATION

Sectarianism, or the conflict associated with religious differences, is a real consequence of religious prejudice.

> A mole in the midst of communities, as one of the principle villains in history's cast of characters. It is responsible for a misrepresentation of nations and religions other than one's own, as well as an uncritical appraisal of one's own religion and nation, using as a weapon, sheer unadulterated ignorance (Ustinov, 2003: 19).

A study of sectarianism in Glasgow shows that most people continue to see sectarianism as a current and prevalent problem regardless of their religion, sex, social class and ethnicity; and they see it as an individual issue (NFO, 2003). Whilst 60 per cent of respondents feel there is some prejudice or a great deal of prejudice against Catholics and Protestants, 79 per cent of people in the study feel there is prejudice against black people and Asians and 85 per cent feel refugees and asylum seekers experience prejudice. Making inappropriate jokes and using sectarian terms to describe people are the commonest forms of sectarianism. However, 65 per cent feel sectarian violence is commonplace and 58 per cent feel that sectarian threats and harassment are commonplace – all of which underlies how and why different groups of people find security in their own defined neighbourhoods and communities, something which Murtagh (1994, 1999) discovered in his studies of the peace lines in Northern Ireland.

Gebler (1991) tells his 'House with the blue door' story to illustrate how we often find it hard to recognize sectarianism in ourselves.

> If you believed what you read in the papers', You'd think civil war was raging everywhere in Northern Ireland. But if you live here, and you think of trouble, you think of it as happening in certain towns. And if you live in those certain towns, you think of it as happening in certain districts. And if you live in those certain districts, you think of it as happening on certain housing estates. And if you live on those certain housing estates, you think of it as happening in certain streets. And if you live in those certain streets, you know that the trouble is being caused by the man at the end of the road in the house with the blue door (Gebler, 1991: 73).

Psychology shows that, whatever the context, people have a tendency to favour their own self-defined grouping. The maxim that the more you look the more you see is true of people and so the more we know a social group the more we see diversity within the group (Brown and Wootton-Millward, 1993). People of other groups or races seem to look more alike than people of one's own group or race. When someone in a group is conspicuous, others tend to see them as the cause of whatever happens (Taylor and Fiske, 1978; Cohen, Cox and Moss-Kanter 1980; Taylor, 1981). Carli et al. (1990) argue that people can show indifference to social injustice, not because they do not believe in the principle of injustice, but because they see no injustice and fail to see and understand the situational forces determining their position.

Prejudice extends to disabled people. At the time of writing, a student, disabled by a car accident whilst studying to be a doctor, is fighting the British Medical Council for the right to complete her course. As she is now a wheelchair user, she cannot complete one of the resuscitation procedures deemed compulsory for every doctor, even though she wants to become a pathologist. This kind of thinking underpinned the inquiry into the police handling of the death of Stephen Lawrence in England, which concluded that institutional racism was at the heart of the problem (MacPherson, 1999).

INVISIBILITY

One of the consequences of this emphasis on race and sex is that other differences such as disabilities become less invisible. Standard sociological texts such as Giddens (2001) include chapters on gender, race and sexuality but nothing on disability. Regeneration processes exclude disabled people (CLES, 2004). This exclusion of disabled people, on many levels, has encouraged the creation of solidarity groups and the evolution of a 'disabled culture' common to all individuals who define themselves as disabled (French Gilson and Deploy, 2000: 209). Gays and lesbians in many societies are another 'out-group' which struggles to gain acceptance and recognition despite legal protection. Recent studies in Northern Ireland show the extent of homophobic violence and harassment. 'Homophobia doesn't have the same shock value for people that racism does in that it is still broadly tolerated' (Jarman in Battles, 2003: 2; Jarman, 2003).

MULTIPLE IDENTITIES

People tend to have more than one set of identities; largely as a result of either/or dichotomies or an over-reliance on binary forms of analysis. Disability rights movements and feminism have often been presented as homogenous and unified movements, with feminism appearing to speak for all women, and disability rights, based on the social model of disability, appearing to speak for all disabled people (Fawcett, 2000: 39).

Multiple identities play out in different ways. During the 1970s, at the height of the troubles in Northern Ireland, the gay and lesbian community created a non-sectarian set of identities which in effect set aside those means of identity which the rest of the community was using. In doing this they created a cocoon liberating people from the sectarianism of both sides. Finally in 1982 the Government decriminalized homosexual activity in Northern Ireland. Gays and lesbians did not then or now decide friendship by the same rules as elsewhere in society and set aside an imposed identity of religion for something more meaningful (Presley, 2003).

Local politics can lead to particular areas of discrimination being ignored, as one set of differences dominates the political and social agenda. In the case of race in Northern Ireland where up until 2001 the census collected no information on ethnicity (McKittrick, 2003), discrimination faced by the traveller community is still largely unrecognized (Ellis, 2003). The Community Relations Council has developed a range of material to help young people understand cultural diversity and its insidious effects (The Community Relations Council, 1999). The year 2004 has seen an increase in the level of racially motivated violence in Northern Ireland.

With the creation of devolved government in the United Kingdom and the creation of the Scottish Parliament and the Assembly for Wales, notions of national identity have come to the fore. This has afforded an opportunity to look at the way in which disability and national identity relate to one another. The new parliament buildings have afforded the opportunity to see how national identity is conveyed through the designs for the new iconic buildings (Hastings, 2001). In addition the study sets out to discover what the provisions for disabled people say about the sense of national identity and the status which disabled people have in the two nations. Drawing on the work of Yack (1999) and MacCormick (1999), Hastings took a sense of national identity to mean identifying with a nation, a political entity which exists because of present-day consent, shared memories and practices and a shared sense of the future (Hastings, 2001: 36). The definition also acknowledged that beliefs undergo reconstruction over time in response to social and political forces. This study of the design and development of the Scottish Parliament in Edinburgh and the Assembly for Wales building in Cardiff examined the way in which the states and their new representatives perceived disabled people and what this means for the national identity of the Scots and Welsh. The study of the design process showed that the Scottish Parliament and the Welsh Assembly treated access issues differently. Despite the fact that disabled people make up a higher proportion of the population of Wales than any other part of the UK (Disability Wales, undated in Hastings, 2001), Hastings discerned a 'more inclusive construction of national identity in the Scottish Parliament building design process, including the building user brief, designs, and the apparently powerful role of the access consultant and involvement of the consultation group from the outset' (Hastings, 2001: 65).

DIVERSITY, EQUALITY AND THE MODERNIZATION AGENDA

Governments the world over are modernizing. For some this means democratization, for others it means maximizing the potential of Information Technology (IT). The modernization agenda is a central part of government strategies across Europe and beyond. It is associated with the need for governments to respond to global trends, the pressures on public sector finance and the need to maximize efficiency and improve social cohesion.

Difference, diversity and equality are dynamic concepts. The driving forces include population growth and urbanization, economic growth and consumption and the persistence of poverty and economic inequalities (World Resources Institute, 1998). Prejudice need not persist indefinitely. As new social norms develop, prejudice against a group can diminish. We tend to associate with different groups at different times. Perceived differences between groups of people change over time. At one time, people actually found gender role differences hard to see. It did not seem to occur to people that women survive and indeed prosper outside the kitchen. The behaviour of women and men was explained solely in terms of their innate dispositions and not to the gender roles assigned by society. Once established, prejudice of this kind is maintained largely by inertia. In an essay, in 1891, George Bernard Shaw said that:

> If we have come to think that the nursery and the kitchen are the natural sphere of woman, we have done so exactly as English children come to think that a cage is the natural sphere of a parrot – because they have never seen one anywhere else (cited in Myers, 2001: 197).

One hundred and ten years later, on a trip to New Zealand I overheard the following joke admittedly in a bar: 'Why is a wedding dress white?' – answer: 'To go with all the other white goods in the kitchen.'

To see what lies ahead we tend to look to the work of futurists. Recent studies show some worrying trends which may themselves become self-fulfilling prophecies. Futurology texts tend to take a common approach to difference and diversity (McRae, 1995; Mercer, 1998; Matathia and Salzman, 1999; Margolis, 2001; Salzman, 2003). All refer to the changing role of women and men and the ever-increasing role women will play in society. The growth in power, and especially the influence, held by women in the twenty-first century cannot be overestimated and there are those

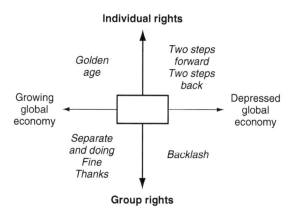

Figure 1.2 The four futures of women (Source: McCurdock and Ramsey, 1996: 16)

who argue that the impact has been much greater than formerly appreciated (Mercer, 1998: 93, 96). In the future, 67 per cent expect gender equality to be global by 2030 and 70 per cent expect a notable rise in the feminine value of co-operation by 2015. All the futurist books reviewed refer to the impact of the ageing society. The invisibility of disabled people, however, is striking. Only one mentions disabled people either as a serious consumer group or as a force for change, in the context of redefining beauty (Matathia and Salzman, 1999: 101). Because of the ageing population, there has been a swing away from youth culture to middle-age culture with a contradiction between the rights of young people and the power they have. Race is seen as synonymous with ethnic tension and problems. The term 'asylum seeker' does not figure in the books written in the mid-1990s.

McCurdock and Ramsey (1996) depict 'A Golden Age of Equality' in which economies grow and individual rights, the rule of law and personal privacy prevail (Figure 1.2). Societies accommodate different traditions and it is recognized that war is an irrational use of resources and environmental protection is acknowledged. In this Golden Age, women are recognized as different from but not somehow less than men. Fertility control is accepted and available. A critical mass of educated women shape the workplace rather than perpetuate the existing workplace. Work smart replaces work long. The one-dimensional man whose life collapsed when he retired is no longer. The stressful stereotypes men felt forced to live up to dissolve. Legislation exists mandating 50/50 representation in national parliaments with knock-on effects on education. Pandemic violence against women becomes a public issue. The so-called women's issues are recognized at last to be important to society. Women and girls continue their education into the cyberspace. A generation of women exist at international level who want change and are prepared to work together to achieve it. Equality in the workplace leads to family-friendly policies that people are not afraid to ask for because it might be seen to reflect on their commitment. In the Golden Age, work is looked at through a family lens. By 2015, workaholics are seen as socially handicapped as the chronically unemployed. Hiring more women is recognized to be not enough. Business operations recognize the need to change – hours stretched to weekends and evenings but working hours dropped. Harnessed as a positive feature, diversity is no longer a problem.

One of the consequences of difference and diversity for planners was summed up by Healey, 'if we live and form our life-worlds in different cultural communities within which we develop different languages and different systems of valuing, how do we get to talk to each other about matters of common concern? And when we get to talking across these divides, how do we get to decide what is right? Are there any absolute priorities, such as a duty of environmental stewardship or natural justice which should override our little local differences?' (Healey, 1997: 63).

PART 2   SUSTAINABLE DEVELOPMENT

Sustainable development offers a way forward and has become an explicit goal of planning, although there is no agreed or universal template. Planners, like other professionals, need to chart paths towards sustainable development which respects and takes account of the needs and values of different groups of people. For some, sustainable development is characterized by internal contradictions in that it urges us to use less while development seems to say to use more. Urban sustainability seems a contradiction when we have global cities with millions of people which on the face of it seem to function (Soja, 1999). Look closer and you will see that expert commentators report that the best examples of cities with sustainable energy and waste management are medium-sized and that as the conditions for their growth are reversed, they should actually contract in size again (Girardet, 2001).

While only a third of the population of the United Kingdom claim to have heard about sustainable development, only 7 per cent appear to understand what it means (Planning, 2003). This is not surprising when research shows that the public's knowledge of topical science issues only slightly improves as a result of their education or consumption of news media (Hargreaves, Lewis and Speers, 2003). One of the reasons why sustainable development is not understood is that it has not achieved the political attention it deserves. It needs to become part of the debate about priorities and spending alongside and integral to health, education, jobs and housing. As a cross-cutting theme, sustainable development has relevance for each of these traditional policy areas. Another reason why many people have difficulty with the concept of sustainability is that it seems to have so many different definitions. This lack of precision, however, has not lessened the importance of the concept. In a sense, attempts to provide the ultimate definition go against the pluralistic nature of sustainability. Several key ideas are common to many of the ways of thinking about sustainability. Whole systems' thinking integrates the social, economic and environmental dimensions, and integrates the notions of social justice, environmental justice and the economy. Long-term thinking creates an understanding of the consequences of actions over time. Traditional cultures can teach us much. For instance, the councils of the Iroquois and other Native American groups evaluate each decision by asking what impact it will have on the seventh generation from today (Washington State Department of Ecology, 2003). Thinking about limits creates an appreciation of the finiteness of the ecosystem. Finally, the idea of improving livelihoods and creating a better quality of life, both for today and for future generations, creates a sense of motivation to change.

Despite being contested and debated, pulled and tugged and manipulated, the concept has remained remarkably robust. Despite numerous definitions, it is possible to categorize the approaches to and models of sustainability in a manageable number of ways. Each conceptualizes people and sources of power differently. In some, the source of power is explicit, in others implicit. Five types of graphical model are commonly in use. The first depicts three interlocking circles representing the social, economic and environmental dimensions of sustainable development. It sets out to show that the environmental, economic and social aspects all interconnect, that to achieve social justice involves addressing environmental justice and economic distribution (Figure 1.3).

Sustainable development involves creating as much overlap as possible between all three circles. Although widely used and conceptually useful at an introductory level, this model quickly becomes too simplistic and one-dimensional. The three components are usually depicted with the same size circles, each overlapping to the same extent, implying the equal importance of each dimension. On the positive side, models like this have helped create a wider understanding of the interlinkages between each dimension. However, in their simplicity, the social dimension becomes equated with the generic notion of community and social justice with inequalities between groups becoming subsumed and invisible.

An alternative to this model nests the economy within society and the wider environment (City of Seattle, 2002). The model says that the environment forms the basis of everything else and if we mess with the environment, this affects us socially and economically. Cynics might interpret it differently and say that it shows government putting the economy at the centre of everything and placing environmental issues at the margins. As a result of the ambiguity it creates, the model is less helpful than the first one (Figure 1.4).

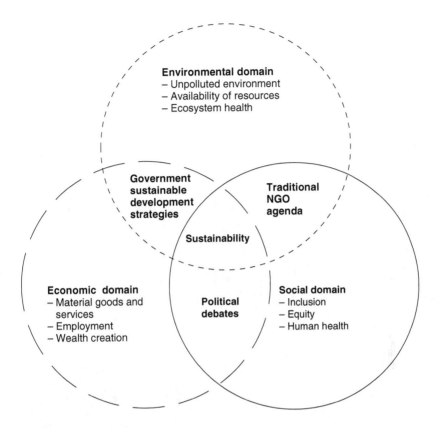

Figure 1.3 Sustainable development – Venn diagram

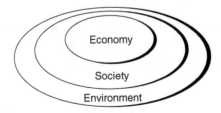

Figure 1.4 The Nesting model of sustainable development

The model put forward by Baker *et al.* (1997) includes four dimensions and sets out to reflect the stages of sustainable development (Table 1.1). However, only the ideal model embraces the social dimension positively and constructively. Redistribution is defined in terms of inter- and intragenerational equity and it is not clear whether gender, race and age form a component of this social perspective. Most current models of sustainability see equity in global terms and, consistent with the original

Table 1.1 Four dimensions of sustainable development

Approach to sustainable development	Philosophy	Policy instruments and tools	Redistribution	Civil society
Ideal model	Ecocentric/ biocentric	Full range of policy tools, sophisticated use of indicators extending to social dimensions	Inter- and intra- generational equity	Bottom-up community structures and control of new approach to valuing work
Strong		Advanced use of sustainability indicators wide range of policy tools	Strengthened redistribution policy	Open-ended dialogue and envisioning
Weak		Token use of environmental indicators; limited range of market-led policy tools	Equity a marginal issue	Top-down initiatives, limited state– environmental movements dialogue
Treadmill	Anthropocentric/ techno-cratic	Conventional accounting	Equity not an issue	Very limited dialogue between the state and environmental movements

Source: Baker *et al.* (1997).

Brundtland definition of sustainability, focus on the inequalities between generations. The UN development programme reports that over one quarter of the world's population, 1.3 billion people, live in poverty and 500 million are chronically malnourished. According to the measure of 'capability poverty' developed by the UN, 1.6 billion people, one-third of the world's population, lack the three basic essentials: of being well nourished and healthy, capable of healthy reproduction and of being educated and knowledgeable. Trends are getting worse not better and this can be seen within the UK as well as the rest of the world. The UK has become one of the most unequal societies in the world.

The fourth model separates out social sustainability, economic and environmental sustainability as independent domains of action, implying the possibility of attaining environmental, economic or social sustainability independently of the other two (Figure 1.5). It closely mirrors the compartmentalized nature of government organizations, and could be said to depict the current model of public policy making. Critics argue that it creates false gaps between the three domains and contradicts the

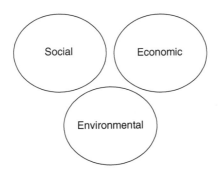

Figure 1.5 The Mercury model of sustainability

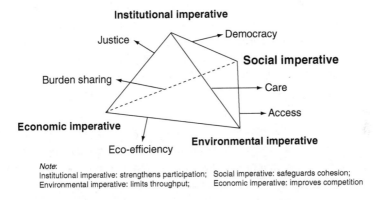

Note:
Institutional imperative: strengthens participation;   Social imperative: safeguards cohesion;
Environmental imperative: limits throughput;   Economic imperative: improves competition

Figure 1.6 The Swedish prism model

underlying assumption that one aspect of sustainable development cannot be achieved at the expense of another.

The Swedish prism model explicitly acknowledges the importance of government and other organizations with its four dimensions (Figure 1.6). Along with the economic, social and environmental dimensions is the institutional dimension (Eden, Falkheden and Malberet, 2000). Through the prism, we can approach sustainability from any dimension without losing the links between the other dimensions. Local situations can be built in and appropriate actions developed. With its long tradition of top-down environmental management, where the role of the state is recognized as crucial, the Swedes consider the prism model mirrors the sentiments of the Rio declaration, linking institutionalism with participative decision-making (Valentin and Spangeberg, 1999).

Common amongst all these models is the recognition that a sustainable project, plan, goal or objective must address environmental, economic and social issues over the long term. Things become more contested when the assumptions underlying the various approaches are considered. At one extreme are those who argue that sustainability can be achieved without seriously impeding economic growth. The economy and the environment, advocates say, are not in conflict and environmental improvements actually depend on economic prosperity. An example of this is ecological modernization. At the other extreme are those who argue that the ecosystem should take priority and that sustainable development can only be achieved through alternative modes of production. An example is risk society theory which suggests that the relationship between the economy and the environment is irreconcilable (Beck, 1992). Planning for sustainable development involves acknowledging and finding common ground between the 'ecological modernization' and the 'risk society' theories (Davoudi, 2002: 127).

The ecological modernization concept introduced in the mid-1980s (Hajer, 1997) has its roots in both the radical environmental movements represented in the Blueprint for Survival (The Ecologist, 1972), and the technocratic approach of environmental scientists reflected in the Club of Rome's Limit to Growth Study (Meadows, Randers and Behrens, 1972). The 'risk society' theory, introduced by Beck (1992, 1998) and building on the work of Carson (1962) in *Silent Spring*, argues that the unintended consequences of industrial modernity have created a need to deal with social and environmental risks. Social and environmental justice are core objectives. Environmental economists see the sustainability problem as quite simply 'managing economic activity to address inequality and poverty in ways which do not undermine the base for future economic activity' (Common, 1995: 31). Within ecological modernization theory, the concept of sustainability is more market-orientated with the environment seen as a stock of assets which can be quantified, priced and traded in quasi-monetary terms. The USA Council on Sustainable Development reflects this approach when it says that 'to achieve sustainable development, some things must grow – jobs, productivity, wages, capital and savings, profits, information, knowledge and education – and others – pollution, waste, poverty – must not' (Council on Sustainable Development, 1994/1999).

The European Commission's (EC) model of sustainable development is about much more than minimizing the environmental impact of economic growth. It has three objectives: sustainable economic growth; social cohesion, through access for all to employment; and the maintenance of the environmental capital on which life depends. The guidance produced by the EC integrates the environmental aspects of sustainability within regional employment and economic growth, with the target groups including existing workers, long-term unemployed, young unemployed, new labour force entrants, low-skilled, skilled and high-skilled (EC, 1999). To track progress, tests of sustainability have been developed. For instance, the Eastern Scotland European Partnership created an Access and Opportunity test which involves an assessment of the extent to which the project actively promotes the full and equal participation of individuals and social groups in the *local* economy (EC, 1999: paras 11, 13).

Within risk society, the concept of sustainability is both radical and moral. Here the protection of ecosystems has priority over any other demands. This earth-centred approach emphasizes the need to constrain human activity within the carrying capacity of ecological systems (Davoudi, 2002: 129). According to the ecological modernization theory, the state has an enabling role, facilitating market operations whereas the risk society promotes a more interventionist state which is based on the power of collective action. Both theories assume 'intervention', but different kinds of intervention with different intents. The ecological modernization approach implies a light touch form of intervention, leaving things up to the market, while risk society implies a form of intervention which emphasizes the need to constrain human activity within the carrying capacity of ecological systems. The risk society approach emphasizes the need for greater democracy and participation whereas the ecological modernization approach relies on a techno-corporatist approach to decision-making. What we see today is the domination of the ecological modernization approach in public policy with pressure from Non-Governmental Organizations to make public policy more risk-aware. Although apparently irreconcilable, these approaches provide a basis for the debates which need to happen and which planning needs to facilitate.

Sustainability is a political vision which seeks to tackle increasingly global problems of environmental degradation and poverty within specific locations (Eden, Falkheden and Malberet, 2000). To drive the political vision forward, the UK and other governments recognize the importance of creating a statutory duty to promote sustainable development for all authorities and agencies responsible for planning, implementing or investing in public services (ODPM, 2002a). Right now, most governments in the world are experiencing what they see as a crisis of democracy. So to achieve their goals, governments are engaging the active participation of society to bring about sustainability as envisaged at the UN Conference on sustainable development in 1992 to:

- Fair access to a clean environment (in other words, everyone needs to contribute to a sustainable environment and everyone has a right to a clean environment).
- Maintenance of public health and elimination as far as practicable of environmental risks.
- Equity in the use of environmental resources. (This would ensure that the current generation takes into account the needs of future generations. It would also imply that the current generation is not seen as homogenous and that a more equitable distribution of resources takes place between constituencies.)
- Full access to education and information regarding the environment.
- Sustainable planning, development and human settlement policies (UN, 1992).

Active participation is at the heart of sustainable community development. A sustainable community is:

> A community that uses its resources to meet current needs while ensuring that adequate resources are available for future generations. A sustainable community seeks a better quality of life for all its residents while maintaining nature's ability to function over time by minimising waste, preventing pollution, promoting efficiency and developing local resources to revitalise the local economy. Decision Making in a sustainable community stems from a rich civic life and shared information among community members. A sustainable community resembles a living system in which human, natural and economic elements are interdependent and draw strength from each other (ODPM, 2002a).

Sustainable development does not have an agreed or universal template, so the very process of planning must provide the necessary forums for defining sustainable development in different communities (TCPA, 1999: 11). Planners need to chart paths towards sustainable development which respect and take into account the needs and values of different groups of people. The Seattle city website does just this and the stories which make up the site provide examples of the small steps Seattleites are trying to make the city a more sustainable place (City of Seattle, 2002).

Most of the approaches to sustainable development are human rather than earth-centred. However, as yet there is little evidence of a fusion between equality, diversity and sustainable development. Studies in general tend to be gender-neutral and portray little sense of the effect of ethnic and cultural diversity. Some commentators argue that the grass-roots bottom-up 'urban ecology' approach has the potential to ensure that different groups of people are engaged in the process of achieving sustainability, whereas the top-down environmental management approach which is much more mechanistic and techno-corporatist tends to exclude ordinary people. However, the Swedish experience seems to contradict this. Some commentators consider the two approaches mutually exclusive although both could usefully recognize the ways in which different groups of people use and perceive the environment (Eden, Falkheden and Malberet, 2000). Whatever approach is taken, sustainable development objectives can only be achieved if the diverse characteristics of populations are acknowledged and people's rights to a healthy environment recognized.

PART 3   SPACE AND PLACE

Space and place, social relations and environment are all core concepts for planners and for those engaged in planning, the publics, business and enterprise, lobby groups to name but three. What are needed are a language, literacy, an understanding of place and space which respects difference and diversity and promotes equality (Gehl, 1996).

The Schumacher Society defines the sustainable city as one where:

Safety in public places, equal opportunities, freedom of expression and the needs of the young, the old and the disabled must be adequately provided for.

The sustainable city is

Organised so as to enable *all* its citizens to meet their own needs and to enhance their well-being without damaging the natural world or endangering the living conditions of other people, now or in the future. This emphasises *people* and their long term needs. These include good quality air and water, healthy food and good housing. It also encompasses quality education, a vibrant culture, good health care, satisfying employment or occupations and the sharing of wealth (Girardet, 2001: 13).

At the heart of a sustainable city lie the principles of equity and equality as well as respect for difference. Inequality, it is argued, dissolves the social glue; vital to the collective action needed to stimulate the active participation of a sustainable community. Decision-makers have responsibility for creating the context for this social glue. If we properly understand the expectations of those who make decisions, we can predict what they will do. If expectations shape the future and if you can influence expectations, then you can influence the shape of the future (Mercer, 1998: 239). To move towards the sustainable city, we need to give decision-makers and those who influence them the space to reflect on their expectations. We need to persuade them of the benefits of providing everyone with opportunities to be involved, thereby tapping into local expertise. This belief, this contention, is at the heart of change. Spatial planning should create sustainable places and spaces by recognizing difference and diversity and equality.

A place is a particular point or part of a space or surface. It could be a town or city, a place to live, a riverbank or a park, a favourite hideaway for children, a spiritual retreat. Where we live defines us. Where we live affects how we live, whom we interact with, and what we eat, our moods and feelings, our health and well-being. Places shape the way we live our lives, our access to water, whether we have electricity, the opportunities we have to get a paid job, how easy it is to get to school or to health care, how to keep in touch with friends and relatives. Places are for experiencing (Hiss, 1990).

If our sense of 'who we are' is based on our personal and social identity, our sense of place also reflects this. Some have argued that a sense of place is part of what it is to be human (Tuan, 1990, 2001). However, we know that humans are not the only species with a sense of place. Birds, fish and other mammals have a homing instinct. A place can mean a home, neighbourhood, community and city. It may be linked to emotions and memories (Jacobs, 1961). However, a place need not be just a physical location. A place can exist in the mind, somewhere to go to meditate or reflect, an intersection of sets of social relations, functional places, knowledge cities, intelligent cities and learning communities. The future is a place, and as the trend-spotters of the 1990s found, people 'don't look to the future as the place to be anymore' (Popcorn, 1991: 6). The horrors of the Aids epidemic and the prospect of constant war mean that societies have grown wary, anxious and often frightened of the future which should bring hope and a better life.

No matter what the culture, it seems that people put enormous value on place and this sense of value is not always measured in money but in terms of physical and spiritual worth. Putting something unique up for sale does not guarantee buyers, particularly where people believe the place should not be owned by anyone. The lack of interest in buying the Cuillins mountain range on the Isle of Skye in Scotland, when it went up for sale in 2001, so that the owner John McLeod could raise money to refurbish his castle, reflected a belief held by the community that mountains are not for sale. Equally, land which cannot be developed excites little interest amongst those who need to make a return on that capital. The mountains were then offered to the nation in return for money to refurbish the castle. This time, the state was decidedly cool. In July 2003, the owner finally gave the Cuillins mountains to the nation and handed the castle to a charitable trust responsible for the restoration (D. Ross, 2003).

Whereas a 'place' is a particular point, space is 'the three-dimensional expanse in which all material objects are located'. This means that space contains tangible objects such as beautiful buildings, natural landscapes and real people. Space becomes the intervals of distance between points, objects or events; between places, people and buildings. The objects need not be real in the sense that we can touch them. In the space of virtual reality created through computer programs for instance, images represent reality and space becomes representational – open space, green space, personal space, corporate space, state space, contested space, gendered space, racialized space and disabling space, cyberspace (Dodge and Kitchen, 2001). Relative space attributed to Haggett and Chorley (1969) provides a basic tool for understanding and ordering the environment. We look at how cities relate to one another in terms of the economy and communications. The European Spatial Development Perspective (ESDP) (2003) reflects the use of relative space and the traditions of spatial patterning. As well as relative space, planners work with absolute space or the physical reality. Most professionals still like to think that this notion of absolute reality exists and can be seen, mapped and photographed although it is clear to many that the lens or conceptual frames of references we use determine what absolute space we see and what space others see. Planning should reflect these different conceptions of space.

Table 1.2 The characteristics of a sustainable city

A just city	Where justice, food, shelter, education, health and hope are *fairly* distributed
A beautiful city	Where art, architecture and landscape spark the imagination and move the spirit
A creative city	Where open mindedness and experimentation mobilize the *full* potential of its human resources
An ecological city	Which minimizes its ecological impact, where landscape and built form are balanced and where buildings and infrastructures are safe and resource efficient
A city of easy contact and mobility	Where information is exchanged both face to face and electronically
A compact and polycentric city	Which protects the countryside, focuses and integrates communities within neighbourhoods and maximises proximity
A diverse city	Where a broad range of overlapping activities create animation, inspiration and foster a vital public life

Source: Rogers (1998) *Cities for a Small Planet*.

Some of these conceptions of space and place have become reflected in current models of thinking about sustainable cities. Rogers (1998) identified seven components of a sustainable city set out in Table 1.2.

THE SAMENESS OF PLACE OR FAMILIARITY

Globalization has led to criticisms of the sameness of cities. On the one hand this sameness provides a sense of the familiar although on the other hand it can lead to the destruction of those characteristics responsible for the uniqueness of a place. Urbanization has led to debates about the ideal size of cities as sustainable places to live. In a series of articles for *Highlife*, Will Self talks about urbanity being the most delusive experience of place in the sense that you can have the same urban experience wherever you go in the world. 'In creating environments that are so large, they can but be apprehended in the same way as we perceive the natural world, mountainous Manhattan, oceanic Los Angeles, riparian London, we have precipitated ourselves into a topsy-turvy world' (Self, 2002: 94). Picking up a cab at an unnamed airport somewhere in the world, he clearly allowed himself to be seduced into not looking for the special or the unique, for each place retains its uniqueness.

Visionaries help create special and unique places. Tim Smit talks about the Eden project in Cornwall, England, as a space created in a particular place which explores 'development in the fullest sense of the word: the sustainable development of human potential and the achievement of the optimum quality of life for all, across economic, social and cultural boundaries' (Smit, 2001: 302). The creation of this space in a disused place or quarry demonstrates the transformative nature of sustainable development. Not only has it transformed the landscape, but also it will transform the way in which many people see their relationship to the world around them.

Studies have shown that 'urbanisation and industrialisation decrease the likelihood that supportive social relationships can exist even though they have created the conditions for a higher standard of living in material goods and improved sanitation' (Lindheim and Syme, 1983). The number of social contacts a person has and whether they are part of one or more cohesive social groups help determine a person's health. Adults who live together live longer than those who live alone; members of churches or other social groups live longer than those who have few social contacts (Bunker, 2001). Loss of social networks forces people to turn to public assistance and then vie for adequate shelter. Identity and Social Action, a new major multi-disciplinary research programme seeks to deepen our understanding of the processes involved in the making of selves, groups and communities (Wetherell, 2003). The study focuses on how identity practices create social spaces and conflicting and cohesive patterns of social relations.

The quest for the ideal community appears at odds with the way many people actually choose to live their lives. The current belief, reflected in the ideal of the sustainable community, seems to be that cross-cultural co-operation can be brought about through the creation of social heterogeneity. This could include a mix of racial, religious and socio-economic groups. Social psychology does not lead us to question the efficacy of planning for diversity. However, it does show that if we know people are predisposed to in-group bias and privileging their own, we need to highlight the problems this can create by putting ourselves in others shoes (a point developed in Chapter 7). If inertia maintains prejudice, then legislation may be necessary to act as a catalyst for the change in society. It does not seem to be a simple matter of integration as the current models of sustainability advocate. There needs to be a choice. Planners and public policy analysts today increasingly need sharper tools and concepts with which to understand and shape a future which works for everyone. Murtagh (1999) found, in Northern Ireland, that segregation provides people with the sense of security they need to live their lives. In his travels to the east coast of the USA to seek out successful black Americans, Professor Henry Louis Gates Junior (2003) found that many middle-class black Americans want to live together. Studies show that the segregation of older people provides much more efficient places for the delivery of home care services than residential areas, which house people from all age groups, but it may not be the way in which many older people want to live (Rosenberg and Everitt, 2001). If we advocate integration, we do not want planning to perpetuate containment and marginalize already disadvantaged communities

(Duhl and Sanchez, 1999). We want to make sure that everyone has the opportunity to access all they need to live their lives fully and productively. Spatial planning provides one of the tools for doing this.

SPATIAL PLANNING

Planning can contribute to the new world by making new spaces and meaningful places (Castells, 1996: 13).

'Influencing the future distribution of activities in space to create a more rational organization of land uses and linkages between them' is the ESDP's definition of spatial planning (ESDP, 2003). This makes planning sound overly technical, distant and almost inhuman. We know it is not. The human face of spatial planning recognizes that at one and the same time we live as residents of one or more communities, neighbours, business entrepreneurs, parents or carers. The young child goes to school and plays with friends. The parent negotiates caring, paid and/ or unpaid work. The environment in which we live may reinforce a sense of identity, it may alienate and at worst discriminate. So mobility and accessibility are spatial issues. Design and the quality of places are spatial issues. Discrimination and inequality are spatial issues. Spatial planning therefore has an important role to play in tackling social exclusion – when individuals or areas suffer from a combination of linked problems such as environments, poor skills, low incomes, poor housing, high crime rates, bad health and family breakdown. Poverty is gendered and racialized (Oxfam, 2003). Mobility and accessibility are particular issues for disabled and older people.

Spatial plans can show how places connect and how these connections and links can be improved, what needs protecting in terms of heritage, what development is needed in terms of housing, work places, leisure and recreation. The beauty of a spatial plan lies in the fact that we can configure it in different ways. Political boundaries are not always appropriate. River catchments, neighbourhoods of a few streets which make up an identifiable community, a whole town or city region may form the basis of a plan. Anyone can produce a plan; although its legitimacy depends entirely on the level of support and ownership it has gained through community and legal processes. A spatial plan should communicate ideas we can see (visual), ideas we can feel (kinaesthetic) and hear (auditory). Yet plans are generally communicated in the visual mediums (Reeves, 2002a).

Spatial planning offers a way of mediating between competing objectives by offering an understanding of the spatial implications of different decisions. It is about the creation of places and spatial relationships. It is an activity undertaken by communities and agencies in the public, private and voluntary sectors which lead to outcomes at a range of spatial scales. As an activity, it leads to tangible outcomes. The need to develop an effective framework to ensure that planning policies eliminate inequalities between women and men has been recognized for some time (Hayden, 1980; GLC, 1986; Morris, 1995; Booth and Gilroy, 1996). Critiques of planning have highlighted deficiencies caused by gender-blind approaches and the historic male gendering of knowledge (McDowell, 1983; Sandercock and Forsyth, 1992). In the same way that Sandercock (1998: 72) referred to Mannheim's critique of the class-based nature of planning knowledge still prevalent today, the work of Little (1994a,b) highlighted the problems associated with a gender-blind approach in the UK context. The lack of a children's perspective has long been recognized (Ward, 1978) and their right to have a role in shaping their future is now acknowledged (UN, 1989; Driskell, 2002).

All primary and secondary planning legislation, whether in the UK or New Zealand, the USA or South Africa, should require agencies to build in considerations of equality at all levels and stages of spatial planning – from the national spatial framework level to the regional strategies and local development documents. The spatial dimension is important when looking to achieve equality. Spatial issues relate to the:

- location of activities
- interrelationship of activities
- way in which activities are connected
- condition of places
- sustainable development
- quality of places.

Without a consideration of the social dimension of society, it is not possible to develop adequate strategies for sustainability through spatial planning. This takes time for political recognition, as the experience in Scotland shows. Speaking in the debate on sustainability in the Scottish Parliament as Minister for Transport Boyack (2000) said 'Last year, the Secretary of State for Scotland's advisory group on sustainable development submitted its final report. It had worked for five [col. 782] years to bridge the gap between the aspirations of Brundtland and the action that was needed in Scotland. The report sets out ten key action points.' Sarah Boyack moved: 'That the Parliament places sustainable development at the core of its work and commends the Scottish Executive for its commitment to integrate the principles of sustainable development into all Government policies for the benefits it brings to the people of Scotland, now and in the future' (Boyack, 2000: col. 786). Some small nations have already shown the way; where they have led, we must aspire to follow. The Netherlands, for example, has sustainability written into its constitution. Its commitment is exemplified by Article 21 of the constitution which reads:

> The public authorities shall endeavour to ensure a good quality of life in the Netherlands and to protect and enhance the living environment.

The Local Agenda 21, the agenda forged by the United Nation (1992), is a dynamic programme evolving in the light of changing needs. As a result the social dimension, which interacts with the environmental and economic, has come to mean achieving social equity (Blowers, 1997; TCPA, 1999).

FUTURE TRENDS

There seems to be a number of trends which are mapping out the decade ahead from a human perspective and anyone planning for sustainable development in the USA and Europe would do well to reflect on them (Table 1.3). Only five trends

Table 1.3 Trendsetters up to 2010

People in the community	
99 lives*	Too fast a pace, too little time and multiple roles
Anchoring	A reaching back to our spiritual roots
Being alive	Awareness that good health extends longevity and leads to a new way of life
Cashing out*	Working women and men, questioning personal/career satisfaction and goals, opt for simpler living
Save our society*	The country rediscovers a social conscience of ethics, passion and compassion
Clanning	Belonging to a group that represents common feelings, causes or ideals; validating one's own belief system
Cocooning	The need to protect oneself from the harsh, unpredictable realities of the outside world
Down ageing*	Nostalgic for their carefree childhood, baby boomers find comfort in familiar pursuits and products from their youth
People as consumers	
Atmosfear	Polluted air, water and tainted food, fuel, consumer doubt and uncertainty
Eveolution	Women's impact on business
Egonomics*	To offset a depersonalized society, consumers crave recognition of their individuality
Fantasy adventure	The modern age whets our desire for roads untaken
Icon toppling	Pillars of society are questioned and rejected
Pleasure revenge	Consumers want to cut loose again
Small indulgences	Stressed-out consumers indulge in affordable luxuries to reward themselves
Vigilante consumer	Frustrated, often angry consumers are manipulating the marketplace through pressure, protest and politics

Note: *Trends continuing from the 1990s.
Source: Popcorn (2003).

continue from the 1990s, others appear for the first time. In the context of planning for sustainable development, one group of trends relates to the way people relate to their community and another group relates to the way people see themselves as consumers. Whereas we might be forgiven for thinking that people are motivated entirely by greed and selfishness, these trends demonstrate a belief in society and a need to work to make it better.

There is a potential gap between how the public sees equality issues and how the professionals see it. The Equal Opportunities Commission (EOC) in the UK commissioned a piece of research to look at people's perceptions of equality issues (Howard and Tibballs, 2003). Although a small exercise, it highlights the potential gaps between how equality professionals and the public view equality. The public are aware that social inequality and discrimination are widespread and yet they do not talk about it in the same way equality professionals talk about it. They seem to like rights-based language and recognize institutionalisms. They talk about fairness, tolerance, having the same life chances. They identify the groups who they 'know' to be unequal – ethnic minorities, gay men and lesbian women. In the UK, women, as a group, are not seen as unequal in society and most people do not see sex inequality as a priority issue. However, it seems that younger women in particular like the idea of promoting women's rights (Howard and Tibballs, 2003) and online discussions have shown that men and boys see more benefits than disbenefits to gender equality (UNDAW, 2003).

CONCLUSION

Something very important happens when you start to look at sustainable development and spatial planning, diversity and equality side by side. You start to see the interrelationships. Equality and diversity are integral to sustainable development and spatial planning. A full consideration of equality and diversity should lead to an increase in the effectiveness of spatial planning for sustainable development. For this to happen a shift in thinking and new tools are needed. The concepts of difference and diversity themselves are dynamic and context specific. Through continuous learning and development, professionals and those engaged in planning develop their knowledge and expertise.

On reflection, I started the research for this chapter with the belief that if policy can achieve an ideal mix, communities will sustain themselves. However, this is too simplistic and the conclusion I draw at this stage is that the picture is more complex. Difference and diversity are highly contexualized and many people want to feel safe in their own self-defined space. In Northern Ireland, people know that if they do not learn to live side by side they will fall into the abyss again (Orangeman, Channel 4, 2003). But 'side by side' means different things in different contexts.

I also started research for this chapter with the view that disability had a high profile in the minds of social policy experts as well as planners and futurists. The reality could not be farther from the truth, particularly in the UK context and this is reflected in Europe and Canada. The question is how can this change?

Chapter 2 looks at what shifts would be needed to the various strands of planning to achieve a sensitivity to diversity so that inequality and discrimination can be tackled. Planning has tended to see the people affected by planning as one-dimensional. A common building block for all the traditional strands of planning has been class and income and this is reflected in the kinds of statistics presented in strategic and local plans documents, processes and outcomes.

CHAPTER 2

DEVELOPMENTS IN PLANNING

> One thing we can be certain: the meaning of planning in the twenty first century will depend on how planners intervene with other political actors in the emerging social struggles of our time.
>
> – Milroy (2003: 1)

Spatial planning today is a composite and a fusion of a range of different approaches. Whether in Europe, USA/Canada, Australia/New Zealand or South Africa, you can recognize the key approaches which influence the way planners work and the tools, knowledge and theoretical understanding they use. You may have graduated from a course which identifies itself completely with one tradition. As a non-professional, you may come into contact with professionals who have been trained in and think in a particular way. This chapter sketches the principle approaches to and traditions of planning evident in the literature and in practice. Seven main approaches are identified: (1) the economic, (2) physical, (3) public administration, (4) social, (5) environmental, (6) collaborative and (7) sustainable. The chapter shows how the different strands of planning conceptualize people, what social divisions and sectoral groups the different approaches use, how they consider difference and diversity. The chapter offers a broad overview and is structured around a simple outline of each approach with one or more illustrations. The aim is to raise questions and stimulate thinking rather than provide a definitive model. By viewing them through different lenses, the impact of the approaches on different groups of people can be examined. For instance, the notion of the gender contract is used to test some of the assumptions behind the economic approach. The biological and social models of disability test the assumptions behind the physical model. In addition, the critique of the plan for Birmingham (England) using the lens of race provides a fresh insight into physical planning in the 1960s in the UK (Chan, 2003). The example of Berlin shows how physical planning has been used to express the city's identity, through qualitative improvements and in-fill projects, by applying the theory of 'critical reconstruction' which allows traces of historical development patterns to become exposed. The example of the South East Queensland plan by Margerum (2002) gives an insight into the application of the collaborative approach. Walby's (1990) theory of patriarchy is used to test the social approach to town planning. To effectively meet the needs and expectations of society in the future,

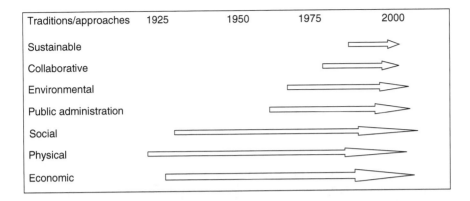

Figure 2.1 Approaches to planning – timeline

approaches to planning need to be explicit about their approach to difference. As a result, the analysis of problems and proposed solutions needs to become more relevant to the diverse communities of today and tomorrow. Situated in a particular space and time, each approach to and tradition of planning influences and is influenced by its socio-political context (Figure 2.1).

The issues planners identify, how problems become defined and what planners understand as their legitimate knowledge base, all relate to their socio-political contexts. Public health issues shaped modern planning in Western Europe from the late nineteenth and early twentieth centuries. Cullingworth and Nadin (2001) provide an historical overview of the origins of planning in Britain while Hall (2002a,b) takes a more international perspective. Urban regeneration has dominated the planning agenda since 1945 in Europe, and throughout the world since the 1990s sustainability has started to shape the process and content of planning. Wider currents of change affect the way in which governments respond. Since 1990, information technology, globalization, AIDS, climate change and continued urbanization have all impacted on planning issues, policies and possible outcomes.

Healey (1997) identified three strands of thought from which spatial planning has been woven: the economic, physical and the public administration traditions. Healey herself went on to map out her preferred, collaborative approach to planning. Inspired by the demands of the environmental and sustainability agendas, it provides an integrated and holistic response to planning issues and public policy. Included here is the social approach to town planning advocated by Greed (1999a) after Jacobs (1961). Sustainable development is seen as a distinct approach and the reader is also referred to Chapter 1. In reality, the planning adopted at any point becomes a fusion of a number of approaches.

THE ECONOMIC APPROACH

The economic approach to planning, as conceived during the late nineteenth century, focuses on and takes as its starting point the productive assets of nations and regions, their location and accessibility. Raw materials, sources of energy and transport form the heart of this approach, typified by the coal mining regions of Germany, the UK and the Eastern seaboard of the USA. Chicago – Illinois, the Yorkshire coalfields, the Ruhr region of Germany (Figure 2.2), all provide a legacy

Figure 2.2 Ruhr Valley, Germany

to the physical and economic growth as well as the environmental destruction often associated with this growth. The approach was driven by industrial invention and innovation.

The exhibits by major companies at the 1939 New York World's Fair reflect the consumerist future we have today (Corn and Horrigan, 1984). The public was encouraged to associate the image of the city of the future with high-tech transportation systems, the dominance of the car, highways and motorways, all of which would provide routes of escape from the city.

Table 2.1 indicates the vocabulary associated with the economic approach and the assumptions, both explicit and implicit, which it has made about equality and diversity.

The economic approach taken depends on the way countries organize and promote their productive assets. Centralized economies, represented by the Eastern Europe of the early twentieth century, controlled what and how much got produced through tight regulations and bureaucracies. In contrast, communitarians maximized productivity by creating company towns for workers next to factories and places of production. The world heritage site of Saltaire (2003) outside Bradford in England provides a fine example as does Guelph in Ontario, Canada, although it was never built as originally planned (Galt, 1985). Other economic approaches are more consumer-based and seek to increase the demand for products through fiscal and financial mechanisms. Using the vocabulary of neo-classical economics and the notion that science can help objectively develop policies, the economic approaches share a common goal of increasing people's demand for more material goods, euphemistically termed enhancing people's material well-being. The approach defines people as workers or non-workers, productive or non-productive, part-time or full-time. Class, as defined by income and type of paid work, has been a key identifier. Non-waged work (in the home) has gone completely unrecognized by the state. Those working part-time have a much lower status than those who work full-time. Those in poverty are not seen as representing a significant market for goods. Disabled people are seen as a cost to the productive sector with only limited buying power and their employment only possible with subsidies from the state.

Those who have highlighted the inequities of the traditional economic approach have stimulated some transformative thinking about the way in which organizations can operate in the marketplace. These have won widespread recognition. The 'In Business' programme on BBC Radio 4 featured the work of Prahalad (2003) who advocates the need for companies to recognize the scale of the cumulative buying power of the poor. Using India as an example, he showed how companies can adjust their production techniques to meet the needs of the poor by packaging goods in small quantities to match the income of the poor. Henderson (1995, 1996)

Table 2.1 The economic approach summarized

Aims	To manage the productive assets of nations and regions	
Vocabulary	*Categories*	*Classifications*
	Sectors	Socio-economic
	Workers	Income
	Employees	Sector
	Waged and unwaged	Productive/
	Full-time	unproductive,
	Part-time	market segments,
	Zero hours	supply factors,
	Class	demand factors
Assumptions	Unwaged work has no economic value	
	For the economy to function, the immediate extended family does the childcare	
	Those in poverty, including disabled people, do not represent a market for goods and services	
	Disabled people are a cost to the productive sector. The medical model predominates	
	Immigrants are seen as a source of labour or investment capital	
	Economists dominate as professionals	
	Power is located in the treasury and finance ministries	
Conceptions of space and place	Economic space	
Characteristics of space and place	Importance of relative space, time–distance–cost elements	
Policy responses	Strategic	
	Infrastructure solutions	
	Congestion reduction	
	Creating homes where jobs are	
	Infrastructure solutions	
	Clustering	
	Edge cities	
	New town expansion	

and Elson (1993) have long campaigned for models of the economy which recognize the contributions of the un-waged who, across the world, are mainly women (Johnson, 2001; Oxfam, 2002). Porter (2003) speaks about the need for business to become more proactive in economic development. He envisages businesses moving away from, what he terms, corporate social responsibility programmes. These, he says, amount to handouts to inner city poor communities. Instead what we need is a working partnership with communities to achieve sustainable economic development and regeneration.

THE ECONOMIC APPROACH THROUGH THE LENS OF THE GENDER CONTRACT

Using a feminist analysis, the traditional economic approach can be seen to rely on an unwritten contract between the state and households, and between women and men. The concept of the gender contract recognizes that at any particular time a tacit agreement exists between the genders, which defines what the different sexes actually do and what they can and should do. The social policies pursued by government then reflect the contract. In Sweden, between the 1930s and 1960s, Hirdman (1990) identified a 'housewife' contract which institutionalized separate gender roles. During the 1960s, as a result of the insecurity of the male wage, women demanded the right to work for a wage and involvement in the political process. The resulting political solution involved the promise of full employment for men or a state wage, while women received good housing and schooling. The 1950s and 1960s saw more women entering the labour market and experiencing the double role of housewife and paid worker. The unwritten equality contract of the 1960s which lasted until the mid-1980s was based on the state's desire to enable all adults to become economically independent. However, despite the increasing availability of universal childcare facilities, men and fathers have still not become more active in the home, even when further demands were made by women and men about balancing work and family to achieve a more equal status. Men who take time out are afraid of being perceived by management and colleagues as less committed. The concept of the gender contract does apply elsewhere. Observing the UK during the mid-1990s, Duncan (1994) saw a transitional phase in which the so-called 'housewife' contract had broken down with, as yet, no long-term replacement. Many women in the labour market, with families, experienced the double workload of paid work and homework, and single parents were excluded wholesale from the labour market as a result of inadequate childcare facilities (Yeandle, 1996). Almost a decade later, in the UK, there has been some shift in the relationship between women and men, and between women and the state, with the development of new fiscal tools, incentives and support for parents. The UK Women's Budget Group (WBG, 2003) lobbies the Treasury to highlight the requirements for a more equitable relationship between women and men taking into account socio-ethnic differences.

Although widely used, the term 'gender contract' is misleading in that it implies a mutual agreement between the sexes. However, the power relationship is anything but equal (Greer, 2000). If parliaments lack representativeness, in the sense of not having a gender balance, then social policy is likely to become less a mutually agreed contract between the sexes and more a contract in which one group imposes their will on another. The notion of the contract extends beyond the sexes. If parliaments and legislatures do not represent the ethnic diversity of a country, policies may well reproduce existing inequalities. So it is possible to see how the notion of a contract can apply between different ethnic groups and how the balance of power is crucial in determining who develops the stronger negotiating position. One of the key issues for the current decade is the political response to international population movements. The contract being offered in the UK is one where immigrants are welcome if (1) they are legitimate, (2) they fill gaps in the labour market ranging from low-paid service work to nursing and teaching or (3) they bring entrepreneurial enterprises and funding, and finally affirm a sense of Britishness.

The kind of changes brought about by planning policies and programmes can reinforce outdated notions of the relationships within households and between different communities. It can reinforce stereotypes of different ethnic and cultural groups. The need to ensure that policies do not simply re-enforce inequalities between women and men has been recognized for sometime. McDowell (1983) and Ford and Lewis (1984) wrote about the gender relations created by the new towns in the UK. The Greater London Council (GLC, 1986), Morris (1994), Booth and Gilroy (1996), Reeves (1996b) and more recently Darke, Ledwith and Woods (2000) have all illustrated the specific needs of women which planning needs to address. To date, however, much equality work in the field of spatial planning has focused on the implementation of policies at the local level. Useful checklists and guidelines have been produced to aid the work of policy makers (RTPI, 1995). The GLC in 1986 produced its Changing Places document; the Royal Town Planning Institute (RTPI) in 1989 produced Planning for Choice and Opportunity and in 1995 produced Planning for Women. As a consequence, many local authorities developed reputations for gender-sensitive policy work (Higgins and Davies, 1996).

Much of post-1945 planning in Europe and the USA reflects the economic approach and you can see the influence on regional and sub-regional planning with policies which, in effect, determine which groups of people can contribute to the economic well-being and social sustainability of their region. Studies have shown how the gendered nature of both regional planning (Ridder and Modderman, 1991) and the distribution of structural funds in Europe operate (Horelli, 1996; Horelli, Booth and Gilroy, 1997). These studies found that projects targeted towards or representing women's interests have aims and objectives different to those which are not women-orientated. In order to address some of these difficulties, it has been argued that strategic planning at the regional level should develop a multi-sectoral and integrated approach and ensure complementarity between environment, economic and social goals. The development of a more holistic approach exposes the conflicts between different sets of goals, actors and policies.

Studies of comprehensive planning and the regional policy process in Sweden found that male participants in the debate firmly believed that regional policies ought simply to focus on economic growth (Friberg, 1996; Friberg and Larsson, 1998). Environmental quality, a high priority for women, received less attention. The studies showed that a women's perspective is difficult to find in strategic planning because

Table 2.2 Developments in consciousness, movements and spatial planning

Types of consciousness (Cott)	Women's movements (Wekerle)	Relationship to spatial planning
Female consciousness	Maternalist movements	Estate design
Community consciousness	Place-based movements	Neighbourhood planning
Global consciousness	Solidarity movements	Agenda 21 strategies
European consciousness	Gender-based movements	Structural funds Strategic planning

it has become associated with 'low level' planning of the neighbourhood or community. This analysis confirms the work of feminist historians and others who explain the local focus in terms of the role women tend to play in the family (Cott, 1989; Wekerle, 1998). They developed a triptych typology of women's movements, which show that, in the past, gender issues focused on the level of the individual and the family as a result of the social constructions of the role of women and men. Hence, the 'maternalist movement', based on Cott's female consciousness, focuses on the survival and well-being of families and communities and so includes projects relating to women's violence and food security. Over time this local focus widened to the community, and the second of the typologies presented by Wekerle (1998), the 'place based movement' extends women's caring to the wider community. Based on Cott's communal consciousness, it includes projects which highlight the problems of pollution, contamination and objections to development proposals. The third typology, the 'feminist locality based movement', which relates to Cott's feminist consciousness focuses on achieving access to resources and participation in the local state. During the 1990s, as the perspectives continued to widen in scope, the fourth UN World Conference on Women in Beijing signalled a new level of global consciousness (UN, 1995). The 1990s have seen a continued growth of European consciousness (Table 2.2).

Despite sustainable development and the recognized importance of the environment, the drive for economic growth has all but superceded environmental and social considerations. The economic conception of space creates an emphasis on the need to reduce time spent transporting goods and materials as well as journey to work times for commuters.

PHYSICAL APPROACH

Based on the skills of architects and engineers from the nineteenth century, the physical approach focuses on the development of towns and cities to promote

Table 2.3 The physical approach summarized

Aims	To manage the physical development of towns and cities to promote health, economy, convenience and beauty	
Vocabulary	*Categories*	*Classifications*
	Citizens	Households
	The public	Jobs
	Residents	Market segments
	Business people	
	Visitors	
Assumptions	The family unit is made up of a heterosexual couple with two children	
	Equality means treating everyone the same	
	The medical-biological model dominates	
	The architect and engineer as professionals dominate	
	Technical solutions are needed	
	Power located with developers, landowners and lawyers	
Conceptions of space and place	Three-dimensional space	
Characteristics of space and place	Importance of function and aesthetics	
	Technical responses	
Policy responses	Master planning	
	Land-use planning	
	Creation of order	

health, economy, convenience and beauty (Table 2.3). Often called the classical movement, the approach evolved to create functional and aesthetically pleasing environments or social utopias. By the 1920s, many countries had already become essentially urban with over half their populations living in cities or towns of 2,500 people or more. Following the First World War, Corn and Horrigan (1984) document a new spirit inspiring a radical vision for urban design which was to be crystallized by architects such as Courbusier, Walter Gropius and Ludwig Mies van der Rohe. Commentators agree that by the end of the 1920s in the USA, there was unanimity about the form of the future city; towering, complex and rational. Courbusier's City for three million created the definitive modern image of the city: 'stretching across vast, flat space – resembling more a game board than a real landscape – the city was filled with widely spaced, rigorously modern skyscrapers of uniform height' (Corn and Horrigan, 1984: 38). The antidote to this almost hysterical drive for urbanism came from Frank Lloyd Wright, who in the 1930s designed Broadacre City for 1,400 families set in open countryside. Lois Howe, who came second to Sophia Hayden in the Women's Building Competition in 1893, played an increasingly important role in the design of domestic scale architecture (Torre, 1977).

In many parts of Europe, the modernist physical tradition was more muted, leaving at least some remnants of the historic and valuable physical heritage, beloved of tourists and communities today. Surveys have shown that 80 per cent of tourists to Edinburgh come because of the townscape and heritage. The success of the BBC TV programme 'Restoration' shows the depth of feeling people in the UK have for their heritage (BBC, 2003). However, the physical approach to planning has tended to see people as homogeneous, able-bodied, white and male. It depicts the family as the basic unit of policy and more heterogeneous households only later becoming recognized units. In this approach equality means treating everyone the same, without recognizing that the norm to which everything is referenced is often the male norm in terms of average size, height and reach. The biological-medical model of disability dominates, meaning that people who cannot function in society as it is become confined to their homes or institutions. It is only relatively recently that legislation has given disabled people some rights to an accessible environment, although the legislation still reflects a strong medical as opposed to social model of disability (Crookson, 2003). The biological-medical model which developed during the nineteenth century still plays an influential role in the way we, as individuals and members of society, respond to disability rights, gender and race equality. The biologically based models evolved in the nineteenth century with the development of scientific knowledge and the gradual predominance of the scientific approach over religion. The application of the biological model to disability leads to a medical response to the effects of disability and the treatment of impairments as diseases. When we see disease or a health condition as the root cause of an issue or problem, then we use a medical model of understanding. By viewing disability as a medical issue, the management of the disability at the political level involves modifying or reforming health care policy. Society places the onus on the individual disabled person to access this medical support. When we see the social environment and culture as the root cause of disability, we use a social model of understanding. Using this model, disability becomes a problem created by society in terms of the way in which people think about and perceive disabled people. The management of the issues then requires broader social action to raise awareness and change attitudes and behaviour. In relation to race, the biological model associates with a scientific response which looks at the relationship between physical attributes and mental abilities and the subsequent pigeon-holing of people into particular social roles. In relation to gender, the biological model leads to responses which deal with physiological differences between women and men. A very topical example of the biological-physiological approach can be seen in the lack of consideration given to the design and provision of public toilets. If physiological differences between women and men were taken into account, a greater provision for women would result than is currently the case (Greed, 2003).

A key challenge for planners is to understand that their professional activity affects equality and diversity. Perhaps because of past failures, planners and related professionals feel wary about reflecting on the ways in which planning could promote equality. A survey to find out how planners in Northern Ireland think they should be addressing issues of cultural identity for instance, as set out in the Good Friday Agreement (NIO, 1998), showed that most believed they should get involved, although most were not sure how, and a number took the view that the key determinant of issues (in area plans) are concerns of environmental amenity and accessibility – not cultural issues. Over half of those responding stated that issues of cultural identity should not be dealt with more explicitly in development or area plans, and a typical response reflecting this view can be paraphrased as follows: 'the development plan is a regulatory process for controlling development on land as a finite resource. How can cultural identity infiltrate this process?' (Neill, 2000).

BIRMINGHAM'S CITY DEVELOPMENT PLAN 1960 REVISITED

Some academics have started to re-examine the kinds of assumptions made by physical development plans of the 1960s (Chan, 2003). The analysis of planning in post-war Birmingham, England, reveals evidence that physical plans treated racial groups as 'others' (Figure 2.3). Chan's (2003) study re-evaluates the assumptions underlying post-war planning and reconstruction and challenges our understanding of the relationship between immigration and the city. During the post-1945 era, cities in England were rebuilt after one of the most destructive world wars. Chan uses the notion of privileging to highlight the way in which different groups of people were given an enhanced status in planning and housing policies. Birmingham published its first official post-war planning agenda in the form of the Development Plan (City of Birmingham, 1960). Although described as essentially 'a rationalization of conflicting land uses' (Cherry, 1994: 194), Chan argues that the CBDP did more than rationalize existing land uses and that:

> both the presence and absence of new British citizens were a persistent part of the
> rebuilding of the city, and furthermore, that they became a definitional, yet
> sometimes elided [omitted] limit to the ideal of land use planning. Post-war planners
> were already dealing with different entities – including overseas migrants – but as
> an antagonism to it (Chan, 2003: 79).

Two concepts underpinned the plan – congestion and spaciousness. The defining concept was the notion of congestion: housing congestion, congested inner city, traffic congestion, the need to relieve congestion with respect to shopping and business areas. The second concept, spaciousness, meant creating a green

Figure 2.3 Birmingham

setting with house and gardens, wider roads and parkways set amongst green and open land. The conurbation report produced by the West Midlands Group stated that spaciousness would be dependent on a 'balance between immigration and emigration' (West Midlands Group, 1946: 200). Spaciousness and congestion 'were never simply about land use ... the design of the city involved a number of interwoven assumptions made by planners and policy makers of an idealized population size of urban agglomerations' (Chan, 2003: 70). In this context Birmingham underwent a policy shift from expansionism to retrenchment. The 1947 Town and Country Planning Act required local authorities to define a target population figure which then made it possible to calculate population overspill. The strategic guidance for the Birmingham plan reflected a particular view of post-war migrants.

> to avoid the danger of congestion, the population should be allowed to continue to grow only to the extent that is equivalent to the natural excess of births over deaths. Policy should therefore be directed to effecting an even balance between immigration and emigration (West Midlands Group, 1946: 84–85).

Despite the calculations which showed that natural increase would far exceed increases from immigration, it was the latter which planners sought to check. This 'privileging' of the social process of natural increase over immigration reinforces the notion of 'the other'. The Conurbation report frequently positions immigrant as a synonym for social disorder and overcrowding. For Chan, 'this categorical split (natural increase and immigration) encourages the reader to consider the way in which planning persistently composes its ideals through privileging and relegating different identities in a multiple field of uneven social relations' (Chan, 2003: 79). Chan draws two implications from this: 'firstly that in this differential marking, identities co-exist and secondly that each identity becomes mutually constitutive of its other in a syntactic play between absences and presences. The posing, privileging or normalization of natural increase, spaciousness and physical planning alludes to the existence of a heterogeneity, which may be silenced in the planning language' (Chan, 2003: 79, forthcoming). 'The evocation of uniformity by planners in this way should be read as an attempted closure and or a contextual privilege given to a certain aesthetic and its visualisation' (Chan, 2003: 79).

BERLIN AND THE PHYSICAL APPROACH

Berlin provides a contemporary example of a plan illustrating the physical approach (Neill, 2004). The Planwerk Innenstadt, drawn up in 1996, was eventually adopted by the Berlin Senat on 18 May 1999. The opening of the Berlin wall in 1989 revealed the two separate cities which had developed under two very different socio-political structures over 50 years. Planwerk Innenstadt was seen as one way of integrating the two cities into one, re-creating and strengthening relationships between the two city centres to re-expose a common history and future through the use of bold strategic concepts. Planwerk aims to create an attractively urban inner city that reaches from Alexanderplatz to the west of the city centre and which offers an overarching structure with an interconnected network of attractive public spaces. The plan aims to express Berlin's identity, improve the conditions for living and for retail, culture, hotels and services. It proposes to do this through qualitative improvements and in-fill projects applying the theory of 'critical reconstruction' which allows traces of historical development patterns to become exposed, thus ensuring that the redeveloped structure does not disown any phase of Berlin's development history. The kinds of questions dealt with through the public Stadforum illustrate the physical planning tradition at work. These included: re-examining post-war design in the east and west; analysis of public spaces and traffic in the inner city; and new development and building types – public, open and green spaces. Critics of the master plan see it as a means of destabilizing present building and land-use arrangements and re-imposing the pre-war street layout with no regard for the existing residents. They stress the historical significance of Berlin – the international conflict between two systems in the second half of the twentieth century which should be made perceptible for present-day tourists and future generations. This plan is based on a concept of history which sees the post-war historical period as abnormal, historical and ultimately destructive (Hain, 2003: 78).

The optimism surrounding re-unification which inspired the 1992 spatial development plan for the whole of Berlin was short-lived. The predictions for new build and private investment foundered on a collapsing economy and increasing unemployment rates.

Berlin uses physical planning to protect tangible memories of the history of the divided city in the future structure. The physical planning of post-1945 Birmingham reflected assumptions about the immigrant communities which are now being explored for the first time.

PUBLIC ADMINISTRATION

In addition to the economic and physical approaches, the public administration approach has been identified as a key planning tradition (Healey, 1997). The public administration or policy analysis approach evolved in the United States of America and has since been adopted with enthusiasm in Europe. It aims to achieve both efficiency and effectiveness in the goals of public agencies. One of the consequences of this has been that the public and politicians have tended to see planning more as a bureaucratic and negative process than a truly visionary activity. Table 2.4 summarizes the characteristics of the approach.

The development plans produced by most cities in the UK during the 1990s reflect the public administration approach. The drive to provide a coherent and up-to-date statement for cities as a whole led planners to create a policy document which would first and foremost manage development in a consistent way and provide a series of statements headlining a physical vision. The project management of the development plan process was one aspect of the managerial approach which was less well developed in the early 1990s, although it is now a common feature (ODPM, 2003d). Fusion has led to plans and planning exhibiting a combination of approaches. The Glasgow City Council (2003) fuses together the managerial and physical approaches with the strong urban design tradition of planning in Glasgow based on the city's rich architectural traditions. The production of a single plan for Glasgow is a significant step. It provides a focus for private sector investment and aspires to facilitate the convergence of all relevant public sector programmes for physical change in the coming years (Glasgow City Council, 2003: 1).

As planners have come to understand the city as a complex social system in which only some aspects express themselves in terms of physical buildings or locational arrangements, they have argued that it is no longer possible to talk about the physical city versus the social city or the economic city, or the political city or the intellectual city (Horrock et al., 1972). It is a synthesis of all of these.

Table 2.4 The public administration approach summarized

Aims	To achieve both efficiency and effectiveness in the goals of public agencies	
Vocabulary	*Categories*	*Classifications*
	Customers	Units
	Clients	Inputs
	Internal markets	Outputs
	Publics	Performance targets
		Quality regimes
Assumptions	Equality seen as incompatible with efficiency and effectiveness	
	Equal opportunities seen as a human resource management issue	
	Both the medical and social models are recognized	
	The planner as a professional must use their expertise to create an efficient system	
	Power lies with lawyers, finance specialists, chief executives and professional managers	
Conceptions of space and place	Institutional space	
	Importance of virtual space	
Characteristics of space and place	Importance of networks	
	Informal and formal structures	
Policy responses	Performance management	

SOCIAL TOWN PLANNING

The term 'social planning' was first used in the early 1970s to describe the support provided in the new towns for new incomers and residents (Horrock *et al.*, 1972; Mayer, 1972). The need for community planners was recognized in the UK at the time when new towns developed and whole communities were decamped from inner cities to outlying towns in the 1950s and 1960s (Rein, 1970). Given our better understanding of what makes communities strong, resilient and sustainable, these social engineering projects would happen in a very different way today. The social model has, in the past, been associated with a welfare charitable approach or an individual rights approach. The social model of race leads to a focus on cultural diversity, bi-culturalism and multi-culturalism. The application of the social model to gender, in the first instance, leads to equal rights (to work) and more recently a right to work which takes account of responsibilities and the need for work/home balance. The social model advocated by Oliver (1995) made possible a profound and radical shift whereby disability was no longer seen as a 'function of an individual's material impairment and her supposed lack of a normal body, but instead is viewed as the result of socially imposed barriers such that disablement resides in ablest environments and not in the disabled body per se' (Fawcett, 2000: 34). With the development and acceptance of the social model came the recognition that disability or the loss or limitation of opportunities to take part in the everyday life of the community is the result of discrimination (Campbell and Oliver, 1996; Oliver and Mercer, 2002). The Person Centred Planning approach (Table 2.5) developed by professionals and people with mental impairments and learning disabilities helps illustrate the key differences between approaches led by and controlled by professionals and those which evolve as a result of a partnership between the individual and the professional (O'Brien and O'Brien, 2000).

Feminists and medical sociologists have highlighted the weaknesses of the medical and social models. Feminist disability theorists such as Fawcett (2000) critique the way in which the social model overlooks the role of the body and experience in its concrete, material manifestations of impairment. The model positions disabled people in ways that force a public/private split of their bodies using the concepts of impairment (biological) and disability (social construction) – a split that leads to a fragmented self-conception of a person's disability. For example, seeking medical attention for an impairment ends up a personal and private medical matter, one that is independent of and inconsistent with the notion of disability as a socially constructed, public matter. Shakespeare and Corker (2002) argue that the very success of the social model is its weakness in that it has become so much of a sacred cow of an ideology that to criticize it amounts to challenging the very foundation of disability

Table 2.5 Understanding diversities

	Medical/rehabilitation view	Social/independent living view
Terms for defining problems	Impairment Skill Deficiency	Dependence on professionals, relatives and others who take over control of life
Where are the problems located?	In the person	In the environment and the way services do their work
What's the solution?	Professional intervention	Removal of barriers, advocacy
Who is the person?	Patient/client	Person/citizen
Who's in charge?	Professional	Citizen
What defines results?	Maximum possible individual functioning as judged by professional	Living independently (being in control of your life regardless of how much assistance you need to do so)

Source: O'Brien and O'Brien (2000).

Table 2.6 The social approach summarized

Aims	To integrate the physical planning and policy making to solve a wide range of social problems	
Vocabulary	*Categories*	*Classifications*
	Communities, individuals	Social class
	Winners and losers	Social status
		Stage in family cycle
		Disadvantaged groups
		Life-stage
		Life-course
Assumptions	Many social ills do derive from the environment in which people live	
	Professionals work with and articulate community concerns through plans	
	Equality constructed as social justice with an emphasis on poverty	
	Social model predominates	
	Power lies with communities and politicians	
Conceptions of space and place	Social space/perceptual space	
	Personal space	
Characteristics of space and place	Importance of relationships	
	Paternalistic	
Policy responses	Integration or segregation	

rights. Whereas Shakespeare and Corker advocate a replacement of the social model, Fawcett (2000) argues that, in the very least, disability theorists need to reconsider the tendencies of the social model to speak for all disabled people.

Today social planning means something very different. Social town planning (Table 2.6) represents the position taken by a growing number of practitioners and academics who call for an approach to planning which takes into account more fully the diversity of human beings who live in communities, whether large cities or tiny villages (Greed, 1997; Friedman and Douglass, 1998).

The social identities of sex, race and age become more than descriptive categories. People's experience of issues such as crime are structured by age, race, gender and disability (Pain, 2001; Priestley, 2001, 2003). The social approach to planning builds on a whole series of critiques of the status quo. Mannheim's (1950) critique of the class-based nature of planning demonstrates the location of power and why certain communities are forced to live next to noxious activities and developments. A whole series of commentators and interest groups provide critiques of the disabling environments created by planning, urban regeneration and urban design. The racialized nature of space and place has been criticized by Thomas (1997).

WALBY'S FEMINIST CRITIQUE

Walby (1990, 1994) provides a powerful feminist critique of society and during the 1980s and early 1990s was influential in providing the theoretical reasoning for women's input into the budget process, now well established through the International Women's Budget Group (*Financial Times*, 2003). The feminist critique is based on the notion that patriarchy is a system of social structures and practices, in which men dominate, that oppress or exploit women. It is a collective framework and does not infer that every man acts in a dominant way (Duncan, 1994). Walby (1990: 1178) named six arenas in which men's domination of women manifests itself in society: paid work, household production, the state, male violence, sexuality and culture. They recognize the heterogeneity of women's experience, although they require interpretation in different cultural contexts. Paid work has for a long time been seen as a measure of women's emancipation and independence. The extent to which policies and programmes genuinely facilitate women's access to the labour market has become one of the key measures of success of the EUs structural fund programmes. As Walby argues, paid work is only emancipatory if it is linked to the availability of childcare and if jobs exist near to or are accessible to people's homes. Paid work is not emancipatory if it is low-paid, insecure and so dangerous that it is likely to maim and disable. Applied to planning and the built environment, which after all creates the physical manifestation of patriarchy, the question is how to create opportunities for paid work which are easy to get to and involve working in well-designed work places inside or outside the home. It means creating work opportunities accessible by public transport and with appropriate social facilities. Sensitive change can be brought about through the integration of transport and land-use policies and recognition that childcare facilities have a status at least equal to car parking in national planning guidance. Computer technology and new communication systems may provide more people with access to paid work, provided relevant training is available (Wilkinson, 2002; Reeves, 2002c). The second arena through which men exercise their power relates to household production and the nature of households in terms of size and make-up. This is determined by many social and economic factors as well as the availability of suitable properties. Future housing needs are assessed through an analysis of population and household trends. Traditionally this has involved providing a figure for all new housing. However, the failure of the housing and planning systems to provide for the needs of women and men in terms of house types and designs illustrates Walby's patriarchy at work. For practical purposes housing projections should provide details of the need for specific types of housing to meet the needs of a whole range of households taking into account the work on the suitability of existing forms of housing whether suburbia or high-rise living (Weisman, 1992; RTPI, 2003).

The third arena is the state. If equality between women and men does not exist at the political level, the 'state' may be representing gendered political forces which reflect the nature of patriarchy operating at national and local level. Policies may then simply reflect political priorities defined by men. Where political forums are gendered, the potential to perpetuate patriarchy remains. The Welsh Assembly and Scottish Parliament both have a better representation of women than the UK Parliament. Studies are underway to assess what benefits these political changes have brought to women and men (MacKay and Chaney, 2003). Planners need to consider whether the approach taken to transport, shopping and housing reflects the priorities of people throughout the community. For instance, the traditional emphasis on the car and the current emphasis on high-technology transport systems such as the tram and light rail reflect a form of patriarchy where large capital infrastructure responses to problems are put forward as the only solutions. Other examples could include:

- policies supporting out-of-town shopping centres which have led to a decline in town and local centres;
- the promotion of cities as sports capitals which leads to the closure of many local facilities;
- the promotion of owner-occupation at the expense of social rented housing.

A further arena in which men's domination of women manifests is through male violence. Feminists have long campaigned for women to have adequate protection against violence perpetuated by men, especially in the home. Violence manifests itself in a number of ways in the private and public spheres. At the extreme, violence leads to death, rape and physical abuse, although attacks need not have a physical manifestation, if they involve mental abuse. The environment can play a key role in creating opportunities for crime to take place. Environments which have surveillance and good lighting can minimize the possibility of attacks occurring. The safer cities campaigns have encouraged the creation of environments with fewer subways, better lighting and landscaping (Leicester City Council, 1991; Wekerle and Whitzman, 1995; Dame and Grant, 2002).

Feminists contend that women's sexual practices are generally controlled by one man in the private sphere and in the public sphere by what Walby termed 'subjugating discourse' which leads to male censure of forms of sexual conduct (Priestley, 2001). Public consultation exercises need to recognize that women are a diverse group and that the needs and views of as many representative groups as possible will provide a richer picture of community needs. The domination by men of the media, educational management, the church, theatre and the arts, leaves these institutions open to criticism that they reproduce inequalities between women and men and fail to identify positive opportunities to meet the needs of women as well as men (Williams, 1994; Brierley, 2003). The physical manifestation of this in the physical environment is much more prevalent than people might think and takes many forms. Attacks on the senses in the form of insensitive public art or the continued existence in the public realm of statues which reflect the historic dominance of men, the monumental design of many public buildings and spaces, all reflect a particularly patriarchal approach.

Some may find Walby's analysis too radical and too extreme. If so, then the next time you visit your nearest town centre or city start to look at it through her eyes. Look for places, which could be much more sensitive to the people who are actually using the space. Think about the people who are not represented in the places and ask yourself why this might be. You will find yourself starting to look at environments more inclusively and as a result come up with different design solutions. In this way we can ensure that those involved in the planning and design of cities do so in new ways. Walby also distinguished between private and public patriarchy as well as the type and degree of patriarchy. These concepts and dimensions are helpful in the context of planning, regeneration and sustainable communities. To take transport as an example, private patriarchy affects the ability of women to gain access to the 'family' car; public patriarchy affects the nature of the transport system, highly car dependent with an emphasis on big engineering projects, strategic links and high-technology public transport systems as opposed to dial a bus and minibuses which are much more flexible and responsive and in some cases run by volunteers. The 'degree' or level of intensity of patriarchy affects the extent of choice, control and access to new high-technology transport facilities and their ability to match day-to-day needs. Private and public patriarchies influence shopping, the kinds of leisure facilities available, the location of work places, the design of town centres, the nature of open space and the design and location of housing. Private patriarchy has a generational aspect to it in that older women in the UK are less likely than men to drive. Out-of-town shopping centres are by their nature less accessible by public transport. Where the shops locate on the edge of town, shopping trips for many older households are still controlled by the driver who is more likely to be male (Bowlby, 1984, 1985; Reeves, 1996b). Public patriarchy affects the nature of the shopping experience; for example, the unwillingness, until the last ten years or so, for stores in Britain to provide childcare facilities. The gendered shopping experience reflects the operation of private and public patriarchy. A 1994 study by Omnis for the Consumer Association looked at out-of-town and town centre shopping and revealed that women found town centres more accessible than out-of-town centres and women looked on town centres as better sources of bargains with more choice than did men (Taylor and Nelson, 1994; Reeves, 1996b, 2002a).

ENVIRONMENTAL PLANNING

While economic planning and social planning put the economy and people respectively at the centre, environmental planning puts the natural environment at the core. Historically, the approach was associated with Native Americans and Native Aboriginals and Maori people who, with their deep understanding of the natural world, tried to protect areas sacred to their way of life. The approach is also associated with individuals who campaign to protect wilderness areas in the USA, under threat from increasing urbanization and the development of highways, through the creation of National Parks. Similar movements in New Zealand, Canada, UK and mainland Europe led to the creation of National Parks which provide protection. Voluntary organizations like The National Trust (founded by Octavia Hill in 1895) and the Royal Society for the Protection of Birds (RSPB, 2003) in the UK are successful charities which own and manage large areas of protected land. Alongside these are campaign organizations such as Greenpeace (2003) which monitors the activities of governments and private sector companies. Countries which practice an integrated environmental approach to planning are in the minority and include the Netherlands (CEP, 2000).

Commentators in the UK have interpreted environmental planning as a regulatory process which runs parallel to and very distinct from spatial planning (Cullingworth

Table 2.7 The environmental approach summarized

Aims	To protect the natural environment from degradation and destruction	
Vocabulary	*Categories*	*Classifications*
	Protector	Voluntary
	Exploiter	Charities
	User	Campaign and
	Eco-warriors	lobby groups
	Eco-consumers	Radicals
	Eco-babies	Activists
Assumptions	That development does not affect everyone equally That the poor and vulnerable are likely to experience relatively worse environmental conditions	
Conceptions of space and place	Green space, open space, protected space	
Characteristics of space and place	Openness, greenness, biodiversity, wilderness	
Policy responses	Protection, enhancement, green belts, national parks, site designation	

and Nadin, 2001; RCEP, 2003). The legislation relating to air pollution, clean water and noise pollution are seen as material to decisions about the use of land but not central to planning legislation. Environmental planning is something which is much more evident in mainland Europe, Scandinavia and countries such as the Netherlands, where wilderness planning forms an important part of regional spatial planning. The EU Directives on environmental assessment have been crucial in ensuring that the environmental impacts of economic proposals are considered. The 1992 UN Conference on the Human Environment was a key event and in the same year the EC determined that economic expansion should not be an end in itself and that special attention be paid to protection of the environment. The approach to environmental planning outlined here and summarized in Table 2.7 pre-dates and is distinct from sustainable development as set out in the Brundtland Report (1987b) and the UK Sustainable Development Commission (SDC, 2004).

COLLABORATIVE APPROACH

Collaborative planning is a normative approach and in this sense has similarities to sustainable development. Its strengths are that it recognizes the need to make use of expertise from both professionals and communities of interest in order to identify key planning problems and appropriate solutions which are owned by everyone. The key features of the ideal collaborative approach are people-sensitive, sharing of power, listening and building consensus. It involves recognizing the complete range of knowledge and experiences available. To do justice to collaborative planning, the reader is urged to study Healey (1997). It is often seen as an unachievable ideal and yet to illustrate how it works, Healey has pointed to the planning approaches of many local planning authorities including the GLC and Sheffield which undertook extensive public involvement as part of the process of creating their citywide plans (Alty and Darke, 1987; Reeves, 1996b).

Critics still say that collaborative planning focuses too much on process rather than outcomes (Harris, 2002). Yet by doing so it highlights how outcomes can be influenced by process. The traditions of economic and physical planning had become discredited in many arenas as a result of the outcomes being imposed on communities and there was seen to be a serious need to consider how planning outcomes should come about. In this sense, planning is seen as a style of governance rather than a technical profession. There is a need to focus on process not only to ensure that the range of interests are involved at each stage of the process but also to effect changes in the nature of outcomes – for example, by ensuring that those disabled by environments are involved in creating solutions. Collaborative planning represents a consensus-building approach to urban and regional change (Healey,

Table 2.8 The collaborative approach summarized

Aims	To develop a consensus approach to urban and regional change by viewing planning as a style of governance	
Vocabulary	*Categories*	*Classifications*
	Clients	Cultural
	Stakeholders	Public/private
	Publics	agencies
	Communities	Business
	Agencies	Community
		Political
Assumptions	Public policy and planning are seen as social processes through which ways of valuing and ways of acting are constructed by participants (Healey, 1997: 9) As such, collaborative planning recognizes the diversity of stakeholders and that much work happens outside the formal agencies of government Communities are diverse and live in one or more relational worlds	
Conceptions of space and place	Shared, multi-dimensional, socially made, institutional	
Characteristics of space and place	Multiple meanings Pluralist Changing, opening out Formal and informal	
Policy responses	Inclusive, open, accountable, involving power sharing, social learning, listening about experiences	

1997). It has a very practical orientation in that it is concerned with how communities organize to improve the quality of places. The approach is designed to provide a framework for understanding as well as a framework for practical action (Table 2.8). It has the potential to be inclusive, open, transparent and transformative and as such potentially more receptive to diversity and equality issues.

SOUTH EAST QUEENSLAND (SEQ), AUSTRALIA

The Australian South East Queensland Regional Planning process illustrates aspects of this approach (Margerum, 2002). South East Queensland (SEQ, 2003) is one of the fastest growing regions with a population of 2.2 million, set to increase by a further 1 million by 2011. The rapid growth and urban sprawl threaten the very amenities which attract people to the region. When the Premier of the South East Queensland launched the regional planning process in 1990, he pledged a collaborative approach. Margerum's study looks at the process five years on and focuses on the planning and land-use policy relating to habitat and conservation, recreation and open space.

Drawing on the literature, interviews with local government and state officials and a review of plan documents, Margerum (2002) assessed the SEQ collaborative process using the following criteria:

- including the full range of stakeholders;
- including public participation and involvement;
- supporting and facilitating the process;
- establishing a common problem definition or shared task;
- organizing the process in terms of ground rules and agendas;
- engaging participants, jointly search information and invent new options;
- reaching agreement through consensus.

The evaluation involved looking at whether the goals were clear, and whether there was evidence of the use of sound theory about intervention. In addition, it was evaluated in terms of whether planning objectives were integrated with other object-ives, whether there was support from stakeholders and the public, and whether the structures maximized interaction between stakeholders and the public. The researchers concluded that the planning process was conducted in a collaborative way with ongoing co-ordination between councils particularly for implementation purposes, shared understanding of data and a regional perspective among local governments. However, the study showed limited public input and the concentration of power in the highest-level committees in the regional government. This particular example of the collaborative process was not as inclusive as the process envisaged by Healey, and Margerum's evaluation revealed no explicit evidence of ethno-cultural perspective.

SUSTAINABLE PLANNING

The sustainability agenda embodies the ideas of the Rio Declaration (UN, 1992), and reflects what many planners have sought to achieve for decades in shaping future places and spaces, whilst taking a measured look at the economic, environmental and social implications of proposals. Promoted through the UN, this approach has gained international recognition relatively quickly with a common language which planners across the world can understand and relate to. Many hoped that the promotion of sustainable development would lead to a thorough consideration of the environmental consequences of development although many argue this has not materialized. Today there are a number of different models of sustainable development, and the key approaches have been discussed in Chapter 1. As Table 2.9 shows, the

Table 2.9 The sustainable approach summarized

Aims	*Shaping future places and spaces taking a measured look at the economic, environmental and social implications of proposals*	
Vocabulary	*Categories* Social Economic Environmental Institutional	*Classifications* Degrees of disadvantage, capital Income/household type Resources base
Assumptions	This will depend on the model being used One model will start from the premise that economic development can bring about environmental improvement Another model will start from the premise that the environment provides the basis for all economic and social development	
Conceptions of space and place	Local Global Glocal	
Characteristics of space and place	Holistic Interrelated Stewardship	
Policy responses	Environmentally driven response will tend to be more protective An economically driven response will tend to look on the environment as a resource and society as the culprit A socially motivated response will look to improve people's quality of life by reducing the environmental impact of economic development	

interpretation given to sustainable development will determine how diversity and equality issues are treated.

The UK approach is based on the notion of sustainable growth and the need to accommodate growth. The Deputy Prime Minister launched the Communities Plan (Sustainable Communities: Building for the future) in February 2003 (ODPM, 2003e). It sets out a long-term programme of action for delivering sustainable communities in both urban and rural areas. It aims to tackle housing supply issues in the South East, low demand in other parts of the country and the quality of our public spaces. Sustainable communities are seen as meeting the

> diverse needs of existing and future residents, their children and other users and contributing to a high quality of life and providing opportunity and choice. They achieve this in ways that make effective use of natural resources, enhance the environment, promote social cohesion and inclusion and strengthen economic prosperity (Egan, 2004).

NEWCASTLE, NORTHERN IRELAND

The community-led plan for Newcastle illustrates the use of sustainability as a framework for local planning. Down and Ards Council was in the process of producing a local plan (which was published in 2002) and the community chose to make their contribution by producing their own plan. Newcastle lies nestling on the east coast of Northern Ireland and with a population of just over 10,000, the town has the air of a place which has seen better days and which looks forward to better days ahead (Figure 2.4). The recent Rough Guide, on the one hand, praises the town's setting in the Mourne Mountains and, on the other, describes the main street 'as nothing more than a soulless strip of amusement arcades, fast food outlets and tacky souvenir stores' (Greenwood *et al.*, 2003: 722).

The community chose to use a conception of sustainable development as its starting point because it offered a practical and holistic way of investigating the problems and opportunities facing the town and its setting. 'A town plan which deals only with the physical and visible features which occupy land, cannot itself answer all the desired ideals set out in the sustainable development principles' (Forbes, 2001: 5). In line with the Venn model, the Newcastle community group felt that the town should develop in harmony with its natural environment. The community

Figure 2.4 Newcastle Co. Down, NI

planning exercise used the social, economic and environmental facets of sustainable development. The social principle (quality of life) means

> tackling social disadvantage and meeting the needs of all in the community by a careful study and response to needs for housing, local services, educational opportunities, recreation and personal security. The economic principle means keeping money circulating locally through local businesses, by creating local jobs and training, projects which demonstrate the application of advanced technologies in recycling, energy conservation and building techniques. It also means supporting locally owned businesses and service providers to retain as much income in the local economy. The environmental principle means protecting the environment, and calls for everyone to use this hugely important asset wisely by looking carefully at how to use the exceptional natural surroundings for economic gain in a way which does not damage those surroundings by welcoming development which promotes sustainability (Forbes, 2001: 5).

The participative ethos of sustainability can be seen through the community-based process involving a planner living in the community, working voluntarily, committed to the place, committed to public involvement and committed to sustainable futures. Jean Forbes embarked on the ambitious task of facilitating a vision for the town of Newcastle when she moved from Glasgow to Northern Ireland. Planning Newcastle for 2020 is the result (Forbes, 2001, 2003). Between January 1999 and May 2000, she ran a series of workshops with members of the public, followed by articles in the local paper, the *Mourne Observer* (2001) culminating in a public exhibition in November 2000. She produced at least three drafts of the collected ideas of the community and circulated them widely for comment. First, through the local plan, people voiced concerns about the definition of the town's limits in the interest of protecting a unique landscape of the mountain area, countryside and watercourses (Table 2.10). Second local people expressed concern that the character of different

Table 2.10 Summary of recommendations in the Newcastle Community Plan

1. Define the development envelope and give the town a sharp clear edge and stick to it
2. To preserve the local character within the envelope, apply higher density standards in the town centre and lower densities outside
3. Give priority to the refurbishment of existing buildings and reuse vacant sites
4. Define a green network of paths and green spaces, to link together the town and the country
5. Focus attention on a flagship development to serve the whole community
6. Re-organise vehicle circulation to enable town centre regeneration
7. Focus special conservation measures on the harbour and the historic parts of the town

Source: Forbes (2001).

parts of the town deserved recognition and enhancing with new development, and third the economic and social heart of the town needs special treatment. The community wanted to see the future change managed in a sustainable way using the principles identified to provide a focus for public and private investment.

CONCLUSION

It is important for planners and those engaged with planning to understand the different approaches which may be taken and the assumptions each make about people who make up communities. Readers are invited to explore the types of plans in their areas and to assess their approach to people. What seems certain is that all the approaches make different assumptions about the people who make up the community.

I started the research for this chapter, thinking that perhaps one approach to planning is needed and that sustainable development would be the ideal or preferred approach. I have come to the view that the approach taken will depend on the context and that each approach benefits from an infusion of sustainability and the social perspective which provides a series of lenses through which the needs of a diverse community can be understood. In many countries, where the legislative basis of planning has encouraged the dominance of the economic approach, new legislation needs to rectify the imbalance and ensure that concerns for the environment and social equity are given equal weight.

CHAPTER 3

RESPONSES TO DIVERSITY AND EQUALITY

Many planners say 'we treat everyone the same' and don't (wittingly) discriminate or disadvantage anyone and even if we do, someone would tell us, or as a planner in Toronto said 'someone would scream'.

– Milroy and Wallace (2002: 25)

Professionals who treat everyone the same are likely to be insensitive to and unaware of the diverse needs of different people and their rights to equal opportunities. The conceptualization of diversity outlined in Chapter 1 supports the integration of diversity and equality. Sustainable development can then achieve fairness and equality along with the environmental and economic objectives. This chapter sketches out how different countries address diversity and equality and introduces the strategy of mainstreaming as a means of building in a consideration of diversity and equality to all aspects of planning. Part 1 starts by looking in broad terms at legislative frameworks in a range of countries. Part 2 looks at the current evidence for diversity and equality in spatial planning in the UK. Part 3 introduces mainstreaming as a strategy, showing how it developed, particularly in the European context; how it has been applied to environmental and equality issues and what lessons can be learnt by looking at mainstreaming through innovation theory.

The one thing observers and commentators of equality issues do agree on is the tortuously slow progress countries have made towards diversity and equality at national and local levels. The impacts of racist, disabling, gendered and ageist environments in our cities and towns are all too evident as Chapter 1 discussed and Table 3.1 summarizes.

Many commentators argue that with a larger ethnic minority population, policy makers in the USA have had to pay more attention to racial disadvantage. The very specific managing diversity approach, it is argued, developed as a reaction to the backlash of employers to affirmative action (or what Europeans would know as positive discrimination).

PART 1 CONSTITUTIONAL AND LEGISLATIVE EQUALITY GUARANTEES

Countries may provide constitutional equality guarantees through general human rights legislation or legislation covering specific groups of people. A constitutional

Table 3.1 Some effects of a racist, disabling and gendered environment

Sectoral group	Example of impacts
Disabling environment	Lack of physical or sensory access, barriers, institutionalization
Racist environment	Red-lining, invisibility, lack of cultural recognition
Gendered environment	Re-enforce oppressed social roles, lack of balance between work and home, restricted access to the formal labour market
Ageist	Lack of facilities for young people and older people

approach ensures that equality is regarded as an unequivocal human right applying to all other legislation, as is the case in the USA, Canada, South Africa and India (Nieuwboer, 2003). In the USA, where the constitution provides a very general guarantee that no State shall deny to any person the equal protection of the law (US Annals of Congress, 1787), the Supreme Court generates the principles to decide which groups the law covers. In India, the general equality guarantee is followed by specific articles prohibiting discrimination on the basis of religion, caste, sex or place of birth (Fredman, 2002: 2). The Netherlands constitution establishes everyone's right to a home and so equality and emancipation apply more to social housing than anything else (Spitz, 2003). Article 1 states that: 'all persons in the Netherlands shall be treated equally in equal circumstances. Discrimination on the grounds of religion, belief, political opinion, race, or sex or on any other grounds whatsoever shall not be permitted' (Netherlands Government, 1983). In contrast the UK has taken more of a sectoral approach with the Human Rights Act (HRA) coming into effect only within the last few years (UK, 1998). Here, there is no constitution, the legislature decides when and in what circumstances equality legislation should apply.

Table 3.2 provides a brief overview of the legislative timelines in a range of countries drawing on the work of Fredman (2002) and Nieuwboer (2003). The year 1918 was particularly significant in the UK because this is when women gained the right to vote. Each country has its own set of landmark events. In 1893, New Zealand became the first country in the world to give women the vote (New Zealand, 2003). It was not until the 1960s when the Aborigines in Australia won the right to vote.

Legislation can be ground-breaking and act as a catalyst for change. Legislation may be anti-discriminatory in nature as in the UK or incorporate affirmative action or positive discrimination, as in the USA, to close long-standing inequality gaps which would otherwise never be breached. In 1985, the Belgium government installed a Ministry and a State Secretary for Equal Opportunity and Social Emancipation,

Table 3.2 Developments in primary equality legislation

Country	Primary legislation
USA	1964 Civil Rights Act, 1972 The Equal Employment Opportunity Act, 1990 Americans with Disability Act
Canada	1982 Charter of Rights and Freedoms, Human Rights Act, Employment Equity Act
Australia	1975 Racial Discrimination Act, 1984 Sex Discrimination Act, 1992 Disability Discrimination Act
New Zealand	1993 Human Rights Act
UK	1968 Race Relations Act; 1970 Chronically Sick and Disabled Persons Act; 1975 Sex Discrimination Act; 1976 Race Relations Act; 1989, 1996 The Employment Rights Act; 1995 The Disability Discrimination Act
Ireland	1974 Anti-discrimination (Pay) Act, 1998 Employment Equality Act, 2000 Equal Status Act
Netherlands	1994 Equal Treatment Act, Samen Act Extension 2002–2004

Sources: Fredman (2002) and Nieuwboer (2003).

and since 1994, the electoral list for members of parliament must be at least 40 per cent female (Belgium, 1989).

The first comprehensive legislative measures protected citizens against discrimination on the grounds of race in North America in 1964. In all countries, equality and diversity legislation outlawing discrimination on the grounds of disability has come on stream anything between 20 and 50 years after initial equal opportunities legislation. Most countries have established a sectoral approach to diversity and equality with separate legislation for race, gender and disability, age and more latterly sexuality and religion. In most countries, legislative protection is circumscribed and applies to specified areas. For instance, the EU directives on race are limited to employment and training, although domestic legislatures are free to extend beyond these boundaries, so that equality could apply to all services.

HIERARCHY OF LEGISLATION

Diversity and equality legislation does not cover every aspect of government and often there is a hierarchy of legislation. New Zealand's experience shows how governments seek to subordinate some laws, as well as limit and exempt areas from legal protection. The 1993 Human Rights legislation included a section actually making it subordinate to other statutes and, apart from the race clauses, the law originally exempted the government from complying (Fortuin, 2001). This was subject to a sunset clause that was to have led to its repeal at the end of 1999. By this time, the Human

Rights Commission (HRC) was expected to have examined all government policies, practices and legislation and identified any conflicts with the HRA (New Zealand, 1993). The resulting audit proved so costly and time-consuming that the Government called a halt to the exercise, and proposed instead that the exemption be made permanent. However, after a period of indecision, a compromise was reached and the exemption was extended for a further two years till the end of 2001. The Human Rights Amendment Act 2001 not only amalgamated the Race Relations Office and the HRC, it also introduced a standard of compliance for the public sector and a new method of dispute resolution. Law on equality in the UK is seen as applying only to areas specified in the statutes, due to specific exceptions in the discrimination legislation. So to this extent, equality is subordinate to other interests (Fredman, 2003a).

Countries in larger unions are obliged to work within the rules and comply with directives. As an economic union, the European Union directives developed in response to economic pressures rather than a desire to rectify social injustice. Legislation relating to sex pre-dates race directives. Article 119 of the original Treaty of Rome (EU, 1957) enshrined the idea of equal pay for equal work and arose from concerns by the French Government of the day that French business would suffer and become less competitive because of the disparity in pay between women and men in Spain (Bennett, 2000; Justice Initiative, 2003). The Court of Justice ruled following *Defrenne* versus *The Belgium State* test case that women could rely on Article 119 in their national courts irrespective of whether or not national legislation existed on equal pay. This then provided EU policy makers and women's lobby groups with a legal hook on which to hang their demands for further sex equality legislation. Article 2 of the Treaty of Amsterdam confirms equality between women and men (EU, 1997). Article 3 assigns to the community responsibility for eliminating inequalities and promoting equality in all its activities. Article 13 permits member states to take appropriate action to combat discrimination on the grounds of (interalia) sex. Article 141, which replaces the original Article 119, permits member states to adopt positive action measures on behalf of the under-represented sex. (Positive action means is designed to promote access to opportunities although it does not permit discrimination.) The equality guarantee contained in Article 14 of the European Convention of Human Rights (ECHR, 1950) came into effect in Britain in October 2000 with the HRA (UK, 1998). It is important to realize that the HRA does not give a free-standing right to equality in the sense that everyone has an equal right to any service no matter what their race, sex or age (Fenster, 1999; Fredman and Spencer, forthcoming). Instead the Act states that it is the enjoyment of the rights under the convention which should be guaranteed without discrimination. Although EU directives have focused on employment and vocational training there is no reason why equality should be any less important in education, health care, regeneration, planning and housing. The independent universal equality right established under Protocol 12 of Article 14 of the ECHR (1950) means that equality legislation should apply to all areas rather than to the rights and freedoms under the convention (Enfield and Harris, 2003; European Women's Lobby, 2003). Until this protocol is accepted, as it stands the legislation will continue to cause confusion and inconsistencies with respect to planning and regeneration. In the UK, the Disability Discrimination Act (UK, 1995) and the Race Relations Act (UK, 1976) give much clearer avenues for redress than the Sex Discrimination legislation because they refer explicitly to planning. The Race Relations Amendment Act not only makes it unlawful to discriminate against a person in carrying out a planning function but also requires local authorities to promote equality (UK, 2001). Section 19 of the UK Disability Discrimination Act similarly makes it unlawful for a provider of services such as planning to discriminate against a disabled person (UK, 1995). However, disability legislation in the UK and the USA also provides for justification defence which can be used to excuse detrimental treatment of disabled people. The Sex Discrimination legislation makes it unlawful for any person concerned with the provision of goods, facilities and services to the public to discriminate on the basis of sex. However, because planning is not specifically mentioned in the legislation, legal experts in the UK still see planning lying outside the scope of the act (Fredman, 2003b). Planning is covered explicitly in the race and disability legislation and the government recently imposed a duty on public authorities to promote racial equality. Legislation requires public bodies to produce race equality schemes or action plans but not disability or gender schemes. This places sex equality in a different and weaker position to race and disability. In May 2004, the UK Government recommended a public sector duty to promote equality between women and men – similar to the duty to promote race equality introduced since 2000, and the duty to promote equality of opportunity for disabled people contained in the current Draft Disability Discrimination Bill (Hewitt, 2004). The devolved governments have shown their specific commitment to gender equality. Although not a devolved function, in the sense that only the UK parliament can pass equality legislation through their enacting legislation, the new parliament in Scotland and Assemblies in Wales and Northern Ireland signaled their intention to highlight equality issues.

> Equal Opportunities means the prevention, elimination or regulation of discrimination between persons on the grounds of sex or marital status, on racial grounds, or on grounds of disability, age, sexual orientation, language or social origin, or of other personal attributes, including beliefs or opinions, such as religious beliefs or political opinions (Scotland, 1998).

The Scottish Parliament endorses an inclusive approach to equal opportunities in its enacting legislation and subsequent guidance to officials and politicians (Bennett et al., 2002). Legislation has increased the impetus for local authorities as

Table 3.3 Equal treatment, equal opportunities, positive action and diversity compared

	Equal treatment	*Equal opportunities*	*Positive action*	*Diversity*
Approach	Treating likes alike	Removing barriers	Creating equal outcomes	Respecting difference
Legal formulation	Direct discrimination	Indirect discrimination	Targeting areas of disadvantage	Unspecified
Target	Individuals	Individuals	Groups	Responding to plurality of identities, needs and values
Recourse	Compensating identified victims	Compensating identified groups	Targeting identified groups	Where appropriate targeting identified groups

Source: Constructed from Fredman (2002).

employers and service providers to develop policies and strategies for equal opportunities and to undertake Best Value Reviews as part of their quality management process (Audit Commission, 2003). The Commission for Racial Equality (CRE) developed a self-assessment tool for local authorities called the CRE Standard for Racial Equality (CRE, 2002b). The Audit Commission which acts as a public sector watchdog found that the take up of the CRE Standard was low, with just fewer than 40 per cent of local authorities adopting it (Audit Commission, 2002). The CRE Standard has now been replaced by the Equality Standard for Local Government, developed by the Employers' Organization with the CRE, Disability Rights Commission and Equal Opportunities Council. The new Equality Standard (EOLG, 2001, 2003) allows local authorities to self-assess, on a number of levels, their delivery of diversity and equality to ethnic minorities, women and disabled people. In the rest of Europe, many organizations are striving for the EC's E-Quality kite mark award (EC, 1994; EFQM, 2003).

In summary and as Table 3.3 shows, we have moved from an equal treatment approach to equality to a diversity approach and what is now needed is a wider recognition of the need for these approaches to be seen not as separate but part of an integrated approach to equality and diversity.

SECTORAL APPROACHES

Internationally governments have tended to deal with equality issues in a highly sectoral way under the headings of race/ethnicity, sex and disability (Table 3.4).

Table 3.4 Sectoral groups named in primary legislation

UK	Netherlands	Ireland	Scotland
Sex	Religion	Gender	Sex
Race	Belief	Marital status	Marital status
Disability	Political opinion	Family status	Race
Age	Race	Sexual orientation	Disability
Religion	Sex	Religious belief	Age
Sexuality	Or any other grounds	Age Disability Race, colour, nationality or ethnic or national origin Traveller community	Sexual orientation Language Social origin Other personal attributes, beliefs or opinions, such as religious beliefs or political opinions

This is reflected in the UK Race Relations and Sex Discrimination legislation in the 1970s and was reinforced with the passage of the Disability Discrimination Act in 1995. Guidance provided by governments and professional institutes such as the RTPI has reflected this sectoral approach. At least two access practice guides were produced in the UK during the European Year of the Disabled (DPTAC, 2003; ODPM, 2003a). In 1996, a Practice Advice Note (PAN) on Planning for Women was produced (RTPI, 1996b). The sectoral approach extended to local authorities. In response to the demands of the 1970s legislation, along with lobbying by community and women's groups, many local authorities established race relations and women's units or committees to implement the legislation. Often the approach to each group was separate, with specialist and separate women's and race equality units in some authorities briefed to monitor policy and practice within the local authority (Randall, 1991; Breugal and Kean, 1995; Young, 1997). Subsequent equal opportunity policies instigated by local authorities in the 1980s reflected the legislative framework, using it as a set of hooks for innovative programmes focusing on women and ethnic minorities (Figure 3.1).

Other local authorities implemented strategies and policies via their personnel functions and the implementation of equal opportunities became an increasingly specialist human resource function within local authorities (Young, 1997). In addition to developing equal opportunity policies and new committees to monitor implementation, many local authorities instituted awareness training for their staff on both gender and race. This emphasis on individuals without parallel programmes to tackle corporate and institutional responsibilities led to much criticism (Bruegal and Kean, 1995: 155).

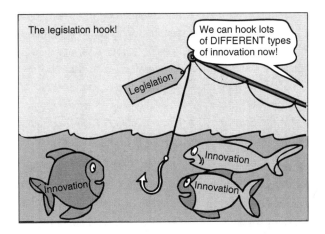

Figure 3.1 The legislation hook

PART 2   CURRENT EVIDENCE FOR DIVERSITY AND EQUALITY

Central government in the UK has tended to be very critical of local government. A literature review commissioned by the UK government shows little sympathy for the weaknesses in the legislative framework created by central government at the time, or the inadequate resources made available to run the Equality bodies charged with implementing the legislation. The literature review shows that many saw the equal opportunities approach to discrimination and disadvantage as London-led and as such problematic (Cross, Brar and McLeod, 1991; Solomos and Back, 1995; Young, 1997). The review points to one commentator who saw the period of the 'loony left councils' as one of 'municipal socialism' (Randall, 1991); another referred to the political impetus to highlight women's issues as 'municipal feminism'. As a consequence, some local authorities were keen to distance themselves from this approach (Solomos and Back, 1995) and so by the end of the 1980s, there was a widespread perception that local authorities had not delivered in terms of either race or gender equality (EOC, 1997).

The political context for equal opportunities in the UK changed in 1997 when Labour came to power. The Government built on the traditional values set out in the Report of the Commission on Social Justice (1994) chaired by John Smith (then leader of the UK Labour Party):

> the values of social justice are for us essential. They are: the equal worth of all citizens, their equal right to be able to meet their basic needs, the need to spread opportunities and life chances as widely as possible, and finally the requirement that we reduce and where possible eliminate unjustified inequalities (CSJ, 1994: 1).

Although central government in the UK has been critical of local government, criticisms can be levied on equal measure to central government. Potentially all aspects of planning have a diversity dimension and so it is important that government guidance reflects this. Guidance for planners has simply stated that plans should have regard to social considerations in their general policies and proposals. This unspecific type of guidance has resulted in very little change on the ground. Government Ministers, for instance, have only been able to point to a limited number of ways in which the government has addressed the needs of women (Jackson, 1999):

- Promote accessibility to public buildings and spaces for people with disabilities and those with pushchairs – Planning Policy Guidance 1 on General Policies and Principles (DoE, 1997).
- Look at ways in which the design of new developments can deter crime and provide security for women – DoE Circular 5/94, Planning and Crime (DoE, 1994a).
- Encourage development in city centres which are accessible by public transport – Planning Policy Guidance 6 on Major Retail Development (DoE, 1996) and Planning Policy Guidance 13 on Highways Considerations (DoE, 2001).
- Use flexibility in applying planning controls on homeworking and the use of homes for childminding – Planning Policy Guidance 4 on Industrial and Commercial Development (DoE, 1994c).

Existing Government policies, guidance and advice treat diversity and equality issues inconsistently. Stereotyping and inappropriate language are evident. Some groups are mentioned, others are ignored; some groups are characterized inappropriately as problems, others as vulnerable. Most of the references in UK Government planning guidance are to disabled people and to people with physical disabilities and specifically wheelchair users. This group represents a small proportion of disabled people, although particularly affected by a disabling environment (Imrie, 1996). There is one reference to hearing-impaired in Design Bulletin 32 (DoE, 1998), no references to sexual orientation, and children are only mentioned in relation to transport. Guidance depicts gypsies and travellers as a problem rather than a group of people with rights to a place to live. Women are stereotyped. The Good Practice Guide 27 on Vital and Viable Town enters talks about 'mothers and prams' instead of parent and paragraph 2.03 talks about shopping 'as a real reason for getting out of the house and a change of scene' (ODPM, 2003b). There is an implied co-existence of ethnic minorities and old city neighbourhoods which means that black and ethnic minority groups outside urban areas are overlooked in policy. The Good Practice Notes contain more references to different groups of people but have a lower status than Circulars and Planning Practice Guidance.

RACE AND PLANNING

The most comprehensive survey ever undertaken of local authority planning practice with regards to the needs of black and ethnic minority groups in England, Scotland and Wales, showed that only a tiny 3 per cent of Local Planning Authorities (LPAs) monitor the impact of planning policies on ethnic minority groups; 14 per cent of LPAs have in place formal mechanisms for direct contact with ethnic minority groups (with 22 per cent indicating they have informal arrangements); 13 per cent of LPAs said they had in place planning policies specifically related to the needs of black and ethnic minority communities (LGA, 1998). Almost a half (45 per cent) of LPAs gave addressing race and ethnic minority issues in their planning work the two lowest priorities; 12 per cent of LPAs gave these issues the two highest priorities. Only 10 per cent of LPAs undertook any research on the planning needs and aspirations of black and ethnic minority groups in their areas. The LGA (1998) survey showed that few LPAs were able to demonstrate extensive links between the operation of the development control system and the needs of black and ethnic minority communities. Development Control is a crucial part of the planning system and involves implementing the development plan policies. The 'colour blind' approach of the planning system identified in previous studies seemed to persist. The LGA report showed that refusal rates of planning applications for 'Asian applications' was much higher than the average. Following changes in procedure, the refusal rate fell but were still higher than for white applications. A total of 7 per cent of LPAs undertake ethnic monitoring of planning applications and planning permissions and 8 per cent of LPAs could identify a planning application determined in the previous 12 months where considerations relating to ethnic minority groups had been an issue.

DISABILITY AND PLANNING

The report on planning and access for disabled people concluded that the success in delivering inclusive environments varies enormously between local planning authorities, developers, occupiers and investors (ODPM, 2003a: 26). The guide stemmed from a recommendation by the Disability Rights Task Group that Central Government should offer guidance to local authorities and developers on how to tackle the issue of access for disabled people through the planning system in a more consistent way. Previous studies have shown that prior to the introduction of the Disability Discrimination Act (UK, 1995) very few local authorities viewed their planning policies from the social model of disability and many were ignorant of the issues (Imrie, 1996; Reeves, 1996c). The UK government has undertaken more recent research which shows that awareness of the issues has increased as a result of legislation but actual practice still has a long way to go (ODPM, 2003c). Further work is due to be published (ODPM, 2004).

The research undertaken to date shows an overall low level of awareness of diversity and equality issues and how they impact on planning. The lack of recognition of the need for LPAs and other planning agencies to consider diversity reflects a low level of awareness of how to apply existing government policy and in some cases a lack of awareness of the implications of equality legislation (Thomas, 2003). This also results from the highly circumscribed nature of equality legislation as it relates to planning. What is needed is a levelling up of equality legislation using the more powerful Race Equality legislation as the baseline, with a requirement to promote equality along with a duty not to discriminate. The UK government has said that the interests of all groups served must carry equal weight. 'It would be quite wrong for any group either to predominate or become marginalized' (Cabinet Office, 2002: 8, 12). Fredman (2002) argues that any new legislation should be based on a set of principles to enable the targeted implementation. She poses four principles which again illustrate the integration of diversity and equality. First, to break the cycle of disadvantage associated with excluded groups, equality laws should target disadvantaged not advantaged groups and target persons or groups who have been subject to historical disadvantage, prejudice or stereotyping, through the redistribution of resources and benefits and also through the facilitation of choice as opposed to equal outcomes (Fredman, 2002: 11). Second, new legislation should promote respect for the equal dignity and worth to redress the stereotyping, humiliation and violence towards out-groups. Dignity is central to the concerns of many groups subject to discrimination and harassment, particularly older people. The third principle, affirming community identities, recognizes that individuals are partly constituted by their group membership. The fourth principle of facilitating full participation in society acknowledges that equality law must compensate for the absence of political power of minority groups. The application of each principle would, Fredman argues, help achieve equality for particular groups. For instance, where equality law starts from the principle of dignity and the free development of the person, discrimination on the grounds of sexual orientation and age would be tackled (Fredman, 2002: 18). Where legislation starts from the principle of confirming community identity, this would support people to express their religious identity.

PART 3   MAINSTREAMING

Legislation is an important instigator of change. At best, it acts as a catalyst for change, helping organizations re-orientate and develop, knowing that the playing field is level and other bodies are required to comply with similar rules and regulations. At worst, legislation can make individuals and organizations defensive, driving discrimination underground and reducing everything to costs and achieving the legal minimum, rather than working and delivering best practice. This is why strategies like mainstreaming are significant. With the development of legislation and better guidance for those involved in planning and sustainable regeneration, equality and diversity can become part of the mainstream for professionals working in the built environment, sustainable development and regeneration. Given that potentially all aspects of planning have an equality and diversity dimension, at every stage of policy making, implementation and monitoring, diversity and equality need to be explicitly addressed. Mainstreaming involves building a consideration of fairness, equality and diversity into all aspects of planning. It involves assessing which groups of people are likely to experience bias as a result of the assumptions underpinning a policy or plan. Bias and discrimination can result from the priorities, which become established, and the way in which resources are allocated. A lack of diversity within the planning profession also plays a part and this will be discussed in Chapter 6.

As a process and as a goal, sustainable development provides a positive opportunity to embed diversity and equality issues into the policy process because as a concept, sustainable development involves rethinking past approaches. Compared with the economic and environmental domains, the social domain of sustainability has proved less well integrated into the whole conceptual framework of sustainability. This reflects the fact that we see a much longer history of economic and environmental impact assessments dating back to the 1960s (Figure 3.2) (Barrow, 2001).

The American National Environmental Protection Agency (NEPA, 1969) visualized that Environmental Impact Assessments would be used not only for federal projects but also for plans and programmes.

The European Union (or the EEC as it was at the time), from 1978, saw the Environmental Impact Assessment applying to plans as well as projects. It was incorporated in the 1985 Directive, now the Strategic Environmental Assessment, which set up environmental assessment of projects (EC, 2001b). The creation of social criteria by Roche (1999: 41–55) and work on social impact assessment in the 1970s only partly addressed diversity (Carley and Christie, 2000). Even the relatively recent standard guidelines and principles (Inter-Organizational Committee on Guidelines and Principles, 1994) have been criticized for their gender and culturally neutral approach (Verloo and Roogeband, 1996; Verloo, 2003). Other expert commentators on equality have expressed concern that developments in social sustainability have anonymized the gender perspective (Greed, 1996a, b). Race and disability issues have found it even harder to gain recognition.

Mainstreaming as an approach has the potential to integrate the social dimension of sustainability into planning policy and enable planners and other related professionals to review their own and their organization's professional approach. If something is not in the mainstream it is in the margins; in a side stream; in a backwater.

Developments of assessment techniques

Economic
1902   River and harbour projects in the USA
1936   Flood Control Act – water resource development
1950s   UK transport
1960s   Public sector projects; urban development renewal, recreation, health,
          economic development and regional policy, urban and regional plans and
          'third world' projects

Technological
1960s   USA; systematic assessment of the effects on all sectors of society

Environmental
1969   US NEP Act; introduced alongside planning and other legislation
          1985 – UK integrated with the planning system
          1986

Social
1984   Social impact assessment

Note:
*In the US 'environment' was meant to be interpreted broadly and include physical,
social, cultural and economic dimensions. But in the early years the environment was actually
interpreted quite narrowly.

Social/community evaluation vis-á-vis environmental/technological evaluation

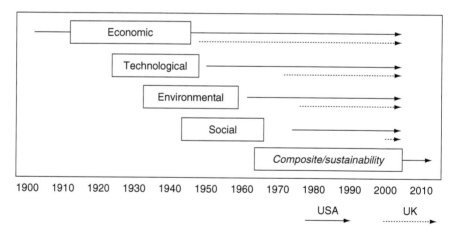

Figure 3.2 Developments in impact evaluations (Source: Derived from Lichfield (1996) *Community
          Impact Assessment*)

Mainstreaming moves beyond legislation to integrate equal opportunities and diversity
principles into everyday policy and practice. Mainstreaming represents a redefined
and broader approach to equality, complementary and yet fundamentally different to
the legislative approach. It is not an end in itself (Beveridge and Nott, 2000). The
potential of mainstreaming to integrate cross-cutting themes such as equality and

environmental sustainability has been recognized for some time by Oxfam (Williams, Seed and Mwau, 1994). The commitment to diversity and equality and a strategy of mainstreaming formed the heart of the preparations for setting up the Scottish Parliament and the Welsh Assembly.

As most governments move towards a more inclusive and integrated approach to diversity and equality, the creation of single equality bodies should make it possible to consider multiple identities and address cumulative discrimination. Innovative work and a sustained effort will be needed to work out how best to deliver guidance in the future. Some good practice will be generic, covering shared needs. Others will need to be very specific to sectoral groups. Following the Good Friday Agreement in Northern Ireland and the setting up of the Assembly (NIO, 1998), the various strands were brought together with the establishment of one Commission for Equality (Equality Commission for Northern Ireland, 2003).

Although some way off in the UK, this could eventually mean a single piece of equality legislation, which could take the form of a revised and extended human rights legislation. Ireland's Equal Status Act (2000) provides a model for such legislation, and Northern Ireland and Republic of Ireland are already working towards equivalence of legislation (Figure 3.3).

As governments move towards a more integrative approach to equality, considering a range of sectoral groups together, professionals across all sectors will

Figure 3.3 Stormont, Belfast

find the strategy of mainstreaming an important tool. The issue is not whether, but how mainstreaming can succeed in effectively integrating issues?

> Gender mainstreaming means moving gender equality concerns from the backwaters and side streams into the mainstream. Instead of having separate policies for gender equality; or adding on gender equality concerns to already formulated policies, programmes and procedures; a gender perspective is introduced from the beginning into all policies, programmes and procedures (Elson, 2003: 1).

The idea of building in a consideration of equality to all policies developed in the global arena of the international women's movement in the 1970s as a strategy for women's equality. Gender mainstreaming appeared in the international texts after the United Nations 3rd Conference on Women (UN, 1985; UNGA, 1985). In the early 1990s the UN, UNESCO, World Bank and Oxfam debated and developed mainstreaming tools (Razavi and Miller, 1995). In 1995, the Platform for Action which rounded off the UN 4th World Conference of Women in Beijing committed the UN and member states to incorporate a gender dimension into policy making (UN, 1995). This international movement has been an important influence on national governments such as Ireland (Carney, 2002).

A mainstreaming strategy involves looking at traditional policy processes and implementation in different ways using a series of lenses. So mainstreaming diversity and equality in urban planning and development involves the application of a set of gender- and age-sensitive visions, concepts, strategies and practices in the different phases and arenas of the development and evaluation cycle (Horelli, Booth and Gilroy, 1997; Horelli, 2003b). Mainstreaming has the following characteristics. It is systematic, proactive, integrative, holistic and transformational. Alongside legislation and positive action policies, mainstreaming ranks as the principal instrument for achieving equality and it has applications right across the diversity spectrum (Rees, 1999). Mainstreaming refers to a multifaceted, holistic and long-term strategy of integrating a gender perspective into all public policies in order to achieve equality between men and women in and beyond the workplace (Mazey, 1995, 2001: 5). The EC adopted mainstreaming to tackle disadvantage between women and men and defines it as:

> 'the systematic consideration of the differences between the conditions, situations and needs of women and men at the point of planning, implementing and evaluation.' It involves 'the (re) organisation, improvement, development and evaluation of policy processes, so that a gender equality perspective is incorporated in all policies at all levels and at all stages, by actors normally involved in policy making' (Council of Europe, 1998).

For many working in day-to-day policy, gender mainstreaming means thinking about gender as a real experience, seeing the consequences of policy for women as well as men – the unintended consequences – and being creative about solutions. Research in Ireland shows the range of ways in which civil servants interpret mainstreaming (Carney, forthcoming). Although the EU was developing tools for mainstreaming sustainability and equality at about the same time during the 1990s, those involved in gender equality felt that environmental sustainability received the most attention. Equally, those involved in and advocating environmental sustainability felt that equality was being taken more seriously. The reality seems to be that the EU has actively supported the integration and mainstreaming of environmental protection into policies for almost 20 years – longer than equality. The Single European Act of 1987 made environmental assessment a legal requirement, further reinforced through the Maastricht Treaty on the European Union (EU, 1992). To achieve this goal, the 5th Environmental Action Programme (CEC, 1992) highlighted Strategic Environmental Appraisal (SEA) as one tool to promote further environmental integration (ODPM, 2002b). Given the goal of achieving sustainable development, it seemed only logical, if not essential, to apply an assessment of the environmental implications to all relevant policies, plans and programmes. However, environmentalists heaped widespread criticism on the structural fund programmes' insensitivity to environmental issues between 1989 and 1993 and, as a consequence, SEAs became a requirement. Since the mid-1990s the EU has used mainstreaming as a strategy to integrate the cross-cutting themes of the environment and it is now a well-established mechanism for integrating environmental concerns. Current structural fund applications (1994–1999) must be accompanied by a form of SEA or environmental profile. Directives require an SEA for 'planning strategies' related to agriculture and forestry, industry (including extractive industries), energy, transport, tourism, water resource management, town and country planning or land use. It was not until 1996 that the EU issued a communication committing the Commission to mainstreaming gender into all EU policies and not restricting efforts to promote equality to the implementation of specific measures to help women (Commission for European Communities, 1996a).

In 1996 the Commission for European Communities issued a communication which stipulated that equal opportunities be incorporated into all community policies and practices (CEC, 1996a). In addition the CEC also issued a guide to gender impact assessment (CEC, 1996b). The EC identified EU Structural Funds and the Employment Guidelines as priority areas for promoting gender mainstreaming. The Framework Regulation for the Structural Funds (2000–2006) incorporates gender mainstreaming as an obligation (EC, 2000a). Since 1998, the EU has required member states to submit a National Action Plan (NAP) to the Commission indicating how gender would be integrated across all the programmes of activity (Mazey, 2001: 49). In June 2000, the Commission adopted the Community Framework Strategy on Gender Equality (2001–2005) with the purpose of establishing a framework for action within which all community activities can contribute to promote gender equality as set out in Article 3(2) of the Treaty of the European Community (EC, 2000b). The strategy operationalizes and consolidates the gender mainstreaming approach adopted by the Commission in 1996 and is underpinned by an annual work programme which includes proactive interventions. This includes adjusting policies by applying gender mainstreaming and implementing concrete actions designed to address the situation of gender inequality in society. Following its work in 2001, the Directorate General Environment undertook to mainstream a gender perspective into all activities related to health and employment. Within this context, it set up a pilot within Directorate General Environment, with the view to assess the gender impact of selected policy areas including municipal waste management planning. The aim of this task is to analyze the extent to which both EU and member state action in relation to municipal waste planning establishes a framework suitable for ensuring that local waste strategies are equipped to take gender differences into account and to assess the impacts of planning policy on women and men.

Individual countries have developed slightly different approaches to mainstreaming. Whether it is Swedish REFLEX (undated; Figure 3.4) or the Canadian SMART, all seek to ensure that equality is built into every stage of policy making and implementation (Braithwaite, 2000; RTPI, 2003).

Figure 3.4 The Reflex Tool, from Sweden

In October 1996, the UK Sex and Race Equality Division of the Department for Education and Employment devised a programme to promote mainstreaming to regional government offices to ensure that equal opportunities and diversity becomes a routine consideration in developing, monitoring, evaluating and reviewing policies (DFEE, 1996). In doing this, they developed Policy Appraisal for Equal Treatment guidelines (PAET) based on the Northern Ireland Policy and Fair Treatment Guidelines (NICCR, 1993: 96), with the intention that all government departments in the UK would appraise the impact of policy on women, ethnic minority groups and people with disabilities. Table 3.5 summarizes the three stages of action identified in the PAET guidelines.

Table 3.5 Three stages of action on the policy and equal treatment approach

Check how the policy or programme will affect, either directly or indirectly, different groups of people – for example women and men, disabled people and those from different ethnic groups	Assessing the potential impact of the proposal: • Make full use of existing research and statistics; if necessary commission new data, ensuring that statistics are separated by gender, race, disability and age • Consult the relevant equality contact on issues specific to their policy areas • Consult established interest groups • Consult those who are likely to use the service • Carry out a differential impact assessment, based on this and any other relevant information
Consider if there may be unequal impact on those groups who do not enjoy specific legal protection, such as older people or groups toward whom specific policy initiatives are being directed, such as young unemployed people	
Identify whether there is any adverse differential impact on a particular group or groups and then decide whether it can be justified in policy terms even if it is legally permissible	Use the information collected to decide whether there is likely to be a differential impact upon a particular group or groups in society and, if so, whether this may be unfair or unlawful, or contradict overall Government policy concerning opportunities or services for certain groups
Take action, if necessary	If some groups will suffer an adverse differential impact: • Ensure the proposed course of action is legally permissible • If not amend the policy or programme • If it is legally permissible, decide whether the difference is justifiable in policy terms • Ensure that Ministers and senior officials are aware that the adverse differential impact of any policy or programme has been assessed

Source: Women and Equality Unit (1998) *Policy Appraisal for Equal Treatment.*

The three stages should be implemented during the development of policy proposals using an impact analysis which clearly brings out the effect on particular sections of the population, and how relevant differences have been addressed (Webber, 1996).

The tools which help mainstream the cross-cutting themes of environmental sustainability and equality are very similar (Braithwaite, 2000). The following section looks at the toolkits to mainstream environmental issues into economic development and the toolkit to mainstream gender into structural funds, both of which provide useful frameworks.

TOOLKIT TO MAINSTREAM ENVIRONMENT INTO REGIONAL ECONOMIC DEVELOPMENT

The current model of development in the EU encourages increased economic activity, accepting that this will lead to more waste emissions and the use of more environmental resources. In 1999 the EC asked consultants to create a model which would help move structural funds towards sustainable development and ensure that economic goals are assisted rather than restrained by environmental sustainability (EC, 1999a). This was done by developing criteria which ensured that:

- 'environmental problems inhibiting economic growth are cleaned up;
- adequate environmental infrastructure is in place to accommodate the waste and effluent from new economic activity brought into the region;
- help is given to existing firms to be more competitive and more eco-efficient by reducing their resource use and waste per unit output;
- support for innovation is at least in part focused on developing sustainable products and processes;
- support for developing enterprises or attracting inward investment is at least in part focused on support for sectors which use few environmental resources;
- the natural assets and cultural heritage of the region are enhanced and protected;
- the transport systems and spatial development pattern are such as to reduce the demand for private travel and encourage the use of mass transit existing infrastructure and the exchange of heat, materials and waste between economic actors' (EC, 1999a: 3).

There appears to have been no further work to develop this model (Healy, 2003). The three tools for mainstreaming environmental sustainability involve:

1. Integrated economic–environment SWOT analysis
2. Development path analysis
3. Key environmental criteria check.

INTEGRATED ECONOMIC–ENVIRONMENT SWOT ANALYSIS

The integrated economic–environment SWOT illustrated in Table 3.6 records the interrelationship between the economy and environment of the region and identifies those aspects of the environment that support or undermine economic development.

The idea is that one sheet is prepared for strengths, weaknesses, opportunities and threats which are subdivided but in the example above all four components are shown as columns. So, for example, an economic strength of a region might be its attractive towns. However, they may be threatened with environmental problems such as pollution from nearby industry which is creating a poor quality environment which in turn may well impact on future economic success.

DEVELOPMENT PATH ANALYSIS

Development path analysis allows a qualitative assessment of the degree to which the programme is helping to move the assisted region towards a more sustainable development path or more eco-friendly methods of production. Using Table 3.7, the

Table 3.6 Integrated SWOT analysis – an example

Environment	Economy			
	S Economic strengths	*W* Economic weaknesses	*O* Opportunities from trends/ demands	*T* Threats from economic trends/ competition
A Environmental assets			Adoption of e-commerce may lead to pressure for dispersed settlements	
P Environmental problems	Attractive towns threatened by poor quality of environment			
F Fragile areas/ scarce resources				Decline of agriculture can lead to loss of landscape management by farmers
R Robust areas/ abundant resources				

Source: EC (1999b: 6 and Annex B: 23–26).

Table 3.7 Development path analyses

Measure	Budget	Development path					
		1 Contribution to economic growth	2 Environmental clean-up	3 Environmental infrastructure	4 Adjustment to existing environmental standards	5 Improve resource efficiency of existing activity	6 New activities using fewer environmental resources
No. 1	500	200	200	100	–	–	–
No. 2	400	–	–	–	300	50	50
No. 3	100	–	–	50	–	50	–
Total	1000	200	200	150	300	100	50
All measures	100%	20%	20%	15%	30%	10%	5%

Source: EC (1999b: 8).

aim is to take each measure or project and allocate the budget for each measure to the development path that it supports.

An indicative breakdown of the budget for each measure may be needed where it contributes to a number of paths. Table 3.7 can then be used as the basis for further discussion to see what can be done to improve the development path for environmental sustainability. So, for example, a budget of 1,000 units may be divided between three different measures which focus on different aspects of development. The measures which are most sustainable will have a spread of expenditure across the columns. Using this framework can help to highlight the areas where expenditure is required for sustainable development to take place.

KEY ENVIRONMENTAL CRITERIA

The third tool involves checking to see how the programme impacts on key environmental criteria set out in the 5th Environmental Action Plan (CEC, 1992). Project leaders can undertake the check at various stages in the development process to help guide and shape the programme. The consultant's advice is to use all three tools, taking care when selecting environmental criteria and drawing on expert knowledge.

TOOLKIT FOR MAINSTREAMING DIVERSITY AND EQUALITY INTO STRUCTURAL FUND PROGRAMMES

The Scottish Executive and Equal Opportunities Commission, Scotland produced a toolkit for mainstreaming equal opportunities into the European Structural Funds (EOC, 1999). Whilst applying a gender lens to Structural Fund management, the introduction to the toolkit recognizes that projects should be used in the broader pursuit of equality across all sectoral groups. This toolkit recognizes the importance of the completeness and relevance of data. Indicators need to describe not only employment rates by gender but also the quality of the employment experience. It relies on:

- sound baseline data about the relative position of women and men across a range of areas;
- clear targets and indicators;
- a comprehensive, responsive and clearly communicated monitoring system and a robust system of evaluation;
- ongoing training and capacity building at all levels;
- impact assessments – sets of questions that help to identify and respond to the different situations and needs of women and men.

The mainstreaming equality toolkit is specifically designed for use by programme managers and the managing authority, and recognizes that programme teams may well need training to work with experts. It recognizes that at each stage of the management and implementation of structural fund programmes, managers need to adopt a gender mainstreaming approach. It also recognizes the need to tackle institutional issues such as the inclusion of women in programme committees. The toolkit also recognizes that an essential first step to developing equality-orientated policies is the identification of patterns of inequality. Regional or sectoral profiles should contain disaggregated data on rates and experiences of unemployment and underemployment participation in the formal labour market, participation in the informal and domestic labour market, education and training and participation in economic development support measures. The regional profile should start to show what issues exist and it should then be possible to develop proposals which address these issues.

The Gender Impact Assessment can then be used to assess whether and how diversity and equal opportunities are taken into account, whether the policy proposal maintains a discriminating perception of women and men and how the proposals should be modified to prevent any negative impacts (Rake, 2000). The toolkit includes a matrix to show the contribution each measure makes towards reducing disparities between women and men (Table 3.8).

Project selection requires the development of targets and criteria which reflect a gender mainstreaming approach. These require project promoters to set out how they have taken equality issues into account. The criteria used in the last round of structural funds programmes is listed in Table 3.9.

During the last round of funding for the 5th framework, there was only limited evidence that these criteria resulted in significant shifts in the way programmes work. The EU and national governments continue to develop mainstreaming capabilities in monitoring and evaluation (Polverari and Fitzgerald, 2002) and the recently commissioned study on mainstreaming gender equality into waste management planning scrutinizes the following aspects of the waste management planning process:

1. The extent to which the local waste planning authority evaluates research data concerning human health in relation to planning on a gender disaggregated basis.
2. The extent to which the executive decision-making process of waste planning takes gender issues into account, including the extent to which a gender balance in decision-making and consultative or scientific bodies is taken into account.
3. The extent to which the aspect of public participation in waste planning is structured so as to take into account its gender impact, notably considering the means and methods employed to ensure public participation.
4. The extent to which the local authority's information and education strategy concerning its municipal waste plan adopts a gender perspective.
5. The extent to which the local authority takes into account the impact of its waste plan in terms of gender, especially in relation to waste collection policies (e.g. kerbside collection or bring bank in relation to recycling, separate collection of targeted waste streams).

Table 3.8 Strategy for achieving reduced inequalities between women and men as specified in the regulations for structural fund programmes

Programme priorities	Employment	Training and education	Enterprise	Reconciliation of work and family life
Transport infrastructure	Improved employment opportunities for women in transport sectors particularly at policy and management levels	Improved equality of participation of girls and women in education and training courses relevant to transport sector professions	Improved access by public transport to enterprise support services Improved rates of female business creation in transport sector	Improved transport access to employment opportunities, services and education and training by women and men
Urban development	Improved equality of participation of women in community development, particularly in decision-making and as project managers Improved participation of women in urban planning	Improved equality of participation of women and men in training opportunities created as a result of urban development initiatives particularly in sectors with marked gender segregation	Improved access to self-employment and enterprise support facilities and services	Improved urban environments which are safe and secure for women, men and children from different cultural and ethnic groups Improved access between living, working and service areas in urban areas Improved accessibility to services in particular to care support for dependants

Source: EOC (1999: 18) and further examples in Commission for the European Communities (1996b) *A Guide to Gender Impact Assessment.*

Table 3.9 Criteria for structural funds

Measure	Gender related selection criteria
Overall principles	All projects will respect equal opportunities principles. Projects which enhance equal opportunities will be preferred The programme is open to anyone in the target groups Projects are required to provide access to public transport or childcare provision where relevant
Skills development (ESF)	Projects with an equal opportunities dimension will be prioritized Training projects must provide for appropriate provision of dependant care
Entrepreneurship (ERDF)	Support to female entrepreneurs – this would apply to start up business
Business development (ERDF)	Integration of women into highly qualified positions Indication of target groups
Care services (ERDF)	Projects benefiting women will be favoured

Source: EOC (1999: 26).

6. The extent to which the local authority accounts for waste streams, including hazardous waste streams, emanating from households and advises and informs householders on their appropriate management (Buckingham, Batchelor and Reeves, 2004).

MAINSTREAMING EQUALITY INTO STRATEGIC PLANNING

The work on EU structural fund programmes is highly relevant to strategic spatial planning. Strategic policies with a spatial planning dimension provide a framework for the allocation of resources and play an increasingly important indirect and direct role in resource distribution. They affect built and natural environments, communities, and the way in which people can contribute effectively to the economic well-being and social sustainability of their region. Strategic plans are one of the key mechanisms for achieving sustainable social, economic and environmental development. Within the field of spatial planning in the UK, strategic policies address issues which have a regional or sub-regional significance. These include the location of large employment, housing, shopping and recreational sites, infrastructure projects, roads, communications and energy networks and urban regeneration projects targeting particular towns and cities.

Since strategic policies affect the way people live their lives, they need to be assessed both in terms of space and the everyday needs of different groups of people. Differences and inequalities between women and men represent one of these sectoral interests. Race, disability and age represent others. The need to develop an effective framework to ensure that policies do not reinforce but eliminate inequalities between women and men has been recognized for some time by GLC (1986) and Booth and Gilroy (1996). Despite developments at EU level, the issue of diversity-sensitive planning at any level has received relatively little attention until 2003. Horelli (1996) found that projects targeted towards or representing women's interests have different aims and objectives to those which are not women-orientated. In order to address this, it has been argued that strategic planning at the regional level should develop a multi-sectoral and integrated approach and ensure complementarity between environmental, economic and social goals (Horelli, 1996). The development of a more holistic approach would then expose any conflicts between different sets of goals, actors and policies. The framework in Table 3.10 can be used to mainstream equality into the strategic planning process. It shows the key issues which need to be addressed at each stage of the plan process.

CAN MAINSTREAMING WORK?

A member of the original EU expert group on gender mainstreaming, Verloo (1999), presented mainstreaming as a policy innovation. By looking at mainstreaming using

Table 3.10 Developing a toolkit for mainstreaming gender in strategic plans

Stage	Requirements for effective mainstreaming
Policy development	Develop policies which meet the needs and desires of women and men
	Establish cross-checking to ensure that policies are complementing each other
Policy appraisal	Ensure that the policy appraisal process involves a duty to demonstrate the extent to which the policy is contributing to the promotion of equality
Proposals	Establish specific outcomes which will meet the needs and desires of women and men
Appraisal of proposals	Ensure that proposals are tested for their contribution to the promotion of equality
	Ensure that interrelated proposals are tested in this way, in terms of content and timing
Monitoring	For a structure plan, the annual reporting process must set out the way in which equality is being addressed and achieved
	The monitoring needs to encompass issues of staff competence and additional training requirements
Evaluation	Formal evaluations of specific key policies or proposals will be required
Review	Establish at the beginning of the structure plan process that a review of the plan will be instigated if equality objectives are not being met

the Innovation Theory developed by Rogers (1995), it is possible to gain a better appreciation of the future potential of mainstreaming to deliver diversity and equality. Having extensively researched and written about innovation since the 1960s, Rogers identified a common set of criteria which he argues need to be present if an innovation is to succeed:

- easily visible to adopters;
- seen to be more promising than alternatives;
- consistent with existing values;
- easy to understand;
- capable of introduction on a trial basis.

EASILY VISIBLE TO ADOPTERS

Would-be adopters of mainstreaming are planning practitioners at local and central government levels, policy makers, politicians, implementers and educators. They must see the relevance of mainstreaming to their day-to-day responsibilities, developing strategies for achieving the goals set by politicians. Mainstreaming was developed in order to make equality issues more visible (MacKay and Bilton, 2000). A series of very high profile symposia in the mid-1990s launched mainstreaming into the European and national policy arenas. Through a process of frame-bridging (using language and ideas with which groups feel comfortable) (Schon and Rein, 1994; Fairhurst and Sarr, 1996), those advocating the approach attempted to present gender main-streaming as acceptable and valuable not only to feminist academics and bureaucrats but also to politicians and policy makers (Verloo, 1999: 5). At the Equality is the Futures Symposium, gender mainstreaming was further promoted within the EC (1999b) and later that year mainstreaming was presented to the planning profession (RTPI, 1999). Although it is recognized as a principal instrument for achieving equality in the EU, mainstreaming has not yet featured in widely used Equal Opportunities training manuals (Clements and Jones, 2002).

MORE PROMISING THAN ALTERNATIVES

For an innovation to succeed, potential adopters need to see that it has more potential than the available alternatives. Adopters tend to take a minimal and compliant approach to diversity and equality based on what needs to be done to keep out of the courts. However, legislation in most countries now requires the promotion of equality and the changed context means that organizations need to look for ways to achieve the legal requirements in the most efficient and effective way possible. The status quo is no longer an option. Managing diversity is a useful tool in the mainstreaming strategy rather than an alternative to it, and mainstreaming does not mean an end to positive action programmes. The advantage of mainstreaming lies in the fact that it has evolved to complement existing approaches and respond to the concerns of various interest groups.

CONSISTENT WITH EXISTING VALUES

To succeed, innovations need consistency with existing values. In the European context, gender mainstreaming is linked to and consistent with the broader and more fundamental goals of human rights and democracy. It is essentially a neo-liberal strategy which does not threaten but accepts the current structures and seeks to transform them (Squires, 1994). However, it sits less easily with social exclusion which, in the UK context, has tended to be defined in terms of poverty and unemployment issues, without a full consideration of who is in poverty and why (Oxfam, 2003). Some feminists who believe that nothing short of an overhaul of institutions will create equality treat mainstreaming with some scepticism. In addition, the values linking mainstreaming and sustainability need strengthening since, in the European and UK context, more emphasis has been given to environmental and economic assessments than equality and gender assessments of policy.

EASY TO UNDERSTAND

Innovations need to be easy to understand, otherwise they will be difficult to communicate and learn. Although a relatively simple concept, mainstreaming is complex to implement, involving as it does the systematic integration of equality issues (Pollack and Hafner-Burton, 2000). As such the implications for organizations and those working in organizations can be far-reaching. Considerable efforts have gone into making gender mainstreaming understandable and meaningful with the development of toolkits (Escott and Dexter, 2002). Mieke Verloo (1999) has argued, and others would agree, that the extent to which gender mainstreaming gains acceptance will continue to depend on the way in which advocates communicate its meaning. In some contexts, the rights-based approach to equality needs emphasizing (Figure 3.5). In others, the notion of fairness and equity will be sufficient. To have a far-reaching and lasting impact, the approach needs diffusing as widely as possible and with the help of toolkits the process can be simplified (Braithwaite, 2000; EOC, 2000).

CAPABLE OF INTRODUCTION ON A TRIAL BASIS

Studies show that innovations spread best when people see they work on a trial basis. The work on mainstreaming gender in European Structural Funds is an example of how this policy innovation is being applied (EOC, 1999). Other examples focus on transport and budgeting. The Department of Transport guidance has led to women's concerns for safety being taken more seriously (DOT, 1997; Hamilton and Jenkins, 2000). The worldwide network of WBG comments on national budgets, to make budgets more gender sensitive (Budlender and Sharp, 1998; Budlender et al., 2002).

A study of the criteria for successful innovation diffusion specified by Rogers (1995) highlights potential problems for mainstreaming. A great deal of work is needed to ensure that mainstreaming is interpreted in very specific contexts and

Figure 3.5 It's people who make the difference

that it remains highly visible. Continued work with the EU Structural Funds is clearly important in this respect.

Rogers (1995) discusses other features which are relevant to the implementation of mainstreaming relating to two important phases: initiating and implementing. Two aspects of initiating are recognized: agenda setting and matching. When a problem is defined in such a way as to need the innovation, organizations are agenda setting. This is well illustrated in studies of companies in the UK and the USA, where particular employment issues such as retention and job satisfaction were solved by recognizing the need for a gendered approach. The need for structure plans to effectively address social sustainability is a particular problem within the planning arena, which should stimulate the need for a gendered approach. Matching is the stage in the innovation process at which a problem from the organization's agenda fits with an innovation. For planning agencies, mainstreaming could be a useful strategy for addressing social exclusion and sustainability. As a holistic approach it involves asking very basic questions relating to power, representation, resources and policy.

Research shows that implementation will succeed when an innovation is re-invented to accommodate an organization's needs and structure more closely and when the organization's structure is modified to fit with the innovation. The involvement of a champion contributes to this process. Mainstreaming as a strategy is helpful but the expression and language associated with it is off-putting to many. Clarifying involves more widespread use of the innovation in the organization so that the meaning becomes clearer to the organization's members. Finally, routinization involves incorporating the innovation into the regular activities of the point where the innovation loses its separate identity.

Experience to date has shown that mainstreaming has become too associated with gender and with women's equality. This is despite the work of agencies to redress the gender perspective through work on mainstreaming men into gender and development (Chant and Gutmann, 2000). There is a need to convey that the strategy has wide application to all aspects of diversity and equality. Barriers to effective mainstreaming have been identified by previous studies (Jahan, 1995) and the research for the RTPI (2003) commissioned Gender Audit Toolkit identified further points (Greed, unpublished). They are in no particular order of priority, although the first four on the list concur with previous studies by the author Reeves (2002b) and Higgins and Davies (1996). These barriers include: lack of gender-separated statistics, attitudes of councillors, lack of political support and lack of central government support.

CONCLUSION

This chapter has sketched the legislative framework for equality and diversity in a number of comparable countries and shown how mainstreaming as a strategy can be used to build in a consideration of diversity and equality into planning and sustainable regeneration. Legislation can ensure a level playing field, particularly important for private sector agencies who need to know that everyone is required to comply with the same stringent social justice standards. Given that planning and sustainable regeneration impacts on transport, housing and the public realm as well as employment opportunities, it is crucial that they are named in equality and diversity legislation so that there is no ambiguity about whether the legislation applies. It is also important that equality and diversity become embedded in planning and sustainable development legislation. Mainstreaming can be an effective strategy to build in diversity and equality to all aspects of planning. I started the research for the chapter believing that mainstreaming was unique to gender and found that within the European context, mainstreaming has been used in the environmental arena prior to its use in the gender arena. I also approached the chapter unsure whether mainstreaming could easily be applied to different sectoral groups. I have come to the conclusion that it can, although extensive development work will be needed. The research for this chapter highlighted the current inconsistencies with equality and diversity legislation for planners. This is particularly the case in the UK. The international comparisons drew attention to the hierarchy of legislation which often relegates equality issues.

The next chapter will examine how public involvement can be made more responsive to the diversity within communities.

CHAPTER 4

PLAN MAKING – MAINSTREAMING IN PRACTICE

If the current rhetoric about handing on a decent living environment to future generations is to have even one iota of meaning, we owe it to subsequent generations to invest now in a collective and very public search for some way to understand the possibilities of achieving a just and ecologically sensitive urbanisation process under contemporary conditions.

– Harvey (1996: 438)

INTRODUCTION

This chapter shows how agencies at the national and local plan level have started to mainstream diversity and equality issues into their planning processes. The first case study looks at London's strategic plan process and how sustainability appraisals have been used to make the plan more sensitive to equality and diversity issues. Plymouth, England provides the basis for the second case study involving a local development plan. The work commissioned by the Irish Department of Justice Equality and Law Reform for the National Development Plan forms the basis of the third case study which is particularly relevant to national spatial development frameworks. London illustrates a city which is mainstreaming equality and diversity issues in relation to a range of sectoral groups whereas Plymouth's local plan review focused, in particular, on gender and takes into account inequalities experienced by different groups of women. Because the Irish NDP is a Single Programming Document used to bid for European funds, it has to comply with European regulations which specifically require an assessment of how plans will address gender equality. The Plymouth and London case studies demonstrate how gender crosscuts other identifiers.

Experience shows that without systematic audits, plans may unintentionally reinforce inequalities and miss opportunities to do more to promote equality. Unless equality and diversity issues are explicitly set out in the policy documents which form the basis of future decisions, officials and politicians will fail to make the progress they can towards a just, fair and equal society.

GREATER LONDON DEVELOPMENT PLAN CASE STUDY

This case study shows how a major world city like London tackles equality and diversity issues through planning and how the city intends to follow this through, as the boroughs develop and implement their policies at the local level. Whether Mayor of London or Chief Planner of New York, the creation of a more 'inclusive city, with economic opportunities for everyone, a healthy environment, and an improved quality of life in revitalized neighborhoods is paramount' (Burden, 2003: 1). Whatever religion, race, sex, age, disability or sexuality, everyone should be able to live their lives free from discrimination. Along with New York and Tokyo, London ranks as a world city and is the financial centre of Europe and the economic hub of the UK. London's recent growth stems from the city's exceptional dynamism, which according to the Mayor is set to continue well into this century (Livingston, 2002). With 7 million people encompassing 14 faiths and 300 languages, London competes with New York and Los Angeles for the title of most diverse places in the world. New York has a population of 8.1 million people representing hundreds of languages and cultures (Commissioner Betty Wu, 2002), whereas Los Angeles is one of the most ethnically diverse city regions in the USA with more than 80 different languages spoken in schools. By way of contrast, Tokyo with over 12 million people is noted for its ageing population rather than its ethnic and cultural diversity (Tokyo Bureau of City Planning, 2001). Many world cities are planning today with diversity as a key context.

In 2000, the Labour Government set up the Greater London Authority (GLA) as the first elected regional government in England to improve the quality of life and develop London as a first-class city for those who live, work, study and visit (Figure 4.1).

The Mayor does not have direct control over all of London's services and it is the 32 London Boroughs which provide education, social support, housing, environmental health, waste collection and street cleaning. The voluntary sector, private companies and the National Health Service provide other important services across London. The GLA provides city-wide strategic government, setting the context for London, with the principle purpose of promoting the economic, social and the environmental improvement of Greater London. The GLA also has an important role in influencing and leading the agendas in London, including equalities (GLA, 2003a,b) and economic development (LDA, 2001). It published the draft plan for London in 2002 (GLA, 2002a) and the final version in February 2004 (GLA, 2004a).

The author's review of the plan process shows that the GLA is tackling equality and diversity issues with the Mayor demonstrating a commitment from the top of the organization:

1. Embedding equality in the legislation which set up the GLA.
2. Embedding equality as a cross-cutting theme in the plan for London.
3. Undertaking gender and race impact assessments as part of the plan process (GLA, 2003c).
4. Making equality a key component of the sustainability appraisal (GLA, 2002b).

Figure 4.1 Greater London Authority, UK

5. Including in the stakeholder group, advising on the sustainability appraisal, representatives from CRE (2003) and RADAR although no umbrella group for women or older people.
6. Including specific policy directions in the draft plan which refer to equality.
7. Undertaking follow-up work with specific sectoral groups not represented at the earlier stages.
8. Producing specific supplementary planning guidance (SPG) on equality as part of the planning process (GLA, 2004b).
9. Producing a gender equality scheme which sets out key outputs for the plan team and related units (GLA, 2003a).
10. Commissioning consultants to work up a set of indicators for use as the plan is implemented.
11. Committing the GLA, through the Gender Equality Action Plan, to monitor and evaluate expenditure relating to equalities (GLA, 2003a: 23).
12. Committing the GLA through its Equality Impact Assessments to evaluate potential policies.

The Act of Parliament setting up the authority for London states very clearly that the GLA must consider equality in the formulation of policies and proposals and their implementation. The Act actually says (GLA, 1999, section 33):

1.   The Authority shall make appropriate arrangements with a view to securing that: (a) in the exercise of the power conferred on the Authority by section 30 above, (b) in the formulation of the policies and proposals to be included in any of the strategies mentioned in section 41(1) below, and (c) in the implementation of any of those strategies, there is due regard to the principle that there should be equality of opportunity for all people.

2.   After each financial year the Authority shall publish a report containing: (a) a statement of the arrangements made in pursuance of subsection (1) above which had effect during that financial year; and (b) an assessment of how effective those arrangements were in promoting equality of opportunity.

3.   The functions conferred or imposed on the Authority under or by virtue of this section shall be functions of the Authority which are exercisable by the Mayor acting on behalf of the Authority.

In other words the legislation requires that, through its policy formulation and implementation, the GLA ensures equality of opportunity. A statute is important in ensuring that resources are made available to meet the legal requirements. The corporate gender equality scheme document provides the framework in which the appropriate arrangements required by the legislation are set out. The equality scheme, although acknowledging the importance of diversity, makes the important distinction between diversity and equal opportunities. It states that by avoiding reference to discrimination and the impact power imbalances have on different communities, diversity can be used inappropriately as an alternative rather than a complement to equal opportunities (GLA, 2003a: 73). We have already seen in Chapter 1 that equality and diversity are not interchangeable and are best seen as concepts and principles which work together.

The GLA Act specifically requires that the plan for London deals with matters of strategic importance and, in his foreword in the plan, Mayor Ken Livingston sets out the strategic direction of accommodating growth within the Greater London boundaries without encroaching on the green belt and inner green spaces (Figure 4.2). His vision is to see London

as an exemplary, sustainable world city based on three interwoven themes:

- strong, diverse long term economic growth
- social inclusivity to give all Londoners the opportunity to share in London's future success
- fundamental improvements in London's environment and use of resources (GLA, 2002a: xi).

The GLA Act also requires that the plan takes account of three cross-cutting themes: the health of Londoners, equality of opportunity and London's contribution to sustainable development in the UK. The law also says that the London plan must

Ken Livingstone
Mayor of London

Figure 4.2 Ken Livingstone, Mayor of London (Source: GLA, 2002a: xiii)

undergo a 'sustainability appraisal' at each stage of the plan process and that it must be published with the draft plan for London (GLA, 2002b). The GLA Act imposes no statutory requirement to produce an equality appraisal or a health impact assessment, although the British Medical Association (BMA) encourages the consideration of health in environmental impact assessments. As a consequence, the sustainability appraisal becomes a key mechanism for ensuring that the plan addresses equality issues. The author examined how the sustainability appraisal of the draft plans addressed equality by examining the appraisal document and the draft plan. Conversations by email and telephone with the consultants commissioned to undertake the sustainability appraisal and GLA staff helped clarify the process.

Government regulations require that a sustainability appraisal forms part of the process of preparing the Spatial Development Strategy (SDS). The legislation requires that an independent appraiser appointed by the GLA must undertake the sustainability appraisal (GOL, 2000). In a qualitative way, appraisals assess progress towards sustainable development by referring to relevant objectives. They evaluate the performance of strategies, plans and projects and provide the basis for their improvement. UK guidance defines sustainability appraisal as:

> A systematic and iterative process undertaken during the preparation of a plan or strategy, which identifies and reports on the extent to which the implementation of the plan or strategy would achieve environmental, economic and social objectives by which sustainable development can be defined, in order that the performance of the strategy and policies are improved (DETR, 1999a: 9).

The words systematic and iterative are important. Systematic means that the appraisal looks at each part of the plan and each policy. Iterative means that it takes place at each stage of the plan process so that the results of the appraisal can contribute to the development of policy. The appraisal should expose any potential sustainability conflicts within the strategy, plan or project.

The Government's sustainable development strategy contains four underlying principles:

1.   social progress which recognizes the needs of everyone;
2.   effective protection of the environment;
3.   prudent use of natural resources; and
4.   maintenance of high and stable levels of economic growth and employment.

The guidelines for sustainability appraisals suggest fairly crude objectives and targets for the social progress theme (Table 4.1). The guidelines do say that 'there may be situations where some disaggregation of impacts by different groups would be appropriate, particularly where there are conflicts to be resolved' (DETR, 1999a: 18). However, the disaggregations suggested include residents, employees, employers, unemployed, visitors, young people, the elderly and non-car-owning households but no mention of gender, race, disability and other sectoral groups, thus making it impossible to establish and assess changes to levels of inequality and discrimination.

The GLA developed three sustainable development objectives relating specifically to equality to create more explicit indicators of social progress.

1.   To actively *challenge* discrimination against all marginalized groups in a consistent and comprehensive way.
2.   To ensure Londoners have *access* to opportunities for employment and occupation.
3.   To *respect* people and value their contribution to society.

Table 4.1 Social progress – framework for targets

Sustainability objectives	Targets and directions of change
To find a balance in the distribution of population, employment and housing	Match housing provision to employment growth at the sub-regional level
	Increase the accessibility to housing for household needs arising within communities and for economic migrants
To reduce disparities in income, and access to jobs, housing, and services between areas within the region and between segments of the population	Implement regeneration programmes in all areas in the top quartile for the region for relative multiple deprivations by 2016
	Reduce unemployment in defined priority areas to X% of the national average by a set date
To ensure good accessibility to jobs, facilities and services	X% of population to be X00 metres from a satisfactory public transport service by a set date
	Y% of population to be within X00 metres of a primary school by a set date
To provide decent housing for every household requiring a home	Match of housing provision to assessed need
	X% of change in mix of house types

Source: DETR, 1999a: 19.

These objectives were developed through a series of round table discussions and meetings involving GLA staff, the London Sustainable Development Commission (LSDC) and other stakeholder groups such as the CRE. The words *challenge*, *access* and *respect* are significant, again reflecting the interplay and synergy there needs to be between equality and diversity. The LSDC is important in that it works to develop a coherent approach to sustainable development throughout London, not only to improve the quality of life for people living, working and visiting London today and for generations to come but also to reduce London's footprint on the rest of the UK and the world. The LSDC is committed to working in open and transparent partnerships and embracing a consensual approach, seeking active engagement and inclusion of citizens, communities and key constituencies. It provides an independent London voice on matters that relate to sustainable development and takes responsibility for advocating, encouraging, supporting and promoting best practice on sustainable development to all sectors. Equity, diversity and inclusivity form core principles of LSDC (2003) and the active challenging of discrimination against all marginalized groups in a consistent and comprehensive way became a key equality objective of the sustainability appraisal. An analysis of the 'Towards London Plan' document, summarized in Table 4.2, shows that 24 policy directions

Table 4.2 Policy directions supporting the sustainable development objectives relating to equality in the Towards London Plan

Sustainable development objectives relating to particular equality themes	Reference number of policy making a distinct contribution to the objective	Reference number of policies contributing to all 3 equality objectives
To actively challenge discrimination against all marginalised groups in a consistent and comprehensive way		10, 12, 13, 14, 15, 17, 19, 22, 23, 24, 27, 29, 30, 31, 35, 50, 76, 77, 78, 82
To ensure Londoners have access to opportunities for employment and occupation	1, 3, 5, 7, 8, 9, 11, 16, 18, 20, 36, 37, 58, 59, 60, 61, 81	
To respect people and value their contribution to society	32, 33, 34, 42, 51, 52, 54, 55, 69	

Source: Extracted from ENTEC (2002: Appendix C and D).

support the objective of actively challenging discrimination against all marginalized groups in a consistent and comprehensive way.

In the subsequent Draft London Plan, 50 policy directions were identified supporting this objective (Figure 4.3).

Table 4.3 lists the policy directions in the Towards London Plan which the appraisal identifies as supporting the objective of actively challenging discrimination against all marginalized groups in a consistent and comprehensive way.

An independent appraisal concluded that the Mayor's vision as set in the draft London Plan 'provides a sound basis on which to develop detailed policies and proposals, consistent with sustainable development principles' (ENTEC, 2002: 31). 'The recognition of the importance of sustainable development by the Mayor of London demonstrates a commitment from the very top of the organisation. This commitment is essential if the vision is to be achieved and London is to have a more sustainable future' (ENTEC, 2002: 32).

The consultants also concluded that one of the strengths of the plan is the policy support given to social inclusion with, for instance, specific policies addressing access to affordable housing and urban regeneration. Nonetheless, the appraisal could still have gone further to tackle discrimination by taking a wider view of planning rather than simply seeing it as a traditional 'land-use planning system' as the following quote illustrates. 'Overall the plan now contains a wide range of sustainability focused policies and the challenge is to utilize the land use planning system in London to contribute to sustainability and hence implement the Mayor's vision' (ENTEC, 2002: 35).

The draft plan has not been without its critics. The examination in public (EIP) began on 3 March 2003 and 10 March saw the consideration of matters relating to

Figure 4.3 The Draft London Plan

London's people. Among those who made written submissions were the Black Londoner's Forum (2003), Women's Resource Centre (2003), Office of Children's Rights (2003) and Age Concern (2003). The groups make a number of important suggestions which would help achieve the strategic goal of accommodating the overall growth within London and at the same time give all Londoners the opportunity to share in London's future success. The assessment by these groups concluded that the plan does not include a strategic approach to ageing, racism, the needs of women, voluntary and community sector and children. They call for standards for the local provision of facilities, whether play space, green space or community space, and stress the importance for health of open space, allotments, community

Table 4.3 Policies which support the objective of challenging discrimination

Economic and demographic growth
P2   Accommodating growth: To ensure that the facilities and services needed to support growth are available
London's role in the global economy
P6   Improving quality of life: To increase the attractiveness and quality of life in London for companies and employees
London's other economic roles
P12   Enhancing local economies: To protect and increase the supply of low cost premises to support viable existing and new small businesses, attract those at the margins of the formal economy into the mainstream, encourage ethnic minority businesses and the economic activities of other disadvantaged groups, and to encourage local employment by local firms
London, city of learning
P13   Enhancing skills and employment opportunities: To encourage provision of training facilities, especially in deprived areas and those targeted at unemployed and other disadvantaged people, and also to facilitate the provision of training that meets the needs of employers from small businesses to global companies
P14   Enhancing skills and employment opportunities: To ensure that boroughs assess the demands for and ensure the provision of school and pre-school educational facilities
P15   Integrating education and business opportunities: To meet the needs of the higher and further education sectors and to sustain London's world city role as a centre for higher education, for example by promoting the provision of student accommodation, encouraging linkages between universities and science parks and supporting centres of academic excellence in key locations
London's communications
P17   Facilitating new styles of living and working: To keep under review the trends towards new styles of living and working, including the effects on transport, demands for office provision and distribution centres for goods, and the size and type of residential accommodation required
London, city of culture
P19   Improving London's attractions as a world city: To recognise the contribution heritage makes to London as a world city by protecting and enhancing conservation areas, listed buildings and heritage sites and ensuring that major new landmark buildings are publicly accessible and make a positive contribution to London's urban environment
P22   Improving London's attractions as a world city: To encourage provision of new facilities which support the identity of London's minority ethnic and faith communities and meet identified needs or deficiencies in provision
P23   Improving London's attractions as a world city: To retain, enhance, maintain and create play and leisure facilities for children and provision for young people
P24   Improving London's attractions as a world city: To promote creative and cultural quarters to enhance local communities and facilitate regeneration
P27   Improving access to facilities: To ensure new and redeveloped arts, cultural and sports facilities are accessible to disabled people

Table 4.3 (Continued)

Housing
P29 Increasing the overall supply of housing: To ensure that the housing stock meets changing needs, for example for single person households and people with special needs
P30 Maximising provision of affordable homes: Subject to an economic impact assessment, to set a target that 50 per cent of new housing should be affordable, including 35 per cent for social renting, and 15 per cent for intermediate housing for people on moderate incomes
P31 Maximising provision of affordable homes: To require an affordable housing element or financial contribution to be included as appropriate in commercial developments
P35 Creating balanced and mixed communities: Within larger residential schemes, to provide for supporting residential facilities, to plan for pedestrians, not cars and to integrate new or existing public transport services
London's urban environment
P53 Enhancing safety, security and accessibility: To promote enhanced accessibility and security in London's buildings and public spaces, especially for pedestrians and people with mobility and sensory disabilities, and to ensure that new buildings and public spaces take account of good practice principles such as those for 'designing out crime'
London's open environment
P62 Providing burial space: To encourage provision to be made for cemetery space in a way that respects cultural and religious preferences and environmental and land use constraints, yet contributes to sustainable land use
London's natural resources
P75 To work with boroughs to ensure that their UDPs are in general conformity with the London Plan and that their other plans, proposals and strategies, including the new Community Strategies, address both London-wide and local concerns
P76 To set out a framework for the consistent application of policies and standards across London
P77 To work with adjoining regions, including regions on continental Europe, to develop more policy consistency and co-ordination with neighbouring authorities and relevant agencies
P78 To set a pan-London framework for borough negotiations with developers on Section 106 agreements
P79 To work with partner agencies to co-ordinate investment strategies in key areas such as transport infrastructure, economic development, housing and regeneration
P82 To take full account of statutory requirements, establish authoritative and co-ordinated monitoring targets and indicators to enable the preparation, implementation and review of the policies contained in the London Plan and related Mayoral strategies

Source: Extracted from the ENTEC (2002). Appraisal of the Towards a London Plan Policy Directions.

facilities and the provision for exercise and formal sports. The Black Londoners Forum calls on the revised plan to set out spatial policies which show how local jobs can be provided for local people without the need for costly travel into central London. They call for compulsory accessibility studies to inform the location of development and transport planning. They also call for a strategic approach to the provision of the spiritual needs of London's diverse communities. The Black Londoners Forum and the Women's Resource Centre call on the revised plan to consider the accommodation needs of the social voluntary and community sector (Black Londoners Forum, 2003; Women's Resource Centre, 2003).

Although the Mayor has a statutory duty to promote equality of opportunity, the plan states that he 'will ensure that the proposals and policies in the London Plan are implemented with due regard to the Race Relations Amendment Act 2000 and the Disabled Persons Act 1981 and relevant government policy advice' (GLA, 2002a: 10). No mention is made of sex and gender, a point highlighted by Age Concern (2003: 2) in their submission to the examination in public. Age Concern call for the equalities section to include an 'equalities framework' showing 'different groups, the common types of disadvantage they share and their unique needs' (Age Concern, 2003: 1). They recommend that boroughs should have regard to the principles and objectives of the equalities framework and ensure they show how they are working to conform to existing legislation on race, disability and gender.

It seems that women as a group were not represented as stakeholders whereas the CRE and RADAR represented black and ethnic groups and disabled people respectively. The sustainability objectives reflect this. In the appraisal of the draft plan there are only a few references to disability and race and none for women or gender. The consultants undertaking appraisals need to have expertise in gender as well as environmental issues. Without the former they will have difficulty working with the discrimination objective. They could not attribute a planning policy to equality or attribute equality to planning policies except in the case of, for example, affordable housing. It is clear that a revised and updated set of guidelines should include a much clearer statement of the need for disaggregated information so that the impact of the objectives can be measured for gender, race and disability as well as age and other sectoral groups.

This case study sets out to show how planners tackled equality issues through the plan for London and in particular to examine the use of the sustainability appraisal as a key means of ensuring that equality issues are built into the plan. There is little doubt that London has proved a world leader although the proof of the plan will be determined during its implementation through the borough plans. It is crucial that sustainability appraisals are not seen as ends in themselves. There are some key lessons for equality. My study of the sustainability appraisal of the draft plans leads me to conclude that the GLA did not assume that every policy direction has the potential to affect equality. Policies relating to waste, for instance, were not seen to have any potential relevance to equality, despite the recognized gendered differences (Reeves, 2003a).

The appraisal of the London plan started from the position that a spatial strategy cannot solve all the problems of social exclusion, but it can help tackle some of the issues. What is needed is an approach which starts more positively with the question how can we use the spatial strategy to tackle social exclusion and inequality. This creates a completely different mindset than before. The Mayor of London is 'committed to ensuring that the planning system is used to its full potential to deliver benefits to all communities' (Livingston, 2002, Foreword). The development of supplementary planning guidance is crucial to this.

CITY OF PLYMOUTH

The second case study relates to planning at a more local level. The case study starts off by explaining why Plymouth went down the route of using a gender audit to assess their plan (Figure 4.4). It then goes on to describe the approach taken. The details of the gender audit and the subsequent evaluation by the planners are presented.

Plymouth City Council commissioned a gender audit as part of the five year review of their 1996 local plan and the framework provides pointers for other local

Figure 4.4 Plymouth City, UK

plan authorities. Plymouth is a coastal city of just under 245,000 people situated on a dramatic waterfront in Devon in the South West of England (Plymouth City Council, 2000a). It is a major urban centre in the Southwest, second only to Bristol and a focus for economic activity in manufacturing, tourism, yachting, business, health, knowledge creation and dissemination. Plymouth City Council addressed equality issues in the local plan process and this case study presents a summary of the gender audit. It is based on the executive summary of the gender audit written by the author for the University of Plymouth (University of Plymouth, 2001). The context for the review of the 1996 local plan was Plymouth's planning strategy produced while the city was Labour-controlled and setting out the key goals for the city. These included tackling inequality, creating a city where everyone is valued, given the opportunity to play a full part in society, have a sense of pride in the city and enjoy an excellent quality of life (Plymouth City Council, 2000a). The objectives support Articles 2 and 3 of the Amsterdam Treaty to make the elimination of inequalities and the promotion of equality between women and men, a central principle of Community policy and action (EU, 1997). These goals also complement one goal of the UK Strategy for Sustainable Development, social progress which recognizes the needs of everyone (DETR, 1999a). When the review of the local plan began in 2000, the planning team recognized that, without a systematic audit, a new local plan could unintentionally reinforce gender inequalities which exist and miss opportunities to do more to promote equality between women and men in the future (Reeves, 2000a). It was recognized that planning has an important role in contributing to equality between women and men. It can shape the environment and the infrastructure for the social and economic life of a community. Men and women do not have the same roles, resources, needs and interests. They do not participate equally in decision-making. The values given to 'women's work' and 'men's work' are often not the same. Land-use planning decisions impact on the location, use and detailed design of buildings, open space and on local environmental quality. In turn, these influence access to and the convenience of facilities and services. Plymouth City Council commissioned Plymouth University to undertake a gender audit, the first of its kind in the UK (Plymouth City Council, 2000b). The main purpose of the gender audit was to identify gender relevant issues for the local plan review and provide an equal opportunities appraisal methodology against which the emerging plan could be tested (Figure 4.5). The consultant was asked to write the audit for those involved in drafting policies for the revised local plan for Plymouth and other strategies produced by and for Plymouth.

The approach taken was based on established mainstreaming tools and techniques discussed in Chapter 3 (Verloo and Roggeband, 1996; Braithwaite, 1998). In addition, the frameworks developed by the European Commission to mainstream gender into structural fund programmes provided important starting points (EOC, 2000;

Figure 4.5 Plymouth Gender Audit

Reeves, 2000b; EC, 2000c). This gender audit of the local plan review process was designed to help planners recognize the nature of the gender inequalities which the plan needed to tackle and shows how this could be used to develop sensitive local plan policies. A gender profile of Plymouth used readily available statistics and the findings from a series of people-based consultations. Through the development of a series of indicators and outputs it provides guidance on how to question existing policy proposals and assess whether and to what extent policies could do more to promote equality. To assess the capacity of planning staff to undertake these tasks the consultants also undertook a survey of staff involved in planning. The complete audit involved:

- scoping of the 1996 local plan to establish the starting point;
- creation of basic indicators for the 2020 vision;
- gender proofing of the planning strategy to identify the gender dimension of the objectives;
- gender profiling of Plymouth using readily available statistics;
- a series of people-based consultations undertaken as a discrete piece of work and incorporated into the audit in August 2000;

- the development of a gender issues matrix to identify the gendered planning issues;
- a survey of staff involved in planning to assess their capacity to implement gender proofing.

SCOPING OF THE 1996 PLAN

The EC distinguishes three types of policy. 'Equality positive policies' which have a specific aim of improving equality between women and men. 'Equality orientated policies' contribute to gender equality objectives. 'Gender neutral policies' make no contribution to equality objectives. To rectify and reverse past imbalances and inequalities and achieve the equality objectives, as many policies as possible need to fall into the positive impact category. A review of the 1996 local plan by the consultants and summarized in Table 4.4 shows some of the areas requiring attention providing an extract focusing on transport and shopping.

GENDER PROFILE

A gender profile shows the differences which exist between women and men and identifies the sources of inequalities. Using the existing local plan as a reference point, the profile presents the key gender gaps and differences, their implications and key questions for the local plan review team. The result was a checklist of questions for planners responsible for each of the following topic areas.

- population and households
- labour market participation and pay
- family and caring responsibilities
- leisure needs
- housing needs
- transport and accessibility
- shopping
- community safety.

Gender gap in population and households

The overall population of Plymouth, like other similar towns, is declining slowly with the numbers of women and men in balance (118,842 males and 124,531 females). However, more women than men fall into the over 40 age group and in the over 70 age group, the number of women (27,900) is more than double the number of men (11,800). The 1991 census showed that a lone pensioner was four times more likely to be a woman than a man with 10,876 female pensioners living alone compared with 2,886 male pensioners. Of a total of 4,331 lone parents in 1991, 294 were male and 4,037 were female and the number of lone parent families had reached

Table 4.4 Gender audit of the 1996 plan

Chapter	Implications of the gender audit for the 1996 plan	How the consultants thought the issues could be addressed
Transport	The gender audit raised questions about the emphasis of transport, which focuses on commuters and visitors as well as congestion. The plan says little about non-commuters many of whom are women and people living in Plymouth	The plan could be much more explicit about the creation of space for bus stops and pick-ups, pedestrian facilities, the need to reduce the stressfulness of shopping which may be resulting from a lack of 'left-shopping' facilities, arcades, some means to transport people up and down the main shopping streets
	The gender audit illustrates the gendered nature of public transport, and its importance for women. Although it raises a number of operational issues, not the immediate concern of a local plan, it identifies issues which residential design guidance could influence	
Shopping	The gender audit demonstrates the importance of local facilities to those who spend time in and around the home	The plan could deal first with local and neighbourhood shopping
	The gender audit suggests a need to re-address priorities and place toilet, crèche and recycling facilities ahead of environmental enhancements	The 'stressful' nature of shopping could be reduced through adequate toilet and crèche facilities and the distances shoppers have to walk to and from public transport stops

Source: Adapted from University of Plymouth (2001).

over 4,800 by 1999. Plymouth has a strong naval tradition with 8,000 families associated with the Navy. In addition 14,800 students are registered with the University of Plymouth. The audit concluded that traditionally local plans have not fully considered the gender differences in population and their implications for the number, type, tenure and location of housing needed, especially when the population profile is taken together with income information (Table 4.5). A key question for the local plan review was whether the technical documents provide sufficient gender-disaggregated information to reveal gendered issues and whether the data is sufficiently rich to uncover the implications of multiple identities.

The analysis of statistical sources provided valuable baseline data highlighting particular gaps in information. To complement this, the people-based focus groups provided more qualitative information and involved interviews with eight groups ranging in size from four to ten people, six groups made up of women, one a mixed

Table 4.5 Summary of the key challenges

Gender gaps or differences	Challenges for the Plymouth Local Plan
Population and households	To ensure that future plans take account of gender differences in population, house holds and income and their impact on all policies
Labour market participation and pay	To help create more ways to improve the relationship between where people live, employment opportunities and facilities such as shopping and create the opportunities for people to access a wider variety of jobs and education
Family and caring responsibilities	To do more to increase the number and range of care facilities for children, young people, older people and dependent relatives, perhaps through planning obligations
Leisure needs	To help increase the provision of leisure facilities for indoor recreation and sport and to increase the provision of childcare facilities associated with leisure facilities, to increase safe and secure cycle paths and increase the provision of allotment space for women
Housing needs	To create more affordable housing with access to employment, shopping and community facilities. It also challenges the plan to create housing areas which are safer, particularly at night and after dark. To make adequate provision for refuges and hostels as well as provide for the housing and community needs of older women and men
Transport and accessibility	To help ensure that public transport is made more accessible and the built environment is compatibly accessible. To help ensure that the city feels safe particularly at night and early morning by encouraging mixed-use areas which can reduce the need to travel. What can be done to create more women-friendly cycle routes
Shopping	To increase the provision of childcare facilities at shopping centers; encourage better provision for public transport in shopping centers; protect and encourage the provision of local shops for those on low incomes; improve the provision of shops near where people work; ensure that the design, location and access to shopping facilities considers the needs of all users
Individual and community safety	To do more to improve the actual and perceived safety of environments, in particular at night and after dark; to design out noises

group, and one consisting entirely of male single parents (Woodward, 2000). Sessions lasted up to two hours and the format was designed to create an interesting and enjoyable context for the discussion. The opening question for discussion was people's everyday life. Following this, participants viewed a clip from a film made in 1946 showing a group of women meeting in a community talking about Plymouth.

Participants were asked about the comparisons between 1946 and today, and at the end they reflected on their initial responses and their relationship with local plan processes in Plymouth.

Women highlighted transport as a major issue. The travel patterns of those interviewed rarely involved a simple work–home relationship. Peak-hour traffic problems were exposed as irrelevant to most of those interviewed. None travelled between the worlds of work and home during an 'average' day. Instead, numerous complicated movements between shops, child pick-up points, launderettes, home and work related spaces, whether in paid employment or not. Women also raised the problems associated with travel to leisure facilities at night and felt that urban space at night was seen as men's space and that women were regarded as irresponsible by being in the city after dark. Parks and play facilities provide the main recreational activity accessed by the participants in these interviews. All considered access to parks in Plymouth good but had a major concern about safety. Most found crossing roads to access parks a relatively minor safety concern compared with the cleanliness and fear of other park users. Parents felt compelled to watch over their children playing. Even older children were asked to report to their parent at regular, frequent intervals. Park wardens, better lighting especially in the winter and detailed redesign were suggested as ways to remove areas where people can hide and improve safety fears. Likewise seating design and location ought to ensure that areas where children play should be easily observable.

Issues matrix

Plans are complex documents with many cross-cutting issues and policy inter-relationships to deal with. Drawing on EC work, the consultants set out to develop a series of templates which could be used by planners to compare issues, appraise policy from a gender perspective and develop indicators. To compare issues, an issues matrix was developed (after the work by Greed, 1994) which sets out the key issues raised by the statistics, the literature review and consultation exercise. The topics identified in the draft plan provide the basic framework and these are then considered from the level of the home, the neighbourhood and the city. An extract from the matrix in Table 4.6 illustrates how the issues of housing and waste were considered.

Gender gap in labour market participation and pay

The profile shows that labour market participation and activity rates in Plymouth broadly reflected the UK picture. In Plymouth of a total 95,793 people working in paid jobs 47,971 were men and 47,822 women, 48 per cent of all women worked in part-time paid work compared with 45 per cent in the UK. Twelve per cent of all male workers in Plymouth worked part-time compared with the UK figure of 7 per cent

Table 4.6 Housing

Using the home	Relevant gender issues	Information	Planning implications
Low incomes	Many single women have limited access to housing and less choice than many men	Literature review Consultation exercise Housing statistics	Need for policies to encourage a mix of housing, new build and renovation and appropriate affordable housing options
Social isolation in the home	Older people (predominantly women) and those caring for children and relatives may spend more of their time in the house than other family members. Low incomes and caring responsibilities can make social contact beyond the home difficult	Literature review Consultation exercise	Need for policies to provide for local social and community facilities in all housing areas
The home as a work site	For most women and some men the house is also a work site – even for those in full-time employment outside the house	Literature review Consultation exercise	Need for policies to provide for local job opportunities and services to reduce travel times

Using the neighbourhood	Relevant gender issues	Information	Planning implications
Perceptions of the home	The house for many women may be experienced as a place of stress – at its most extreme resulting in domestic violence. This idea is at variance with the traditional notion of the house as a place of leisure and safety	Literature review Consultation exercise Housing statistics Community statistics	Improve opportunities for social interaction and leisure in the local area

Using the city	Relevant gender issues	Source	Planning implications
Financial limits on wider experience of the city	Many women feel that they have neither the time nor the money to take advantage of facilities distant from their homes	Transport statistics Consultation exercise	Need for policies to improve opportunities for social interaction and leisure in the local area

Table 4.6 (Continued)

Using the home	Relevant gender issues	Information	Planning implications
Waste storage	Problems of storage for recycling. People who spend a large proportion of their time within their house or immediate locality are more likely to be aware of the importance and significance of local small-scale facilities	Consultation exercise	Consideration of waste storage at individual house/housing in new housing development and rehab schemes
Responsibilities for waste generation, disposal, recycling	The gendered nature of household tasks may mean that those planning waste facilities have fully considered the needs of women and men	Consultation exercise	Need to investigate gendered attitudes and behaviours in relation to waste in order to develop more effective policies
Using the neighbourhood	*Relevant gender issues*	*Information*	*Planning implications*
Location of neighbourhood recycling facilities	Their location will determine how easily many groups of women can use them. Access to private cars varies between women and men of different ages and cultural backgrounds	Consultation exercise Housing statistics Transport statistics	Need to ensure that policies provide for accessible, clean, safe waste and recycling facilities
Using the city	*Relevant gender issues*	*Information*	*Planning implications*
District recycling facilities	Gendered nature of access to private cars	Transport statistics	Policies need to ensure that district facilities for the disposal of white goods are accessible for those in rural areas

Source: Adapted from the Plymouth Gender Audit (University of Plymouth, 2001: 105, 108).

(Plymouth City Council, 1997). Women's economic activity rates were about 70 per cent of the female working age population compared with over 80 per cent for men. Nationally, women's economic activity rates was set to rise whilst men's activity rates have been falling and this is linked to the changing structure of the economy. The key sectors of employment for both men and women remained manufacturing, wholesale and retail with the highest levels of part-time jobs in wholesale and retail. The sectors dominated by women include wholesale, retail and health, whereas the key sectors for men were manufacturing and public administration. The earnings gap also reflected the national picture with women working full time earning 71 per cent of male earnings compared with 68 per cent nationally. Men in Plymouth earned slightly more than the average for Devon but less than the UK average whereas women earned less than the Devon and UK average. The earnings gap, which was narrowing during the 1980s and early 1990s, was widening (Devon County Council, 1997). A key implication for the local plan review was that if inequalities between women and men in the labour market participation were to reduce, the local plan needed to consider both the location of new employment sites, their relationship to where people live and the availability of childcare facilities in or near to new employment sites. The audit challenged planners to help create more ways to improve the relationship between where people live, employment opportunities and the facilities such as shopping and create the opportunities for people to access a wider variety of jobs and education.

Gender gap in family and caring responsibilities

In the UK, women's activity rates tend to fall with increasing numbers of children. At the European level amongst women between 20 and 45 years of age with children under 15, the percentage in work was as high as 86 per cent of women with one child and only 65 per cent of women with three children (Eurostat, 1998). In the UK, the figures were much lower. Based on the 1991 census, it was estimated that in Plymouth almost half of all women with children under 15 were in employment. Many of these women worked part-time in order to combine caring and family responsibilities with paid employment. Studies elsewhere showed caring responsibilities to be a serious barrier to starting training and education for three times as many women as men. Caring responsibilities also affected the distance women and men are willing and able to travel to work. One-third of women compared with 11 per cent of men wanted a job less than five miles (10 kilometres) from their home (Yeandle *et al.*, 1999). A more recent survey has shown women more likely than men to highlight balancing work and family life as their most significant issue (Women's Unit, 1998). Statistics showed that a lot of caring is carried out by young people with 61 per cent of young carers being female (South and West Devon Health Authority, 1999a). The consultants pointed out that although the provision of facilities for childcare had been increasing over the last few years, there was still scope to include provisions for childcare in major new developments. The audit challenged the local plan to do more to increase the number and range of care facilities for children, young people, older people and dependent relatives through planning obligations.

Gender gap in housing

Gender gaps in housing tend to relate to the pay and employment gaps. Housing costs in Plymouth were relatively high and Devon was one of the top four housing cost areas of the UK. Low incomes, part-time employment and lower pensions meant that many single women had more limited access to housing with less choice in terms of tenure than many single men. Homelessness was clearly gendered. The largest group of households accepted as homeless were pregnant women or people with children, the latter also includes high proportions of women, which in turn leads to a demand for refuges and hostels. The statistics showed that the different housing needs of men and women and gender-disaggregated statistics formed an important source of information. Table 4.7 provides an example of the framework which could be used by policy planners to assess the gender sensitivity of their policies.

The audit challenged the local plan to create more affordable housing with access to employment, shopping and community facilities. It also challenged the plan to create housing areas which are safer, particularly at night and after dark. In addition it asked what more the plan could do to make adequate provision for

Table 4.7 Framework for appraising policies

Draft policy (equality positive)	Likely policy impact on gendered relations (equality orientated)	Gender issues (equality neutral)	Recommendations
House extensions for dependent relatives (AHR16)	Equality-orientated policy	Gender gap in caring responsibilities with women tending to take on the caring role	Consider how the policy could reflect different needs as well as ensuring good quality housing
	The policy is providing for the housing needs of older women as well as men	Because of the gender age profile, women are more likely to use this type of accommodation	Encourage the production of design guidelines for this type of accommodation to enable more caring to be shared
		Need to cater for a wide range of needs in different cultural communities	

refuges and hostels as well as provide for the housing and community needs of older women and men.

Gender gap in leisure needs

If you exclude walking, more men than women take part in sport and statistics also show that 54 per cent of men take part in sport on a frequent basis compared with 38 per cent for women (Sport England, 1999). Participation rates have been falling for men and increasing for women. Apart from walking, women take part in keep-fit/yoga (17 per cent), swimming (17 per cent) and cycling (8 per cent) on a regular basis. For men, the most popular activities have been cue sports (20 per cent), cycling (15 per cent) and swimming (13 per cent). Men have higher participation rates than women in all sports with the exception of swimming, keep-fit and yoga, horse riding, ice-skating and netball. This helps explain why the rate at which women use outdoor facilities such as sports pitches has been so low. One in three women aged between 25 and 34 years, who are currently non-participants say that better childcare facilities would encourage them to take part, and this figure reaches as high as 35 per cent for parents with children in the 0–2 age bracket. This was also confirmed by the people-based consultation by Woodward (2000).

Allotment allocation was also found to be highly gendered; 78 per cent male and 22 per cent female. Women expressed a desire to run allotments but constraints include lack of facilities such as toilets, play or childcare facilities and perceptions of security. The audit challenged the local plan to increase the provision of leisure facilities for indoor recreation and sport and to increase the provision of childcare facilities associated with leisure facilities, to increase safe and secure cycle paths and increase the provision of allotment space for women.

Overall gender gap in getting around

National surveys show that there are many gender-specific issues which limit women's transport choices and their ability to enter the labour market, look after family, get involved in leisure activities and undertake educational opportunities (Reid–Howie Associates, 1999; DETR, 2000). The Plymouth study showed women more likely to have to make journeys from one neighbourhood to another rather than from a housing area or suburb straight into the city. Because women are more likely than men to have paid employment which is part-time and this often means travelling early in the morning or late at night, issues of safety and security were highlighted. Women rely more on public transport and in 9 out of 20 wards in Plymouth over 40 per cent of households had no car. Women were more likely than men to work close to home and walk to work although many want to be able to work farther from home. Traditionally, plans focused on commuters and journeys to work. Local plans and transport plans need to ensure that they reflect the range of needs and concerns of men and women. Local plans need to work hand in hand with local transport plans to ensure that the land use and environmental design aspects of people's transport needs are met. It may be easier to get from the suburbs and peripheral estates into Plymouth than to get from neighbourhood to neighbourhood. So the audit challenged the plan to help ensure that public transport is made more accessible and the built environment is compatibly accessible. Planning also needs to help ensure that the city feels safe particularly at night and early morning by encouraging mixed-use areas which can reduce the need to travel. Plans should also look at what can be done to create more women-friendly cycle routes.

Gender differences in shopping

The audit found that women who work full-time or part-time in paid employment were more likely than men to include shopping for household essentials such as food and children's clothes as part of their journey to or from work. Although women of all ages were more likely to use public transport, older women are even more likely than men to be dependent on public transport to get to and from shops. The Internet has become increasingly important over the last few years but in 2000 accounted for less than 20 per cent of shopping nationally. Local shops within easy reach of housing areas provide an invaluable source for day-to-day items. Shopping is an essential activity and shopping facilities help create a vibrant local community. A lack of adequate facilities can make shopping a stressful and time-consuming activity intensified by the wet and windy weather, heavy shopping, lengthy walks between shops, public transport facilities, parking and a lack of childcare facilities. The people-based consultations showed that those shopping for essentials want to minimize the stress involved. The audit challenged the plan to:

- increase the provision of childcare facilities at shopping centres;
- encourage better provision for public transport in shopping centres;
- protect and encourage the provision of local shops for those on low incomes;
- improve the provision of shops near where people work;
- ensure that the design, location and access to shopping facilities considers the needs of all users.

Gender differences in safety and neighbour issues

Personal safety is key to individual and community well-being. If people do not feel safe, they will not use city centres and local facilities. Statistics show that women were more concerned about rape than any other offence. They were more worried than men about burglary and violence and not so worried about car crime. As victims of crime or fear of crime, older people experience most fear, with 60 per cent of women and over 25 per cent of men feeling unsafe on the streets at night. Only 17 per cent of women living in cities go out after dark. Within the community, noise was frequently reported as a nuisance to environmental health. This ranges from noisy neighbours, loud music, commercial and industrial noise, burglar or car alarms, construction and transport noises (Plymouth City Council and Devon and Cornwall Constabulary, 1999). They all increase stress and ill health and those who spend more time in and around the home are more likely to be affected. The audit challenged the plan to do more to improve the actual and perceived safety of environments, in particular at night and after dark, to design out noises.

PLYMOUTH'S SELF EVALUATION

The planners reported to committee in November 2001 on how the draft plan had responded to the issues raised in the gender audit. In response to the need for access to a wider variety of jobs and education, the planners stated that the draft plan is supportive of economic development, promoting manufacturing and service sector jobs, and tourism. It is also supportive of training and childcare proposals. It was recognized that the sustainability appraisal would help identify any particular constraints on the nature of development which may need addressing at the revised deposit stage (Plymouth City Council, 2000b). The report went on to say that the draft plan actively promotes the creation of places where people want to live, with a range of accessible services. It includes policies and proposals to protect and enhance services. The report highlighted six policy areas for comment; social facilities, housing, leisure, getting around, shopping and safety. In terms of social facilities, the planners state that the draft plan is generally supportive of the need to provide for the number and range of care facilities for children, young people, older people and dependant relatives within the context of environmental and social safeguards. It enables planning agreements to be used to provide for such facilities. As to housing, the report states that the draft plan includes site-specific and overall targets for affordable housing, and has regard also to locational criteria. The draft plan includes stronger policies than previously on urban design and community safety. The draft plan supports the provision of such uses in appropriate locations and at the same time being sensitive to environmental and social criteria. The draft plan sets targets for the provision of lifetime homes. In terms of leisure, the report states that the draft plan includes policies and proposals to protect and promote sports and leisure facilities. The provision of childcare in such facilities may be negotiated through planning agreements but it could be difficult to achieve this, given that this is seen as primarily a management issue. The draft plan has strong policies on community safety in the design of schemes which would include cycle-ways. The provision of allotment space for use by women is a management issue outside of the scope of the plan. Planners state that the draft plan has addressed the transport issues and has strong policies on community safety and accessibility of the environment. The draft plan actively promotes mixed-use development and includes many mixed-use proposals.

Shopping was highlighted as a key area and planners state that the draft plan does set out a positive planning strategy for childcare facilities in shopping centres. It also enables the negotiation of childcare facilities in major shopping schemes. The planners recognize that the local plan can only influence the provision of improved public transport in shopping centres in a marginal way. Its policies and proposals do take account where appropriate of the need to promote public transport opportunities. The draft plan contains provisions to improve shopping facilities in deprived areas and to safeguard existing shopping uses. The approach to shopping taken in the draft plan is to safeguard and enhance shopping centres (local, district and city centre). Together with policies which protect corner shops, this is considered the most effective way of maximizing the accessibility of shopping. One of the objectives of the draft plan is to take account of the needs of all sectors of the community through the planning and design of new development. The design and locational policies seek to reflect this principle. The draft plan promotes environmental improvements in shopping centres through new schemes. Finally in terms of safety, the report states that the draft plan includes policies on community safety. Planners feel that:

> the concept behind undertaking a gender audit of the local plan remains a valid one consistent with Government planning guidance and best practice. The work remains ahead of its time in that the need to assess and understand more fully the equality issues associated with land-use change is increasingly influencing the national planning agenda. It has assisted in identifying issues to which the local plan has responded. In addition, the ability to show the gender audit to funders who now require equality and gender auditing of project plans associated with regeneration projects should assist in securing funding from a variety of sources (Plymouth City Council, 2001: 3).

Further monitoring exercises will need to take account of multiple identities.

IRISH NATIONAL DEVELOPMENT PLAN CASE STUDY

This case study shows what structures have been set up to mainstream equality in the Irish National Development Plan (NDP) and the implications this has for spatial strategies at the national level. The case study sets out the background to the NDP and the requirements to mainstream equality. A key aspect of this case study is the insight it gives into the barriers to mainstreaming experienced in Ireland and elsewhere.

The NDP sets out the seven-year plan for the investment of 51 billion euros in regional development for infrastructure, education, training, industry, agriculture, forestry, fishing, tourism, social inclusion, rural and regional development. This is organized into six operational programmes – Economic and Social Infrastructure, Employment and Human Resource Development, Productive Investment, two regional operational programmes (one for the Border, Midland and West region, and

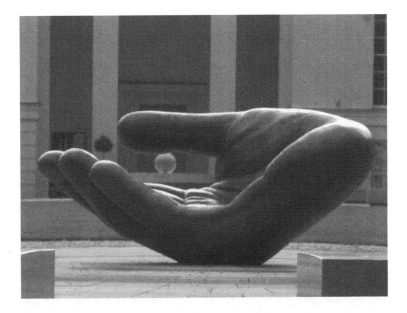

Figure 4.6 Dublin, Ireland

one for the Southern and Eastern region) and the Peace operational programme (to promote peace and reconciliation between communities in the border region with Northern Ireland). The three strategic priorities for the community policies of the EC; (1) regional competitiveness, (2) social cohesion and employment and (3) development of urban and rural areas are underpinned by two horizontal principles – sustainable development and equal opportunities. Under the Treaty of Amsterdam, the Union's financial instruments are required to work simultaneously and in the long-term interest towards economic growth, social cohesion and protection of the environment – in other words sustainable development (Figure 4.6).

In 1999 the Irish government established the Gender Equality Unit in the Department of Justice, Equality and Law Reform to provide advice and support to all bodies working on the NDP. By doing so, the government in effect committed itself to mainstreaming gender in particular. To help meet the requirement to mainstream gender, the unit commissioned a series of fact sheets and good practice guides which outline the main gender equality issues in different policy areas (Figure 4.7).

They have been designed for use both by policy makers in central government and implementers both in local government and their private sector partners, along with strategists in the County Development Boards, social partners and evaluators. As a result of all this activity, gender equality has evolved from being a marginal issue to becoming an integral part of all policy making in Ireland (Carney, 2002: 27). The women's movement in Ireland is credited in playing a central role in achieving

Figure 4.7 Ripple effect

this shift, by using international organizations to introduce policy change at the national level. Although there had been a major government Commission on the Status of Women in 1993, it had resulted in no policy commitment and no spending for the implementation of the report. Between this Second Commission on the Status of Women (1993) and the National Plan for Women (Department of Justice Equality and Law Reform, 2001), gender equality policy in Ireland underwent a transformation. 'It developed from a liberal feminist base to a complex, integrated approach to equality, in line with global standards' (Carney, 2002: 24).

In March 2000, the government passed guidelines on gender impact assessments (GIA), which means that GIA is a requirement for all measures unless exempt. In October 2001, the Department of Justice Equality and Law Reform launched the Draft National Plan for Women or, what many see, the gender mainstreaming policy document. Following this, the NDP gender equality unit set out clearly the requirements in relation to gender mainstreaming in the NDP:

- that equal opportunities, particularly gender equality, be incorporated into the criteria for selecting projects to be funded;
- that indicators to assess progress be broken down by gender 'where the nature of the assistance permits;
- that equal opportunities, particularly gender equality, be a criterion in all terms of reference for evaluation;
- that a balance of women and men on the monitoring committees which oversee progress in the projects being funded be promoted;
- that a representative of the equal opportunities interest, from a relevant government department or statutory body be on all monitoring committees' (NDPGEU, 2001a: 1).

The Government chose not to extend the obligation to mainstream equality to all the grounds covered by the Equal Status Act (Ireland, 2000); marital or family status, sexual orientation, religious belief, age, disability, race, colour, nationality or ethnic or national origin or traveller community. The Employment and Human Resources Operational Programmes does extend to three other target groups: people with disabilities, refugees and travellers. However, the Economic and Social Infrastructure Operational Programmes provide for the encouragement of general efforts to support equal opportunities.

ACHIEVEMENTS SO FAR

There have been two sets of achievements relating to representation of women in the policy process and the development of the fact sheets to inform policy makers. A number of fact sheets are available, covering topics such as transport, housing, rural issues, infrastructure, information technology and the Internet, waste and the environment – topics which are still seen by many as gender neutral (Figure 4.8).

The key gender issues for each topic are summarized in Table 4.8.

The shared issues relate to access, facilities, design, consultation and barriers. The key issues identified in the IT, e-commerce and Internet usage are common across all the areas (Table 4.9) (Reeves, 2002c).

Training sessions held in 2000/2001 to support the dissemination of the fact sheets, brought a range of users together and showed that many of the relevant issues could be thought through from first principles with adequate baseline information in the form of gender disaggregated statistics and qualitative studies. Problems do exist where gendered information is not consistently collected or, if collected, not actually reported. The workshops showed that by taking a much more segmented client-based approach, service providers would ask about the needs of women as well as men. Well-designed consultation mechanisms would provide much of the information needed. In many instances, discussions revealed the need for specific information. The involvement of users in project groups would ensure that the needs of women and men are taken on board.

In parallel, the Equality Authority in Ireland has taken steps to develop an integrated approach to proofing that covers poverty, gender and the wider equality agenda. An integrated proofing process would have a number of advantages. It would (Equality Authority, 2003:1):

- minimize the administrative burden for those involved in the policy process;
- acknowledge the overlapping factors that lead to poverty and inequality;
- highlight the multiple disadvantages suffered when the factors such as gender, race and disability are combined;
- guard against the tendency to treat disadvantaged groups as homogeneous groups;

Figure 4.8 Irish National Development Plan fact sheets

- allow for a more coherent and integrated approach to capacity building within the policy process; and
- maximize the resources available to the policy proofing process.

The Irish experience so far has highlighted the barriers to the success of mainstreaming gender, in the top of the list being a lack of willingness on the part of policy makers to address even basic gender equality issues. In part this is due to a lack of

Table 4.8 Headline issues by topic

Topics	Key gender issues
Housing	Affordable housing, access to owner occupied and rented housing, house design, making communities work, involving users, role of women in housing management, partnerships, development, and funding agencies
Infrastructure	Women and men have different needs and requirements. Surveys in Ireland and elsewhere in Europe show that users, and in particular women, want Public Transport Services to focus on bus and train reliability; improvements to routes, frequency and hours of operation particularly to hospitals and the airport
IT and the Internet	Women were more likely to say that courses were too expensive. Women more likely to cite childcare as a major barrier to learning more about ICT
	Women are more interested in undertaking training. 54 per cent of all respondents expressed an interest and of these 57 per cent were women
	Studies in the USA have shown that only 4 per cent of high tech start-ups that received funding had women CEOs (Muther and Robbins, 2000). Experts agree that the primary reason for this dearth is not lack of business savvy but a weak network for gaining information
	'The computer games business is recognized as being very male dominated. The games industry appears to have settled into its current imbalance without overt masculine intervention or explicit feminine allowance' (Davies, 2002). One result is that the majority of games have a male market (Kerr, 2002)
	Technology is increasingly being used for public involvement exercises but the evaluation of a Geographic Information System based public participation exercise shows a strong male: female bias with 70 per cent of users being male and this may reflect different user preferences (Carver, 2001)
Rural areas	The invisibility of women is a major factor that underpins the lack of good equality practice. Women who are in work in rural communities are often in poorly paid and poorly resourced jobs. They are more likely to be in the service sector (if they are off farm working) which is notoriously badly paid and often only offers part-time or casual jobs. Micro enterprises often find it hard to pay staff well, offer childcare, and support organised training or transport for workers. Self-employment often means scratching a living. Also, women with high qualifications often face low level, casual employment and their skills are very under-utilised. Their opportunities for a life time career can be very curtailed (Swann, 2001)

Table 4.8 (Continued)

Topics	Key gender issues
Waste and the environment	The priority given to specific environmental issues differs for women and men. Their day-to-day lives differ. Women do want different things to men and the 'what women want survey' quotes studies over the last 10 years which show that 20 per cent more women than men want a reduction in air pollution and toxic waste. In terms of the environment, global warming is a key area of concern for officials and pressure groups although women focus on a clean and healthy environment, environmental protection and environmental sustainability (Vallely, 1996)
	Women are more likely to carry out food shopping and preparation and in the UK women still make well over 80 per cent of consumer choices (WEN, Green Teacher, 1994). Women and men have different access to resources, opportunities and decision making. So it is important that projects affect the life situation of women and men directly or indirectly
	Studies often take a gender blind approach which means that without knowing who in the household is responsible for certain activities and tasks, it is impossible to develop a targeted and effective strategy. Tucker's (2001) study of newspaper recycling in the UK, examined what would happen if a kerbside collection for waste paper changed from a frequency of two weeks to 4 weeks. It was predicted that 10 per cent of households would switch from the kerbside scheme to paper banks. No gender analysis was provided and yet men are more likely to have a car and most journeys to paper banks are made by car

Source: NDP Gender Equality Unit.

knowledge and data demonstrating gender inequalities and the tendency of policy making not to involve grassroots consultation. The lack of women in decision-making is problematic as often they can have more awareness of gender equality issues and highlight these issues. Co-ordination was also cited as a problem in that the splitting of different areas of funding/responsibility between different departments and their agencies makes it difficult to develop coherent strategies. Perhaps the biggest issue is the current lack of sanctions in failing to address gender equality issues in policies. Finally, the workload of policy makers is already very high and even those willing to engage with gender mainstreaming find it difficult due to lack of time. These issues are common across jurisdictions and ongoing studies of the implementation of mainstreaming strategies in local government in Wales and Scotland have highlighted similar issues (MacKay and Chaney, 2003).

The NDP unit urges policy makers to adopt a 'can-do' attitude in relation to mainstreaming. The EC has written to the managing authorities asking them to formulate

Table 4.9 Summary of the IT, e-commerce and the Internet fact sheet

Need for gendered baseline information and monitoring of access to, use of, education, employment, wages in each ICT area
Need for gendered targets to be set for recruitment of male/females into education and employment across ICT areas
Need for gendered barriers to ICT to be recognized and addressed
Need for gender monitoring of funding for E-Businesses to ensure equity

Source: Reeves (2002c).

a strategy to increase the number of women on the Monitoring Committees. The unit is beginning to gather new gender-disaggregated data to plug some of the gaps. The use of sanctions or incentives has been considered taking gender equality into account in awarding reserve funding. By the time the NDP gender mainstreaming work was available, the national employment plan had already highlighted projects. The next step involves ensuring that the target selection groups for projects are gender proofed. So no matter what stage or how the projects had been arrived at, there is always an opportunity to gender proof.

CONCLUSIONS

These three case studies of a global city, a local authority and a national plan demonstrate how equality and diversity can be mainstreamed at a range of spatial scales. All demonstrate the importance of a strong legislative basis and international pressure and developments within Europe. The political context has been particularly important in the context of Plymouth and London. The consistent pressure from lobby groups has proved significant in Ireland. The incentives and penalties attached to funding streams have proved important in the Irish context and may well need to be tightened.

A mainstreaming approach has been used in environmental issues although, gender equality has been the primary focus of mainstreaming in theory and practice. Ireland has been looking to develop an integrated model which incorporates diversity and poverty. This means that they take into account the realities of women's and men's lives in respect of race, disability and other dimensions of discrimination and disadvantage, including class, sexuality and religion. It cannot be assumed that the concepts, systems and tools developed for gender mainstreaming will automatically apply to other sectoral groups but the evidence to date suggests that the basic frameworks can be applied. An approach needs to recognize that different dimensions may require different sorts of analyses and specific solutions. A generic mainstreaming approach needs to combine equal treatment and anti-discrimination policies and legislation as well as positive action approaches which recognize the historic and current impact of discriminating structures and practices on different social groups, including women. Diversity approaches recognize the impact of gender, the differences amongst women and amongst men and the existence of multiple discrimination.

Policy tools and decisions need to be sensitive to different legislative contexts and take into account the significance of gender as it affects all women and all men; acknowledges the impact of social group disadvantage (based on, for example, race, ethnicity, age and disability); and exposes the existence of multiple discrimination and the realities for those often made invisible by an approach which does not recognize the existence of gender as a division within equality groups (for example, black women).

CHAPTER 5

PUBLIC PARTICIPATION

> Participation becomes more challenging where a society is composed of a number
> of social, ethnic, gender or age groups that differ in interests, needs, skills and ability
> to articulate their opinions.
>
> — Barrow (2001: 56)

INTRODUCTION

If, as professionals, we do not know what communities need and want – then we
need to ask. If we want to develop sustainable communities then we need to talk.
Public participation strategies will work if they take account of diversity and equality
of communities. As we saw in Chapter 2 there are a number of recognized
approaches to planning and although the collaborative approach to planning, with
participation as a core principle, is the approach which would seem to naturally
make use of the equality and diversity lenses, all can benefit from the insight which
an equality and diversity perspective can give. Chapter 4 went on to examine how
equality and diversity issues can be mainstreamed and built into the development
plan process at a whole range of spatial scales. This chapter considers some of the
key issues facing public participation in diverse communities. In the same way that
mainstreaming can enhance the effectiveness of the different approaches to planning, participation is appropriate to and should inform all approaches to planning.
Drawing on interdisciplinary work, the chapter begins with a look at how public participation has evolved the principles of ethical participation and the barriers to
effective participation. Governments look for best practice across the world. Five
international case studies illustrate the use of a range of approaches to engage
different groups of people. They show contemporary examples at different spatial
scales using both low and high technology techniques. The chapter concludes with
a consideration of how the techniques highlighted in the case studies contribute to
effective participation and what the issues are for the future.

Governments at national and local level are reasserting the importance of public
participation and public involvement to the whole process of spatial and community
planning, regeneration and sustainable development (CDF, 1996; City of Liberty,
2003; ODPM, 2003f). There is a link between politics and participation with left of
centre parties more willing to engage with communities. In the UK, the government
has affirmed the importance of participation, requiring authorities to consult with

users, local businesses and the wider community in order to achieve Best Value (Martin, 1999). The White Papers on modernizing English and Welsh local government go further suggesting that a wider duty to consult would apply to every aspect of a council's activities (DETR, 1999b).

The terms 'public consultation' and 'public involvement' are perceived by many as passive and non-interactive while the term 'participation' signals a shift in thinking to more of a dialogue (Darke, 1998). What should public participation achieve? What can we achieve when participation is more sensitive to diversity and the need for equality? How can we mainstream diversity and equality into public participation? Today, communities expect planners to create workable plans and shared visions for spaces and places. Planners can only achieve this by engaging with different publics to develop meaningful plans which have wide support. The implementation of plans relies on the skills, know-how and often the sweat equity of local people (Selman, 2001, 2003). Jacobs (1961: 148) first used the term 'social capital' in her seminal book *The Life and Death of American Cities* to refer to the people within neighbourhoods who represent the continuity with the past in contrast to newcomers and immigrants who come in to enrich communities.

DEVELOPMENTS IN PUBLIC PARTICIPATION

Local planning authorities in the UK have been required to consult the public since 1972 (MHLG, 1972). The milestones towards achieving effective public participation in development plans in the UK date back 50 years (Dean, 1997). During the debates on the emerging planning legislation in 1947, Member of Parliament Lewis Silkin talked of the need to promote public confidence in planning, suggesting that provisional plans be exhibited and submitted to public opinion. The landmark Skeffington (1969) report considered and reported on the best methods, including publicity, of securing the participation of the public at the formative stage of the development plan. Recommendations included the creation of community forums and the establishment of community development officers. In 1980 the professional body of the RTPI set up a working party on public participation and the recommendations in the final report included proposals for community planning councils developed from Scottish community councils and community health councils (RTPI, 1982). Since then there has been huge growth in and appetite for different kinds of participatory planning approaches, although many would argue that planning legislation is still far too limited in scope. Once again, professional institutes and associations have become acutely aware of the need to enhance public participation skills (Warburton, 2000; Illsley, 2002). The RTPI's New Vision for planning sees planning as 'an essential societal activity − an activity that works best when it is truly inclusive of all people, communities and interests involved − a process which is facilitated, but not owned by professional planners' (RTPI, 2001b). It has taken on the task of co-coordinating planning aid to help communities access planning advice and expertise. With its strap line, 'Making Great Communities Happen', the American Planning Association (APA) sets out to provide leadership in the development of vital communities by advocating excellence in community planning, promoting education and citizen empowerment and providing the tools and support necessary to effect positive change (Cogan, 2000; Earthscan, 2000; APA, 2003).

A legacy of distrust exists. Observers and practitioners have seen participation used as a tool for defending exclusionary, conservative principles, rather than promoting social justice and an ecological vision (Sanoff, 2000). The result can be a concentration of 'bad neighbour' developments such as landfill sites and toxic sites in poor areas (Bullard, 1990). Hester (1996) and others argue that powerful local interests tend to dominate, reducing the capacity of participation to address poverty and social exclusion (Gaventa, 1993). These legacies have deep roots and communities have long memories.

The 1960s saw a rise in community activism when whole neighbourhoods were threatened by redevelopment and consultation was minimal. And it was the post-Vietnam War period in the USA that saw many examples of communities rising up against the tide of business (Clarke, 2003). The traditional Pike Place Market in Seattle, Washington State had been under threat at various times during its history and this intensified from the 1950s onwards with proposals to create a giant parking garage followed by further proposals for high-rise office buildings in the 1960s. Crowley's (1999) account gives an insight into the way in which citizens were effectively mobilized into action to protect the historic market and landmark from demolition. It shows the tenacity communities need if they are to maintain the struggle for what they think is right and the importance of supportive city councillors who provided information and advice to assist the campaign. Due to people pressure, the city scaled back its original urban renewal ambitions on a number of occasions and the community succeeded in achieving preservation status for the area (History Link, 2003). Although the city and the friends of the market subsequently made their peace, there was little agreement on what preservation meant in practical terms. Battles continued over plans for the larger 22-acre urban renewal district and the quasi-corporate Pike Place Market Public Development Authority (PDA) was created in 1973 mainly to purchase and manage public buildings in the market. In addition, a non-profit market foundation was established to fund services for the areas' low-income residents: a senior centre, a clinic and a food bank.

London, UK provides a further example of community activism from this period. Coin Street lies between Waterloo Bridge and Blackfriars Bridge on the south bank of the river Thames (Figures 5.1 and 5.2). In 1997, faced with the prospect of regeneration plans which took little account of their needs and aspirations, local residents set up the Coin Street Action Group. After many struggles to convince

Figure 5.1 Coin Street Scheme, London, UK

the authorities of their vision for the area, they eventually decided to develop and manage the site themselves (Bibby, 2003; CSAG, 2003; Poklewski Koziell, 2003).

The arguments for community participation in urban regeneration today centre around the principle that local residents do know best what their needs are (Hastings, McArthur and McGregor, 1996: 5; Hugh and Carmichael, 1998: 202; Appleton, 1999: 114); community participation promotes inclusive regeneration (Atkinson, 1997; Brownhill and Darke, 1998: 18); and participation means that local residents gain a stake in regeneration (Kintrea, 1996: 290; Amos, 1998).

The two examples of community power cited here demonstrate to developers and communities alike that partnership and engagement are vital and can be achieved through constructive participation (Connor, 2001, 2002). Governments are keen that local people should participate actively in the preparation of plans at the earliest stages. However, in practice, in the UK, local planning authorities are required to do relatively little at each stage of the plan-making process, other than publicize the existence of a plan and produce a statement of public involvement. Much guidance on consultation is still ambivalent, sending mixed messages to the public and professionals alike. Performance management tends to value effectiveness in

Figure 5.2 Coin Street, Gabriel's Wharf, London

terms of time taken, rather than the inclusiveness of the process. As a result, public participation experiences real issues of credibility. Probably most governments still see public participation as contributing to the preparation of statutory development plans and commenting on planning applications (Scottish Executive, 2001). In most countries there is no legal obligation, no mechanism, no framework and no resources for considering community ideas and initiatives. Finland provides one possible answer to the question which planning legislation in every part of the UK, the USA and Canada has not addressed and this is what to do with community ideas. The Finnish Local Government Act (1995) includes a 'Right of initiative'.

> (1) Local residents have the right to submit initiatives to the local authority in matters related to its operations. Persons submitting initiatives shall be informed of action taken as a result of an initiative. At least once a year, the council shall be informed of all initiatives submitted in matters within its purview and of action taken as a result.
> (2) If persons submitting an initiative on a matter within the purview of the Council represent at least two per cent of the local residents entitled to vote, the matter shall be considered by the council not later than six months after the matter is instituted (Finland, 1995: section 28; Tiala, 2002).

WHAT DETERMINES WHO GETS INVOLVED

Studies have shown that the biggest determinant of participation in planning is the state of governance and the nature of central and local governments (Stoker, 2000). Compare the direct democracy of Switzerland where referendums decide policy, and the system of representative democracy in the UK where elected members make decisions on behalf of communities. As the Audit Commission confirmed, the role of elected members in the UK is to decide 'what weight to give the results of community consultation alongside other factors, such as available resources, statutory requirements and the views of partner organisations' (Audit Commission, 1999: para. 48). In Ireland, where elected members have found it impossible to make decisions on contentious issues such as waste management, the government has given executive powers to the Mayor or City Manager (Ireland, 2001).

> Voices reflecting passion, experiences, local knowledge, technical expertise, understanding, culture and history. Voices expressed through language, music, art, actions and silence. Loud and powerful voices. Muffled voices – obstructed by class or physical barriers or prejudice or culture or access. All carry a piece of wisdom, a bit of truth. Together they become wisdom (IAPP, 2004).

A culture of non-participation can generate its own inertia and a sense of quiet compliance with people not wanting to be seen as difficult. Commentators argue that public apathy is the result of social conditioning combined with a devaluation of public experiences, thus creating an apparent public consent to their exclusion from decision-making. Others go further, arguing that the public is implicated in the continuation of the situation. What is clear is that LPAs need to find new ways of building on the experience whilst widening participation to new groups.

In their study of New York, Lach and Hixson (1996) found a 'diversity of viewpoints' to be a key indicator of the value of participation (Sanoff, 2000). Croft and Beresford (1992: 82) argued on the basis of their study in inner-city London that 'most community initiatives have a very small and limited involvement that tends to be biased against poor people, members of ethnic minorities, women, old and young people and others facing particular discrimination'.

Table 5.1 summarizes what Sanoff (2000) sees as the barriers to public participation which he has found across the globe in the USA and Japan. They are consistent with other international studies (ODPM, 2003f). At the root of many of the barriers is the professional's perception of their role to plan for people.

Further studies have found that many people lack awareness of the opportunities to participate due to inadequate advertising and inappropriate timing and location of meetings. Lowndes, Pratchett and Stoker (2001b) found that few people seem to know how to find out about council meetings or their entitlement to attend. In

Table 5.1 Barriers to public involvement and responses

Barriers	Response
Some professionals argue that participation is not necessary, and often undesirable in as much as communities do not have the necessary expertise and often get in the way	The technical complexity of planning can discourage citizen participation, particularly without a skilled facilitator. If planning organizations preempt community involvement by defining problems as too technical or complex for non-professionals to understand, they may engender political passivity, dependency and ignorance (Forrester, 1989)
Because everyone has a different opinion, you will get as many answers as the number of people you ask. A pre-diversity argument is that people are so similar that their needs are not differentiated	People are different and preferences may vary. Excluding users from the design and the planning process, based on the assumption that all people are the same, usually results in solutions that are totally uniform, in which everyone is assumed to have identical requirements
Professionals can feel threatened by participative approach since it implies shifting decision control to users	Professionals have expertise that is different from that of users. Users have expertise in identifying problems, not necessarily in solving them. Collaborating is effective when all participants in the process share their areas of expertise with one another
Involving users is time consuming, and therefore more expensive, than relying on professionals who have broad experience and specialized knowledge	The time and effort devoted to involving users is a basic form of community or organizational development. Helping participants resolve conflicts and identify goals that can be widely discussed are invaluable contributions to any community planning process
The lack of professional experience working in collaboration with users can limit the effectiveness of participation	An outside consultant can facilitate the participatory process and train local professionals and officials
Often the people involved do not represent the majority but are rather citizens who represent special interests	Citizen participation has been found lacking because many effected citizens are left out of the process. The influence of those included in the process is minimized, and the process is inefficient in bringing citizen input to the decision-makers. Participation is unequally distributed throughout society because the qualities that lead some to participate – motivation, skills, and resources – are not equally distributed
There is a danger that the entire process turns out to reflect the aphorism that a camel is a horse designed by committee. Everything is likely to end up as a compromise	People can be reasonable. Most people will change their views in the light of new information when presented in a way that helps them to see how the overall scheme fits into their own vision

Source: Sanoff (2000).

discussing the reasons for non-participation in land-use planning, some argue that the system deliberately perpetuates ignorance and fails to address its limitations. Many exercises seem empty because those involved perceive all too well that, whatever they say, the result appears beyond their influence. The biggest deterrent of all seems to be citizens' expectation or direct experience of a lack of council response to consultation. Researchers report a near universal feeling of councils knowing best and as a result being unresponsive to citizens' concerns, regardless of stated intentions (Lowndes, Pratchett and Stoker, 2001a). Many feel that participation is for 'other people' and that some are 'more suited' to the task. Others, including young people, single parents and ethnic minorities feel excluded because of who they are. Marginalized groups, such as those with learning disabilities, may require advocates but often what is required is an ear to listen to the voice being spoken (Batty, 2003; Lung Ha's Theatre Company, 2003; Radcliffe, 2003).

Appleton's (1999) study tracked the involvement of 19 women in the regeneration of the Norfolk Park/Sheaf Valley area of Sheffield, England (Figure 5.3). She found that the level and depth of participation varied between nil, token and active and that there was an inverse relationship between employment and participation with unemployed people more likely to be involved. She found that the arguments for women's involvement in community participation advanced in the literature are contradictory in that women's 'domestic role does appear to affect their motivation for

Figure 5.3 Sheffield, UK

participation but not necessarily facilitate their ability to participate in a significant role, if at all' (Appleton, 1999: 138). The research concluded that participation is a complex concept and may be experienced at a number of levels (nil, token, active and activist) and it can change through time. The barriers faced by women included institutional, attitudinal and circumstantial factors. Appleton (1999: 130) found that women tend to involve themselves in community action as a continuation of their domestic role. Consistent with other studies she also found that age, employment status and location were important factors (Bondi and Peake, 1988; Christie, 1997; Riseborough, 1997; Lister, 1998).

INVOLVEMENT AS A RIGHT

Ultimately, the three key components of involvement – money, time and the commitment to take on board what people say are key constraints (National Consumer Council, 2003). Who gets involved in planning depends on the mutually reinforcing relationship between the way society sees particular groups of people and the shape of planning and related services. If society sees people as dependent rather than independent, professionals will offer a service which fits this model. If society sees women's equality as a low priority, planning professionals will not see a need to address the gender balance of their consultation process. If society continues to use the medical model of disability, professionals will feel less inclined to see the environment as disabling. If society creates stereotypes of asylum seekers, this affects the extent to which this group is seen to have a right to participate. If society respects older people they will automatically be given a voice. If, as in Finland, society sees young people as potential urban planners, professionals will accord them the respect they deserve in the consultation process (Horelli, 2003a).

In today's representative democracy, we expect local planning authorities to engage with the public to identify issues, generate creative ideas, identify common goals and help build a consensus. But how often do we see LPAs presenting draft plans to communities in meaningful ways which allow scope for effective engagement drawing on a community's social capital? How many times do we see creative workshops with officers of Council and members of the public working side by side to develop fresh ideas about how to tackle local planning problems? Public(s) does not want to be consulted in a cursory way by planning authorities. They do not expect, as was the tradition in Finland before the 1990 Building Act, to be issued with 'public announcements' about an imminent development. Public(s) expects to be treated as partners in the plan-making process. Today, people expect to assert their right to involvement and where that right is limited, communities campaign for legislative change. Although the right to be involved is generally enshrined in planning legislation, communities often need to work hard to assert these rights. Communities want to know what information they have a right to see; what meetings they have a

Table 5.2 Participation approaches

What participation should do	Best practice approaches
Promote inclusive planning and regeneration	Equality proofing the design and implementation of the process, equality impact assessment of the policy proposals
Identify issues and ideal end states drawing on local expertise	Diaries (written, video, photo), drawings, observations (hanging out), guided tours, role play, theatre workshops, focus groups, visioning, planning for real, sustainability for real, interviews, questionnaires, surveys, family support networks
Generate creative ideas	Critical problem solving, brainstorming techniques
Build consensus	Constructive participation techniques, place check, citizens juries, community events, workshops, site visits
Create a stake for people in the future	Networking, participative decision-making, participative budgeting, referenda

right to attend and to speak at; who they have a right to lobby. If planning legislation does not respond to community expectations planning looses credibility and communities resort increasingly to the courts.

Based on a general review of the current literature, Table 5.2 identifies the techniques and tools which can deliver effective participation. Successful participation is determined not so much by the tools but the way they are used and the attitude and approach of the facilitator.

COMMONLY AGREED PRINCIPLES

Commonly agreed international principles of public participation developed by the International Association of Public Participation (IAPP) deal specifically with people's rights, the need for credible follow-through, inclusive processes, proactiveness, people-centredness, transparency and feedback.

1. The public should have a say in decisions about actions that affect their lives.
2. Public participation includes the promise that the public's contribution will influence the decision.
3. The public participation process communicates the interests and meets the process needs of *all* participants.
4. The public participation process *seeks out* and facilitates the involvement of those potentially affected.
5. The public participation process involves participants in *defining* how they participate.

6.   The public participation process provides participants with the information they need to participate in a *meaningful* way.

7.   The public participation process communicates to participants how their input affected the decision (IAPP, 2003).

The principle that public participation involves participants defining how they participate is central to effective public consultation, and the principles set out by the IAPP and this can help guard against consultation fatigue (Figure 5.4). This was a key recommendation of the review of the public consultation on the Sheffield Unitary Development Plan (Reeves, 1995, 1997a). The approach chosen depends on a variety of factors including available time, resources and commitment. The basic principles must be to:

•   go to people;
•   use accessible language;
•   listen actively;
•   show you care;
•   commit to giving feedback;
•   show how their comments and ideas have been taken on board.

Consultation has taken many different forms: one-way information given using the media and advertisements, and two-way interactive techniques to create a dialogue and involve people in the plan-making process (Vancouver City Council, undated; DoE, 1994b). Sanoff (2000: 68) identified nine tools for use at different stages in the planning process:

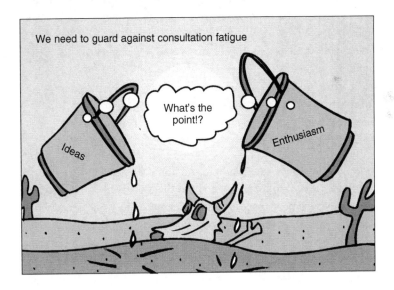

Figure 5.4 Guard against consultation fatigue

1.   Awareness methods – news media, walking tours
2.   Indirect methods – surveys and questionnaires
3.   Group interaction methods – focus groups, charette, design-in
4.   Open-ended methods – participatory cable TV, planning ballot
5.   Brainstorming methods – Gallery, Pin Card, Nominal Group technique, Cranford Slip Method, Ringii Process, Delphi
6.   Interactive brainstorming
7.   Group process
8.   Digital technology, videoconferencing, CU-SeeME desktop videoconferencing, simulation, Sim city
9.   Post-occupancy evaluation to get information about diverse human needs.

Some local authorities see a dilemma in building the competence of those already involved and continuously widening the process to include new groups of citizens. People engage in participatory processes because they appreciate issues and understand the ways in which they can be involved, with a firm belief that their participation will make a difference (Driskell, 2002: 34). Issues which require sustained involvement benefit from approaches which create new and positive opportunities for groups and individuals. People understand that rights and duties do go hand in hand. In their guide to safer communities, Dame and Grant (2002) set out what local people, in particular women and elected officials, can do to create safer communities. Women and women-serving organizations can begin by:

- Calling or writing your local government and letting them know that you are concerned about the need to address women's personal security issues in your community.
- Finding out about planning processes in the community and contacting the community planner.
- Providing, at least once a year, to councils and key staff, information about the current situation of the violence against women.
- Talking to other people in your neighbourhood or community and forming a group that helps women to be involved (Dame and Grant, 2002: 36).

Generally, there has been less public participation at the more strategic levels of planning. The 1980s structure plans in the UK did involve innovative approaches but these never became widespread. A relationship has developed between the scale of planning and the nature of the participation on offer by the state. As the scale increases from regional to national planning, participation tends to take the form of (a) public announcements and (b) invited expert groups. Media advertisements are more limited. Nonetheless, at a national or state level, there has been a trend towards a more consultative approach to the development of government guidance.

The relevant government department decides which areas of policy need to be tackled in the coming one to three years. Research may be commissioned to find out what the issues are and what various stakeholders think the solutions should be. On the basis of the results, the government produces a consultation document and then a final statement of policy. In the UK this takes the form of a white paper if the changes are going to lead to new legislation. Otherwise, the government produces guidance in the form of statutory regulations. The national consultative bodies for equality and diversity such as the EOC, CRE and DRC do not have planning experts, and so input into the development of planning legislation is limited. Single-issue groups and umbrella organizations try to respond. Devolution created fresh opportunities for government to engage with groups and the national women's forum has an opportunity to engage in the development of legislation. With health and education at the top of the public's agenda, environmental and planning issues have received relatively little attention.

The following case studies flesh out what can be done in different circumstances and at different spatial scales. In choosing the case studies, they provide contemporary examples from different spatial scales using different techniques, both low and high technology. I have drawn on the work of planners in the Netherlands where the government involved ordinary people in the national planning process. In addition I have drawn on the work of planners in Finland and Horelli's (2003b) most recent work with young people in Finland to show how networking can facilitate participation. Sanoff's (2000) use of workshops in the USA shows how deaf and blind people have participated in the design of their school communities. Olufemi (1997, 2003) illustrates the level of understanding and empathy gained when she worked with street homeless women in Johannesburg using participatory observation techniques. And finally, the University of Teesside shows the potential use of the very high technology virtual reality tools for planning and urban regeneration (Reeves and Littlejohn, 1999; TCPA, 2003; VRC, 2003).

THE NETHERLANDS WORKING AT THE NATIONAL LEVEL TO INVOLVE PEOPLE

The Netherlands is not noted for its work on mainstreaming equality. However, its approach to the 5th national plan does show how consultation on a national plan can be done (Reeves, 2000c). During a field trip to the Netherlands in 2000, I had the opportunity to meet the consultant who coordinated the consultation on the national plan. Having successfully completed the consultation exercise for the Rotterdam Port authority three years previously, the same consultant was commissioned to take on the ambitious task of consulting on the 5th national plan (Dekker, 2001). This plan sets the context for provincial planning for ten years ahead. Consultation started in October 1999 and in preparation, the consultant examined the issues report, and following discussions with elected officials and interest groups built up a picture of the controversial and contentious issues. These formed the agenda for the public participation. The consultation involved a number of components including newspaper questionnaires published in each of the regional newspapers; an interactive website which attracted over 5,000 responses; 500 randomized telephone surveys made by elected officials and civil servants; public meetings and focus groups. The introduction to the plan includes drawings by young people. The Netherlands example shows that consultation on a national plan is possible and feasible although there are weaknesses. The 5th report contains comments from the consultation report produced by the consultant although it does not show how the comments have been taken on board in the final report, which is a significant weakness. The challenge for the Netherlands will be to show how the public's comments have been taken on board and to help sustain longer term public engagement.

FINLAND – TAKING CHILDREN SERIOUSLY AND USING NETWORKING WITH YOUNG PEOPLE

This case study shows how planners in Finland engage young people. This country has a relatively recent tradition of engaging young people and giving them a legitimate voice in the planning process (Ojanen, 1998). The UN Convention on the rights of a child establishes children's basic right to a healthy and safe environment, as well as to be actors in their own development: to express their views on all matters affecting their lives; to seek, receive and impart information and ideas; and to peaceably assemble (UN, 1989). With its focus on the three 'P's – provision, protection and participation, it has highlighted the need to promote children's participation in many countries. Since the early 1980s and 1990s children's participation in environmental planning and development has increased. The most recent Land Use and Building Act in Finland sees children as official and serious participants (Finnish Ministry of the Environment, 2000). It is recognized that they have a different sense of environmental beauty and a different sense of what makes a place interesting. Children do not simply exist in their environment; they live, grow and develop and they know what they need.

At the Eurofem Conference in Finland, Kaija Ojanen, a planner working in Hameenlina, described the steps taken to involve and take into account the views of children in planning decisions (Figure 5.5) (Ojanen, 1998).

For planners the starting point is the need to recognize and respect the personal values and knowledge of different groups of people. Everyone has a special place – a place with a feeling of belonging, a place with memories. Children have special places which are important. However, a 9-year-old never comes to a public meeting to discuss planning proposals and seldom writes a letter to the bureaucracy. Kaija and her colleagues designed ways of asking children themselves how they experience

Figure 5.5 Eurofem Conference, Finland 1998

the environment, what is important to them and what frightens them. This they called a mental map. At school, children aged 9–12 years are given a list of symbols and a map of the neighbourhood and they work alone with the results collated by the planner. Kaija gives an example of the town plan of Katuma which included proposals for two, five-storey buildings on a particular hill. The children had all said that this was their favourite place – a sunny strawberry field. As a response to this the planner found another suitable location for the buildings and the place was saved from development. Kaija also gave an example of a mast which the telephone company wanted to develop in a park used by children. When it became evident to the company how important this site was to children, another 'uglier' site was chosen. On the mental maps, the children showed that the streets are important to them as places to meet friends although at the same time they are dangerous. To investigate this issue and raise awareness, Kaija arranged a planning walk with children and other members of the community along with planners. At various points, the group would stop and talk about how they saw the environment. The maps have been used by planners and helped to show where further environmental studies would be needed.

The Finnish Ministry of the Interior has also enhanced public participation through networking. Horelli (2003b) has been involved in a project to develop a supportive infrastructure for children's participation in North-Karelia (170,000 residents) in eastern Finland – a sparsely populated region with vast areas of forests and lakes. Once a strong farming region, Karelia has several well-functioning forest and metal industries as well as several high-technology centres. Most residents have free access to Internet services and capacity building for e-citizenship skills. Nevertheless, the unemployment rate is high at around 15 per cent especially among young people who are increasingly moving to the more prosperous parts of Finland. Although the regional council had been aware of the youth problem for a long time, it took three years to negotiate a special project that would seek to create supportive local and regional networks for and with the youth. In the autumn of 2001, the North-Karelian Youth Forum-project (NUFO) was granted 500,000 euros from the European Social Fund and three municipalities (Joensuu, Kitee and Lieksa). This made it possible to hire four young people to co-ordinate and manage the project for two years. They began to mobilize the network, consulted by an evaluator-researcher and the steering committee. The latter comprised major partners, such as representatives from the regional council, the municipalities, some schools, several citizen organizations, and the young people themselves. The vision of the project, created together with the young and older participants, became crystallized as 'A joyful North-Karelia with survival opportunities for young people'. The aim was to create, with young people, a supportive network to provide arenas for meeting face to face and virtually. The objectives included opportunities for work, collaboration in projects, enjoyable events, having a say in local and regional development and sustainable mobility. A variety of enabling methods were used to mobilize the network, one of the most important being the participatory workshop in schools which was also used to launch the project. Each event involved around 100 young people who had the opportunity to discuss their ideas and visions for improving the region with decision-makers. The girls and boys interested in continuing to participate in the work were organized into local or thematic groups. They started to plan and implement events, happenings and new projects. The co-ordination and managing of the project involved considering the outcomes and how the network was to be mobilized and what elements of and connections in the network needed nurturing and caring for. In order to answer these critical questions, a multi-dimensional and partly digitized monitoring and self-evaluation system was carefully developed with the participants. As Horelli outlined, the monitoring instruments consisted of

- a weekly self-assessment sheet for the local project managers;
- a self-assessment notebook for the members of local and thematic teams;
- a monthly self-assessment sheet for the steering committee;
- the monitoring sheet of the process and outcomes of the work plan for the co-coordinator;
- the monitoring sheet of the budget for the co-coordinator.

The collective assessment of the network took place through consultative evaluation sessions, based on adaptive systems theory, after Axelrod *et al.* (Axelrod, 1997; Axelrod, Riolo and Cohen, 2002) and Barabasi (2001). Every second month, the evaluator-researcher and the project managers mapped and discussed the process and outcomes in order to gain an insight into the evolving network patterns. The collective self-assessment involved looking at the structural, spatial and temporal aspects of the project. The supportive network involved people, activities, technology, services, events, institutional actors, concrete and virtual places. The nature and interconnections of the nodes and hubs were assessed through critical dialogue. To make a spatial assessment of the emerging network, the nodes and the hubs were put on the local and regional maps which disclosed the scope and distribution of the support system. Instead of using specific software for the process mapping, a collective memorizing of the significant events of the 'history of the network' was organized after one year. The events were written on stickers, which were then arranged chronologically on the wall and evaluated using a five-point scale in terms of importance. An analytic assessment of the capacity building was undertaken using a matrix of the network actors and this disclosed where and what type of training was needed. The key partners were also invited to discuss the progress of the learning of the network. The network has gathered nearly 2,000 young and adult participants, over 70 per cent of whom are under 25 years old. Four hundred and fifty persons are active agents (two-thirds of them are women) who have the potential to react or pro-act when something happens or is needed in the region. Horelli found that it is the many parallel and consecutive interactions which transform the structure of the network (Horelli, 2005). The long-term challenge will be to see how the network is maintained and whether it becomes sustainable (Figure 5.6).

Figure 5.6 Helsinki, Young and Free

THE USE OF MULTIPLE TECHNIQUES – MINNESOTA ACADEMIES FOR THE BLIND AND THE DEAF (MSAB)

The following example demonstrates how a range of widely used techniques can work with groups who often get left out when it comes to participation, despite the growing protection offered by Disability Legislation and Constitutions. In the USA, according to Article IX of the Constitution, 'no person shall, on the basis of sex, be excluded from participation in, be denied the benefits of, or be subjected to discrimination under any educational program or activity receiving federal financial assistance' (US, 1787). The academies for the blind and the deaf are within a mile of one another in Minnesota, USA, near the State Highway 60 in Faribault MN. The schools which were first established over 100 years ago, sit high above the Straight River overlooking the city of Faribault. They are forty-five minutes south of the Twin Cities Metro Area and an hour northwest of Rochester. MSAB provides comprehensive day and residential educational programmes for blind and visually impaired students from birth through to the age of 22. Both aim to establish and maintain an atmosphere in which individuality and cultural diversity are respected and valued. In 1997, Henry Sanoff was employed to lead a master planning process along with an architectural firm to examine the current and emerging needs of both campuses. The management of both academies wanted to group functionally related areas, allow for the expansion of growth areas and improve pedestrian and vehicle access and movement around the campus. The participation was designed to generate ideas and involve everyone in the planning process. Sanoff and his team asked a sample of staff from both campuses plus representatives of the school community: 23 in the case of the blind academy and 30 in the case of the deaf academy, representing over 20 per cent of the student population. The process involved a series of techniques over three days. Day one started with a walk-through evaluation by staff followed by interviews and an assessment of the major spaces. Following this, a spatial data inventory was undertaken. Day two involved a series of open-ended discussions with a representative group of 23 male and female students. The discussions were led by the consultants and took place throughout the day. In the case of the blind students, ideas were recorded on tape. In the case of deaf students, discussion groups were undertaken and ideas recorded on flip charts. Day two culminated in a workshop. Ten groups of five staff members in each Academy worked together to develop ten proposals for improving the campus. An analysis of current and future activities undertaken as part of the workshop revealed the need to make improvements in academic learning, vocational learning and residential life. In the deaf academy, staff were organized into discussion groups of 30 people each and using the nominal grouping technique each participant was asked to identify and defend his or her two most important concerns for the future of the campus. The actual participation process took place over three days and involved the majority of users. In all, the consultants were involved in the project over a number of months. Eleven projects were identified and prioritized between the two campuses over two years (Sanoff, 2000: 153–155, 2002). This example shows how flexible many of the participative approaches can be for different groups of people. The challenge in this kind of project is to record ideas so that everyone can understand what they mean, and to ensure that everyone understands everyone else's concerns.

USING PARTICIPATORY OBSERVATION TECHNIQUES WITH HOMELESS WOMEN IN JOHANNESBURG

One way of understanding people's concerns is to use techniques which take you into the life world of groups of people. Spatial planners are often criticized for spending too much time at their desks and too little time out and about. Sola Olufemi used participatory observation to increase her understanding of the needs and wants of homeless women in South Africa. I first met Sola at a planning research conference in Sheffield in the late 1990s. We kept in touch and worked on a journal paper together (Olufemi and Reeves, 2004). It was through this process that I could see the potential of the approach to enable planners to understand the communities they plan for better. Street homelessness in South Africa is often perceived as a male issue (Olufemi, 1998, 2000). As part of her PhD research, Olufemi (1997) set out to use an approach which would take her into the life worlds of homeless women. The participative research shows how professionals can build relationships with clients. To understand their life world and day-to-day living, Sola Olufemi lived with a number of the street homeless for a period of two weeks continuously, having built up a relationship with the group over a ten-month period, getting to know key people, networking, establishing a relationship and trust by attending the women's day celebration, visiting those whose shacks were burnt and identifying with their problems. A representative from among the group organized focus group discussions during which street homeless women were able to tell their stories, discuss their life histories and gossip. They described their personal experiences on the street, their daily routines, problems, needs and options. In all, the stories of twelve street homeless women were collected. Four women were randomly selected from each of the categories below for the focus group discussion; (1) pavement/street dwellers, (2) temporary shelters, for example bus shelters, public buildings, open halls, taxi ranks and railway stations and (3) city shelters (organized shelters). The topics introduced for discussion included how people became homeless, their education, their living environment, health, safety and security, their hopes and fears for the future (Figures 5.7 and 5.8).

Here are the stories of three of the women reproduced with the permission of Sola Olufemi:

> Helen is 33 years old, single and lived in Orlando West before she became homeless. She used to work as hairdresser. She has been homeless since 1985

Figure 5.7 Homeless single parent, Johannesburg, South Africa (Source: Photo by Sola Olufemi)

Figure 5.8 Focus group with homeless women, Johannesburg, South Africa (Source: Photo by Sola Olufemi)

when her house was destroyed in violence and due to rape incidents. Helen first stayed in Park station (a shelter for homeless people); she left for Drill hall because of the overcrowding in Park station. Recounting her experience, she said, '...when you become homeless, your life is confused, turned around and negative. You wake up to a new day without a focus nor a plan. You are shut out of the community...'. Helen is of the opinion that '...homelessness is an everyday thing that cannot be curbed.'

Mimi is 38 years old, single mother with three children. She is unemployed and lived in Port Elizabeth before becoming homeless. Mimi became homeless after her husband's death. Her brother-in-law was giving her problems and she lost her job during the period. She left Port Elizabeth in search of a job and ended up in Park station. Mimi recounting her experience said, '...I arrived in Park station on a cold, rainy evening. I stayed in the waiting hall with other women till the next day. The next day and several months to come, I looked for employment, but all to no avail. When it became apparent that I won't get a job, I made friends with the Park station female cleaners, so that they will allow me to stay inside the station when it is cold and raining.'

Nothandile is 27 years old, a single mother with a son. She lived in the Eastern Cape before becoming homeless. She was unemployed. Nothandile has been living on the streets for 5 years with her child. She hopped from one homeless abode to the other before settling in Park Station. She left Eastern Cape to look for a job and good life in Johannesburg. She said, '...I was abused and became pregnant in the course of looking for a job. I had no money to take care of the child and myself. So I met a lady who said I should come with her to Park Station where you don't need money to rent a flat. I sleep on the pavement using cardboard boxes with my child and I scavenge to keep body and soul together.'

Through her research, Olufemi developed a six-stage participatory approach which planners could use to engage with homeless people and other disadvantaged groups in an interactive way. The first step, co-operative encounter, enables the identification and location of people's abodes, their needs, problems and aspirations. Then co-operation is fostered through discussions, brainstorming, workshops or meetings and report backs (feedback mechanism), a process best realized through the street homeless leaders, volunteers or other respected persons. The third step involves co-operative exploration of the street homeless people's ideas for the future, combining this knowledge with the planner's skills. Step four involves an interpretation of the problems, needs and aspirations of the street homeless (women) by the planners after which during step five, they develop themes and strategies based on these interpretations. The planner and the street homeless (women) explore possibilities, options, rank priorities, share responsibilities and set out a plan of action. The last step involves decision-making and practical actions by all those involved to help street homeless (women). This whole approach involves huge commitment and, for many professional planners traditionally trained in clinical analysis, a huge amount of courage to step outside their comfort zones. The challenge for those who advocate this technique is to actually get senior staff to take a lead and act as positive role models to other colleagues.

THE USE OF VIRTUAL REALITY IN PUBLIC INVOLVEMENT

From low to high technology, this last case study shows the potential of computer-based technology for public participation. In 2000, I was commissioned to undertake an evaluation of one of the EC-funded projects being undertaken by the University of Teesside's Virtual Reality (VR) Centre (Reeves, 1999a). As VR technology has become more widely available and increasingly affordable, interest in its potential application to urban regeneration, environmental planning, architecture and related fields has increased. Large-scale VR projects provide extensive models for urban planning with examples from the University of California at Los Angeles and their virtual model of the entire Los Angeles basin (UCLA, 2003) and the University of Strathclyde model of Glasgow (Abacus, 2003). Virtual reality is used to facilitate public participation in regeneration schemes, model town centres, visualize heritage sites, conceptualize environmental reclamation schemes and model pedestrian flows (TPAS, 2003). Virtual reality has a wide application in environmental impact studies to show the likely impact of major developments such as transport or non-renewable energy projects on the natural and built environments. It can be used for housing perception studies to show how people use space and what designs work best for different groups of people. Wheelchair motion platforms for use in virtual environment laboratories allow users to navigate within virtual worlds while experiencing the inclines and changes in surface (Abacus, 2003).

HOW VR WORKS

Virtual reality works by creating the illusion of three-dimensional space where, in fact, there is none. It has been described as a way of building a three-dimensional (3D) model of a particular area using a computer which then lets you move around the area to see what it looks like from any angle. The model can be a reconstruction of what exists already or a proposed area or building. Technologies already used by planners and architects include: line drawing (non-digital), physical 3D modelling (non-digital), digital painting/drawing, 3D modelling and rendering, 2D and 3D computer animation. The distinguishing features of VR over other forms of technology are the powerful sense of realism, engagement and control it creates – the feeling of being there. Other benefits include the ability to interact with the environment by replacing one feature for another. Users can interact with the proposed environment more naturally than simply viewing plans and still images. The use of real-time action can create a sense of actually being there. Many feel that VR helps reduce the conceptual load people experience when faced with two-dimensional plans which require a lot of interpretation. Users actually engage with the environment and gain a deeper perspective. Sound can add to the user's sense of immersion and increase the sense of reality. Inevitably, the more interactive the technology, the more expensive to implement. Virtual reality creates an ability to control the route through the environment. They are increasingly cost competitive with architectural models and in large schemes can be significantly cheaper.

There are two basic types of VR – non-immersive and immersive. Non-immersive VR generally involves three-dimensional scenes being displayed through a conventional two-dimensional display device such as a visual display unit (VDU). Immersive VR allows the user to be surrounded by the image by means of a screen or head-mounted goggles. Head-mounted virtual reality (HMVR) goggles track the users head movement so that the images can move to reflect this movement. Projection-based immersive VR enables 3D images to be displayed on a wide-angle concave video projection screen, often with accompanying sound. This projection-based technology allows users to see their own body in the environment and groups of users can undergo a shared experience and interact with each other in the process and exchange ideas. Users have the option to wear lightweight stereo glasses to view these images in full 3D. In both the non-immersive or immersive systems, the user can explore the environment by moving around and flying through the model using a conventional computer mouse or joystick, interacting with the environment, controlling the speed and direction and viewpoint. Depending on the level of interactivity, the user may be able to change other aspects of the environment, for example replacing one building in a street for another. Immersive VR can only be appreciated fully in a custom-built theatre, whereas other technologies such as 3D computer animation and non-immersive VR can be viewed from stand-alone computers or via the World Wide Web. The Virtual Reality Centre of Teesside Ltd, originally set up by the University of Teesside with European funding, is one of the leading VR centres in Europe. It has two immersive VR auditoria, one with a 7 m × 2.5 m, 140-degree screen with three synchronized projectors and run by a processor Onyx Silicon Graphics computer. The second 6-m Hemispherium™ opened in 1998 with a high-resolution display for single and group interactive floor projectors enabling the user to experience being inside the environment (Stone, 2003).

With planner Anne Goring as project manager, the Teesside Centre explored the use of VR for public participation in regeneration projects which would otherwise have used traditional approaches. Over twenty Teesside community groups involved in the European steel area regeneration projects (RESIDER II) were invited to explore its use. The first group to actively get involved was the Future Regeneration of Grangetown (FROG), a community forum involved in regeneration projects with close partnerships with local industry. This group used VR to model an adventure play area to show the community what their ideas would look like. The community groups saw the VR model as a highly credible and accurate presentation tool for potential funders and the local community. Through VR the community could engage on a more equal level with environmental planners on projects. The South Bank Area of Teesside also pursued the use of VR. Three groups were involved: the South Bank renewal team, the Community Forum and the South Bank single regeneration budget (SRB).

The South Bank renewal team, responsible for private sector housing within South Bank, recognized 'a major potential to have the opportunity to see how proposals will look and affect the area they live in'. The South Bank community forum had the role of ensuring that the community was involved in planning the regeneration activities and strategies and promoting self-sustaining regeneration activities. The group wanted to see the result of planned actions and be able to visualize the benefits of regeneration work. They used VR to assist groups visualize the future, to help groups when their planning is necessary and to help co-ordinate multiple actors in community participation. The benefits of using VR were to enable people to visualize complex proposals in 3D, to generate alternative scenarios and more meaningful consultation (Reeves, 1999a). Meetings, drawings and plans had been used as consultation tools. Virtual reality was used to consult with people over regeneration proposals. The lack of specialist equipment did prove a limitation and the logistics of having to view the VR models in a custom-built theatre was restrictive. Some groups suggested making a video of a 'flythrough' model. The VR centre did pursue the use of portable theatres, which can be taken to the communities, as a result of this feedback. The problem of access to computer equipment on which groups could view models in a non-environment was a problem in the early projects. Web-based access via libraries and schools has overcome this shortcoming.

Community groups were conscious of the need for a continuing programme of briefings, training and awareness raising exercises in order to establish the potential of VR in achieving their objectives. There is a high cost to each model, although the early projects benefited from being part of pilot programmes. Costs increase with the inclusion of all the features which make the models more and more realistic. Community groups were asked to choose which features they considered most important; in other words which features they could do without in order to minimize costs. Beyond the ability to navigate around the VR model, it was felt most important to let the user control the environment, for instance to open doors. Users also felt that the ability to interact with the environment by replacing one building with another was very important. Less important were sound and animation, although the former could be especially useful for visually impaired people.

Virtual reality captured the imaginations of community groups in Teesside (Stone and Hearne, 2004). Even with cheaper options available, the groups found they were taken more seriously by potential funders when using this medium. In order to ensure that the unique features of VR are exploited to the full, groups need to have continuing opportunities to investigate the full potential of this exciting technology. Subsequent projects elsewhere in the UK have also proved very effective in involving older people. Where it is the tool of choice, it seems to draw people in who have not been traditionally engaged in community consultation, and experience has shown that it can make the participation more accessible for people who do not speak English well or cannot go to meetings (TPAS, 2003).

CONCLUSION

The case studies illustrated in this chapter demonstrate techniques which can be used in different international and cultural settings (Driskell, 2002). They can be used with different sectoral groups with sensitive adaptations. The conventions of the IAPP provide important guidelines. The VR technique is not widely available and it is not cheap. However, for major regeneration and redevelopment projects, these costs can be built in from the start. For workshops and participatory observation methods to work well, facilitators need to have well-developed competencies. Networking also requires initial management and facilitation and is most likely to be owned by the clients themselves. Table 5.3 looks at how the approaches rate against the criteria for effective participation.

One of the most important outcomes of effective public participation is that it enables everyone in a community to create a stake in the future. It involves recognizing and valuing local expertise.

Today, developments in Information and Communications Technology (ICT), the World Wide Web, digital TV and mobile phone technology continue to revolutionize our relationship with the state and the possibilities for participation. Ustinov (2003: 19) placed these developments in historical context when he wrote 'we live in an epoch of unprecedented progress. The Internet has opened a yet uncharted ocean far greater than those negotiated by Columbus, Vasco da Gama, Magellan and the like, and now, as then, we are in desperate need of cartographers to bring this immensity down to a workable scale.' Government and state guidance still have to catch up with expectations and the technological potential.

Table 5.3 How the approaches rate

What participation should do	The Netherlands	Finland Networking – young people	USA Work-shops – deaf and blind	South Africa Participatory observation – homeless women	UK Virtual reality – regeneration areas
Promote inclusive planning and regeneration	All the approaches have the capability of being inclusive and the planning and execution needs to be carefully proofed					
Identify issues and ideal end states drawing on local expertise	All the approaches succeed in identifying issues and help people think through what kind of future they would like to see and be part of. The VR model is the most visual. Networking can work on a face to face and virtual level and so is useful where communities of shared interest live far apart or it is difficult to get together					
Generate creative ideas	All the approaches do help generate ideas at an individual and group level, assuming that the VR starts with a blank canvas and the community works directly with the modeller					
Build consensus	Both the networking and workshops prove effective in building consensus. The focus groups used as part of the participatory observation can help assess common issues and solutions					
Create a stake for people in the future	Networking has the most potential to create a stake					

Many countries see IT and the Internet as a means of providing publics with access to information as never before. The Internet has provided a powerful means by which special interest groups galvanize support and communicate with supporters. Although the lobby groups and charities such as Age Concern work to ensure that older people gain access to training about the Internet, it is anticipated that this is the group which will be most disenfranchised by development. Digital TV and community-based TV has yet to become widespread but they have the potential to become the medium of choice. Mobile phones will become an important tool for people to vote in the future. Asked how they would expect to find out about their city's plans for sustainability, first-year students on a sustainable development course unanimously pointed to their mobile phones and the Internet. Third-year planning students in Scotland showed that young people expect to gain most information about planning from the Internet yet also want planners to come and ask them about their ideas for the future (Reeves, unpublished).

Governments need to ensure that the voices of all groups are considered seriously. Participation processes can be equality and diversity proofed by:

- establishing the profile of the community and identifying those who have been discriminated against in the past;
- finding out how people want to participate;
- undertaking research using the equal opportunity guidelines;
- setting up programmes of public involvement over reasonable timescales using the principles established by the IAPP;
- giving feedback in appropriate ways;
- engaging in participatory monitoring with different groups.

'Participation is more challenging where a society is composed of a number of social, ethnic, gender or age groups that differ in interests, needs, skills and ability to articulate their opinions' (Barrow, 2001: 56). Differently abled people have important contributions to make, and the time and resources needed may be very different to those which exist at present. Instead of talking about delaying plans we need to talk about producing inclusive plans. The principles developed by Sandra Fredman, and discussed in Chapter 3, for the future of equality and diversity apply equally to participation as to the provision of health or education (Fredman, 2002).

CHAPTER 6

DIVERSE PROFESSIONS

Hui e, huami e, taiki e
Let it be done
    — Ihimaera (2003)

INTRODUCTION

This chapter examines the importance of diverse professions. Using survey material it identifies the issues and barriers facing under-represented groups and investigates how these issues have persisted over time. The chapter starts by asking why do we have diverse professions. It then goes on to examine the diversity of the planning profession and what issues face under-represented groups. It looks at how main-streaming can be applied to the profession, the institutes responses so far, and considers two specific initiatives introduced by a planning agency to increase the proportion of women and the number of black and ethnic planners.

THE IMPORTANCE OF DIVERSE PROFESSIONS

Leaving aside the fundamental, moral and legal rights individuals have to equality in the workplace, it is generally acknowledged that a profession which reflects the diversity of a community in terms of gender, race, disability and age will better deliver a service which meets the different needs within the community. Healey (1994) wrote about the slow progress to big gains, with the approach of the year 2000; role and representation of Women: urban and regional planning in sustainable development. 'The planning system also needs to be responsive to and better reflect the needs of all communities in Britain. We believe that this will not be achieved without greater diversity in the planning profession itself' (ODPM, 2002a: para. 81). In the UK, following the MacPherson Report (1999) into the police handling of the death of Stephen Lawrence, attention focused on the need for a more diverse police force. The focus in the USA has tended to be on the military and other public sector bodies. Science has been a focus in Europe and the USA, where it is widely recognized that under-represented groups offer valuable new perspectives that are likely to affect both the goals and the practices of technological work and research (WISE, 2003). The case for black scientists remains poorly understood, no more so than in the media. John Humphries (2003), a journalist, in an interview about the need for more black scientists said that he had never given a thought to the idea of black scientists, 'the need for black police officers and black teachers, yes, but not black scientists'. The case for more black planners and architects and a more gender-balanced planning profession has been made since the 1970s in the USA and the early 1980s in the UK. The race relations panel of the RTPI reiterated its position more recently when it stated that 'one of the most effective ways of ensuring the elimination from town planning practice of racial discrimination, both indirect and direct, is to increase the numbers of members of the profession from ethnic minorities' (Ahmed, Couch and Wright, 1998). It was only in 2002 that the government made a commitment to 'pursue initiatives to make the profession more representative' (ODPM, 2002a: para. 81). With the current emphasis on gender and race, what has been missing has been a serious effort to encourage more disabled people to become planners and to ensure support for those who become disabled during their career. Even in countries like New Zealand, with a gender-balanced profession and a clear policy on bi-culturalism and multi-culturalism, the issue of disabled planners has not been considered (Evening, 2003).

THE PROFESSIONAL AND PROFESSIONAL INSTITUTES

Professional status signifies expertness and considerable competence, requiring special training provided by accredited institutions. The promotion of learning and the advancement of knowledge in the public interest is one of the key hallmarks of the modern profession (Grant, 1998, 1999). We tend to make the distinction between professional and amateur status in relation to sport and in the non-sport arenas we are more likely to hear the terms 'amateur archaeologist' and 'amateur astronomer' than 'amateur planner'. A hierarchy of professions exists in most countries with medicine and law still at the apex, and these professions have sought and attracted the most academically talented students. The teaching profession, regarded highly in many countries, has a relatively low status in the UK, and to maintain recruitment levels, attempts have been made to increase its attractiveness. The public perception of the professional has changed dramatically over the last 15–20 years. The esteem and respect which professionals once expected as a right is now hard-earned and this is epitomized in the relationship people expect to have with health professionals. Planners feel undervalued as a profession (Goodstadt, 2003) and civil engineers see themselves experiencing a lower public image than planning (Anderson, 2003). Yet, tens of thousands of people aspire to work in professions because of the perceived rewards, security, career opportunities and apparent social status. Governments have moved to further professionalize areas to improve standards. The finance sector was targeted by the UK government in the 1990s and this decade sees social work becoming increasingly professionalized.

Professional institutes are member organizations in that 'they exist for the purposes of the profession or trade which their members carry on' (DRC, 1999: section 13(4)). They developed originally to control entry to professions and much of the criticism up until relatively recently results from their highly exclusive and clubby cultures. The chief executives of the built-environment professional institutions in the UK are on record as saying that as far as their role in modern industry is concerned, professional institutions have been guilty of 'losing the plot', being 'stuffy', 'very fragmented' and 'living off their past'. They have also been accused of having 'exclusive obsolete culture', which refers to their professional exclusivity (Banbury, 2000). Nowhere in this report is anything said about equality or the need for diverse and gender-balanced professions. Yet institutes are a shop-window for their professions. The image portrayed by an institute affects the perceived attractiveness of the profession as a whole. If a professional body is unrepresentative of those working in the field, the task of addressing the issues of concern to those outside become evermore difficult and the pattern of membership becomes reinforced rather than made more inclusive. Today, professional institutes must be seen to be open and inclusive. Their main role is to set standards for professional education, to help facilitate the dissemination of best practice and ensure that professionals maintain and enhance their professional standards through continual professional development and lifelong learning. The South African Council for Town and Regional Planners (SAPI) is unique in that the Act of Parliament that established it in 1984 (Town and Regional Planners Act, amended in 1993, 1995 and 2002) (SAPI, 2003) stated that 'all levels of the public sector from top to bottom are to integrate the issue of the emancipation of women in their programmes and daily activities' (cited in correspondence with Price, 1994). The UK-based RTPI is independent of government and reliant on its charter and codes of practice to influence its members. It has charitable status, and so must ensure that it exercises itself 'for the benefit of the public' (RTPI, 2003b). This has been a driving force behind the development of planning aid, a service run by volunteer planners who provide advice and guidance to those who otherwise would not be able to afford a planning consultant. The professional institutional structure with charter status is a UK phenomenon. The Royal Institute of Chartered Surveyors (RICS) dates back to 1868 and the RTPI to 1914. Many other professional institutes in the UK date back to the early nineteenth century. Most senior institutions in the UK, and some in the Commonwealth, have sought a Royal Charter by Her/His Majesty in Council – the Privy Council – which has given them not only increased authority but also wide responsibility in a given area. Chartered institutions are empowered and controlled through their charter and bye-laws and the Privy Council must approve any amendments agreed by members.

As well as bodies such as institutes, which set standards for and control entry to their profession, other organizations called associations represent communities of practice, individuals who come together to share best practice and lobby for change. Perhaps the Town and Country Planning Association (TCPA, 2003) is one of the best known. In America, there is a long-established tradition of associations created by women from planning and allied professions. By 1974, there were 12 professional organizations listed in publications. The Cambridge, Massachuesetts, group Women in Architecture, Landscape Architecture and Planning (WALAP) was particularly concerned about the nature of the design professions and campaigned for flexible work schedules and all-women offices (Torre, 1977: 157).

Planning institutes and associations do not necessarily include everyone working in planning because planners do not have to belong to their professional institute to practice. As a consequence, many planners decide not to join their professional body. More planners in academia are probably non-members than in other sectors. More planners in the private sector are members of professional bodies than those working in the public sector. Despite this, the majority of employers, particularly in the private sector, choose to appoint people who have successfully completed courses accredited by professional bodies (Shaw, Pendlebury and Mawson, 2004). Up until the UK Sex Disqualification (Removal) Act, 1919, women could be refused entry to professions and even after this date access to qualifying educational courses and professional articles were limited. Discretionary recruitment and employment practices, or what we would call discrimination, were still the norm. The Sex Discrimination and Race Relations Acts of the 1970s saw barriers tackled, although today, a man in the UK is still twice as likely as a woman to be in a professional occupation, with 29 per cent of working men and 14 per cent of working women in the professions (Table 6.1).

Planners are three times more likely to be men than women. Compare this with 1983, when men were four times as likely to be in professional occupation and a planner was five times as likely to be a man than a woman. A significant change took place in the 1980s but relatively little change took place between 1991 and 1999.

We know that there are at least 20 institutes or planning associations worldwide with over 66,000 members. At the global level we only have a partial picture of how diverse the profession of planning is. We know that most planners worldwide work in the public sector for central or local governments. A smaller, although growing, number work for the private sector. Fewer planners work in the academic sector than either the public

Table 6.1 Women and men in professional occupations in the UK 1983–1999

	1983 (%)	1991 (%)	1999 (%)
Women	5	13	14
Men	22	30	29

Source: Hinds and Jarvis (2000).

Table 6.2 International comparison of professional membership

Country	Name	Number of members
Australia	Planning Institute of Australia 'Creating Liveable Communities'	3,360
Canada	Canadian Institute of Planners	5,000
India	Institute of Town Planners, India	3,600
UK	Royal Town Planning Institute	14,500
USA	American Planning Association/American Institute of Certified Planners	30,000 13,500
Ireland	Irish Planning Institute	381
Netherlands	Beroepsvereniging van Nederlandse Stedebouwkundigen en Planologen	819
New Zealand	New Zealand Planning Institute	564
South Africa	South African Council for Town and Regional Planners – Regenerating Africa through Planning	966

Sources: RTPI (2003a); Eversley (2003).

or the private sector. Most professional institutes have members abroad and it is recognized that the RTPI probably has the widest membership in over 20 countries. The largest professional planning bodies include the American Planners Association (APA), the Royal Town Planning Institute (RTPI), the Institute of Town Planners India (ITPI), the Planning Institute of Australia (PIA) and the Canadian Institute of Planners (CIP) (Table 6.2).

HOW DIVERSE ARE PROFESSIONS?

New Zealand appears to have the most gender-balanced planning profession with 51 per cent male and 49 per cent female over the range of the membership. 'The gender split is indicative of the profession and there has always been a very good representation of females to males in the top jobs' (Inwood, 2003: E-mail). In Sweden, more men than women are involved in physical planning, both as decision-makers and as planners, and amongst citizens who take part in consultation processes. Since the 1980s in Norway, some local authorities have consciously worked to get more women involved in planning and this has resulted in more disaggregated statistics and new working and organizational methods based on co-operation and participation.

The planning profession is one of eight in the construction sector, where the gender contrast is even more marked (Table 6.3).

The profile of planners who decide to become members of their professional body is highly gendered and predominantly white; 73 per cent of corporate members

Table 6.3 Membership in the UK construction professions 2000

Professional institutes	Total membership	Total female	Female (%)	Sector (%)
Royal Town Planning Institute (RTPI)	14,050	3,372	24	3
The Chartered Institute of Building (CIOB)	33,143	903	2.7	5
The Chartered Institution of Building Services Engineers (CIBSE)	15,264	319	2	3
The Institution of Civil Engineers (ICE)	79,480	3,425	4.3	26
The Institution of Structural Engineers (IstructE)	21,636	951	4.4	5
The Royal Institute of British Architects (RIBA)	32,000		12	11
The Royal Institute of Chartered Surveyors (RICS)	92,772	8,062	8.7	35

Source: Greed (2000).

of the RTPI are male and 27 per cent female (Table 6.4) (RTPI, 2000a). Amongst women and men, the proportion of planners from ethnic groups is just less than 2 per cent and only 0.3 per cent of members are registered disabled.

The age profile for women and men in the planning profession is also very different. A total of 57 per cent of women respondents to the RTPI 1997 member's survey were under 35 compared with 26 per cent male. Only 2 per cent of female respondents were over 55 compared with 13 per cent of men. The survey found women more likely to work in local government, twice as likely to spend time out of planning than men and more likely to be job-sharers (two-thirds of job-sharers are women [RTPI, 1997]). Compared with gender and race, professional institutes know next to nothing about the

Table 6.4 The nature of the planning profession through the eyes of the RTPI

Categories	Total number	Female (%)
Corporate members of the RTPI	14,050	24.2
New intake of student members	396	44–45
Proportion of male to female students	66	33
Fellows	395	4
Members of TPI council	56	18
Management board	12	8
Branch chairpersons/convenors	14	29
Directors of planning and related organisations	473	4

Source: RTPI (2000a).

concerns and professional needs of disabled planners. In the UK, disabled planners have no formal network of support provided by their professional body.

VERTICAL AND HORIZONTAL SEGREGATION

Planning as with other built-environment professions is characterized by vertical and horizontal segregation and this has been recognized for some time (Greed, 1996b). Some private consultancies appear more women-friendly than others. The top five ranked consultancies based in the UK are employing an increasing number and percentage of women planners. Data on black and ethnic minority planners is not yet available. The consultancy position is changeable with Arup and Robert Turley both appearing in the top 5 in 2001 but not in 2003 (Table 6.5).

With women making up 47 per cent of all planning students in the UK (Table 6.6) and 44 per cent in Australia (Table 6.7), potentially, the future gender balance of the profession looks healthy.

However, compared with the figures across subject areas, planning in the UK has 10 per cent fewer women than other courses. Figures for all new students, full-time, part-time and postgraduate in 1999 showed that women represented 55 per cent of the 750,000 enrolments compared with the 47 per cent for planning (Major, 2000). Despite the increase in women graduates, the professional membership looks as if it is not changing at the same rate. The gender balance of new RTPI members is 61 per cent male and 39 per cent female (RTPI, 2001a). New members are likely to be male, white, between 26 and 30, living in England, having completed a full-time undergraduate planning course. Six per cent of new members represent ethnic

Table 6.5 Consultants who are major employers of women 2003

UK based consultants	Ranking of consultancy in terms of fee earning capacity 1 September 2003 (ranking in 2000)	Number of women planners 1 September 2003 (number of women in 2000)	Women planners as a percentage of all chartered town planners employed by these organisations in 1 September 2003 (2000)
RPS Group PLC	1(11)	27(7)	24(26)
Barton Wilmore	2(6)	20(10)	27(27)
GVA Grimley	4(1)	21(20)	34(32)
DTZ Pieda Consulting	5(6)	23(10)	41(29)
Drivers Jonas	2(8)	23(8)	50(29)
Total	–	23	35

Sources: Johnston (2000); Dewar (2003).

Table 6.6 Gender breakdown of students on accredited planning courses in the UK

Type of course	1996/ 1997	1997/ 1998	1998/ 1999	1999/ 2000	2000/ 2001	2001/ 2002	Change 1996/2002
UG full-time	2,290	2,175	2,137	2,320	2,385	2,103	−187
Female (%)	33.7	33.6	33.9	32.6	35.3	35.0	+1.3
UG part-time	66	58	61	51	121	89	+23
Female (%)	45.4	39.6	52.4	53.4	53.4	46.1	+0.7
PG full-time	395	404	406	390	354	472	+77
Female (%)	45.8	49.5	54.4	55.6	53.3	52.5	+6.7
PG part-time	509	491	464	436	332	495	−14
Female (%)	44.9	45.0	46.5	49.0	52.1	55.8	+10.9
Total	3,260	3,128	3,068	3,197	3,192	3,159	−101
Female (%)	42.4	41.9	46.8	47.5	48.5	47.4	+5

Note: UG = Undergraduate; PG = Postgraduate.
Source: Shaw, Pendlebury and Mawson (2004).

Table 6.7 The Australian Planning Institute 2003

Category	Number	Female (%)
Corporates	1,897	22
Students	503	46
Graduates	294	44
Associates	303	29
Fellows	254	13
Life fellows	38	0
Honorary fellows	54	18

Source: PIA (2003b).

'minority' groups and the RTPI has no information on disabled planners. The gendered nature of the profession is also reflected in those who leave. Statistics indicate that proportionately more women than men may be leaving the profession. During 2001, for instance, women made up 25 per cent of RTPI corporate membership and over 30 per cent of those resigning or being struck off for non-payment of subscriptions (Table 6.8) (Claydon and Daniels, 2001).

Petrie (2003a) hypothesizes that in the USA, 'many women have left planning and started their own firms'. Her judgement is that they have done this because of the 'frustrations of trying to get ahead in the profession and hitting the glass ceiling'. McCurdock and Ramsey (1996) identified this shift as a part of a wider trend, termed 'separate and doing fine thanks', promoted by long hours cultures, lack of

Table 6.8 Women and men leaving the profession 2001–2003

Categories	2001		2002		2003 (up to August)	
	Male	Female	Male	Female	Male	Female
Retire	134	16 (11%)	118	21 (15%)	83	18 (18%)
Resign	149	60 (29%)	137	72 (34%)	126	55 (30%)
Struck off	117	58 (33%)	117	51 (30%)	98	62 (38%)
Total	400	134 (25%)	372	144 (28%)	307	135 (31%)

Source: Daws (2003).

flexible working and limited career opportunities. Studies of the architecture profession in the UK have revealed similar results (Johnston, Davies and Greed, 2003).

ISSUES AFFECTING UNDER-REPRESENTED GROUPS

Professions have been slow to appreciate the need for diversity. Under-represented groups have worked on the margins of professional institutes with limited support. However, new legislation and government pressure along with market forces have all created the climate of change. In the past there has been a tendency to treat people's under-representation as the individual's problem, to be dealt with first by means of assertiveness training (which does not eradicate entrenched attitudes) and then mentoring (which does not challenge the informal networks). Sensitivity training followed, to enable managers to gain a better understanding of the 'special' contribution that under-represented groups can make. This has often led to even more pigeon-holing of women and other under-represented groups into roles where their supposed skills could be used to best effect, whilst not tackling the issues relating to other colleagues' behaviours and attitudes. Progressive companies and organizations now tackle underlying working practices that reflect outdated cultural norms (Thomas and Ely, 1996; Eyben et al., 2002). So everyone wins, the organization in terms of efficiency and competitiveness, the individuals who feel they can now work in a place where individuals do not feel obliged to conceal family responsibilities or the fact that they have a life outside work.

Under-represented groups in the planning profession have different views about what is being done and what should be done about equality and diversity by their professional bodies. Women in the planning profession are much more likely than men to think that the institute is not doing enough about equality. Black and ethnic minority groups are more likely than everyone else to think that the institute is not doing enough about equality. In the 1997 survey of members, only 29 per cent of women agreed with the statement that the RTPI takes equal opportunity on the grounds of gender seriously compared with 47 per cent of men. The results of the 2001 survey show that on four interrelated counts, women and men take a different view about the extent to which the RTPI encourages women into the profession, or supports members who are women or is effective in raising issues which affect women (Table 6.9).

A review of surveys undertaken from the 1970s onwards does show that the issues affecting women as an under-represented group within the planning profession have remained stubbornly consistent. Discrimination, pay, career prospects, opportunities for job-share and part-time work are all key issues. A 1973 survey in the New York chapter area, cited in Torre (1977: 157), showed that 70 per cent of the women interviewed acknowledged discrimination and 95 per cent of men denied it. The American Institute of Architects (AIA) found that the most serious problems of sex discrimination were found in the area of employment and began at the start of the career. When hired, women were found placed in a few stereotyped positions

Table 6.9 RTPI members survey 2001

Statement	Female		Male		Overall result	
	% agree	Confidence limit	% agree	Confidence limit	% agree	Confidence limit
I am satisfied with the balance between my work and other aspects of my life	59.2	8.2	50.6	5.0	52.8	4.3
The RTPI is effective in encouraging women into the profession	16.9	6.7	31.2	5.8	26.5	4.5
The RTPI provides adequate support for members who are women	12.1	6.1	21.8	6.4	17.9	4.6
The RTPI is effective in raising issues in planning that affect women	17.2	7.0	27.1	5.9	23.7	4.6

Sources: RTPI (2001a); Reeves (1999b).

regardless of their qualifications. The average income of male architects was found to be over 61 per cent higher than that of female architects. Discrimination against married women and women with young children was not uncommon and there was a double standard of part-time work, where men who took time off to teach were encouraged, whereas women who took time off to care for children risked losing their jobs. Pearson's (2003) fictional book *I Don't Know How She Does It* relates the story of a woman working in the finance sector juggling working and parenting. All that is different in 2003 seems to be the computer and the mobile.

The report of the 1969 survey of 211 RTPI members living in the UK and Ireland gives no gender breakdown (Marcus, 1969). One respondent (assumed to be female) talked about bias against women in county boroughs, other respondents (presumed to be women) talked about the difficulty of keeping abreast with the increasing planning literature. There was a plea for refresher courses sponsored by the RTPI and more part-time working. In 1985, two women planners, in Yorkshire, undertook one of the first surveys of women planners (Smith and Kirby, 1986). Fifty-three out of a potential 122 responded. When asked if 'they believed they had ever experienced discrimination at work because you are a woman', 38 per cent said 'yes', and of these 48 per cent said they saw it in 'attitudes at work', 19 per cent said it was a 'gut reaction' and 14 per cent said they had 'sexist questions at inter-views'. Forty-one per cent of respondents were not in paid work at the time of the survey and three-quarters cared for young children. Services provided by the institute, such as continual professional development, were virtually inaccessible to those with caring responsibilities, because of their timing, cost or availability. As for being able to participate in the governance of the institute at regional or national level, this was very difficult for anyone with caring responsibilities. The 1980s saw the growth of women's networks to provide support, undertake surveys and campaign for better services, with the most active groups at this time in Scotland, Yorkshire and London and later the South West. Caring allowances, grants for summer school and conference attendance, promotion of job-sharing and the development of mentoring schemes all resulted (Burley, 2000). Networking has also proved important (MacCarthy, 2003). Almost on the anniversary of the 1986 report, a national workshop was held in Leeds (England) where women identified 'balancing work as a planner and family life' and 'being accepted in the profession' as key issues. Problems negotiating job-share and part-time working were also cited.

> How is it possible to balance work and family commitments? Few women at the top in local government have children. Is it unrealistic to hope to be a good planner and a good mother/parent? The time, effort and commitment required to reach levels of higher management can only be achieved at a cost to the family or with a high level of support (Mid-career women planner).

When you are a student you are unaware of the barriers within the work place and feel you can take on the world. As soon as you start work as a planner, there is an entirely established way of doing things, which is very hard to influence and change. It is a very difficult path to tread to put oneself in a position of moving up the hierarchy (Young woman planner) (Reeves, 1997b).

Rahder's (1998) study of women planners in Canada identifies similar issues and there is increasingly evidence that the issues facing women are similar the world over. Promotion prospects and the apparent reservation of certain areas of planning for women (soft planning areas like social planning) have been identified as issues by women in the Commonwealth Association of Planners (CAP, 2003) network, although a full survey is needed (Olufemi, 2003). Other surveys in the public sector report a range of similar and related problems facing women and under-represented groups. These include: lonely and non-supportive environments, excluding people from group activities because of their differences, failing to help individuals prepare for management, balancing work and personal life issues, and developing organizational awareness (Davidson and Burke, 1994; Hakim, 1996). Anthony's (2001) study of architects in the USA found a profession 'rife with gender and racial discrimination'. Since the first women in the planning conference in Scotland in 1983, women in planning groups have supported and mentored each other and campaigned for gender to be built into all professional activities (Alderson, 2003; Morris, 2003). Twenty years on, there is a need for a follow-up survey to identify the nature and extent of the current issues facing women planners. We simply do not know why women in the UK are choosing to leave planning and if this is greater than in architecture as shown by Johnston, Davies and Greed's (2003) study of surveying (Ellison, 1999; RIBA, 2004). The Department of Trade and Industry study shows that 80 per cent of women who ask are able to achieve job-sharing or flexible working although for many this means a change in conditions and a drop in salary. We do not know what the issues are for women in planning. There are some success stories. Baker (2001) wrote about two women who head up Development Control in Islington, London.

There is a sense that women in architecture fare worse than women in the planning profession (Manley, 2003b).

I was genuinely amazed by some of the experiences that women architects told me about for example office social events being held in a lap dancing club! Or the very strong expectation of women being expected to work all night or a woman being afraid to mention in the office that her child was seriously ill. These are just a few examples. I would be surprised if the same kind of very direct experiences of macho behaviour would be experienced by women in planning – especially in the local government area of work. I suspect that more planners are aware of the need to be geared up to an approach to work based on Equal Opportunities and hence they speak the language of Equal Opportunity. Of course, this would not necessarily mean that sexist or macho behaviour is not part of the experience of female planners (Manley, 2003a).

Pay inequalities are a concern for planners in the UK, ahead of training opportunities and job-sharing/flexible working and they have been so since the 1980s (Walton, 1985). Excessive hours, career opportunities and professional status also figure strongly. Few students think they face the prospect of discrimination, which is why the campaign '15 per cent' targets young women (EOC, 2002). Graduate pay is highly gendered as studies continue to show (University of Strathclyde, 2001; Morran, 2003; Prospects, 2003). In 1999, three-quarters of women planners earned below £25,000 pa ($61,250), the halfway mark for professional earnings overall in the UK (Johnston, 1999). A follow-up survey in 2001 showed that generally male planners earned more than females; the most common starting salary being £13,000–£15,000. The survey by the RICS members, which included members from the Planning and Development Division, showed that more men than women are likely to be in the higher earning brackets (Ellison, 1999: 29).

Things have not fared much better in academia with regard to pay (Ledwith, 1999) and in the 1999 Independent Review of Higher Education Pay and Conditions, the Secretary of State expressed concern about equal opportunities including the lack of women, ethnic minorities and disabled people in senior positions (Bett, 1999). The UK-wide pay gap between female and male academic staff in 2000 stood at 16 per cent, while in Wales and Scotland the gap exceeded 19 per cent (Kennedy, 2002). The Association of University Teachers (AUT) has consistently reported that 'being black or female is an impediment to progression in higher education institutions' (Halvorsen, 2002). Caplan's (1995) women's guide to surviving in the American academic world has still much to commend it. Although education institutions believe they are in the vanguard of good employment practices and centres of tolerance and diversity, current research shows considerable grounds for concern. In 2003, the UK had only eight women vice chancellors and no university leader from an ethnic minority. The AUT and Proud (2001) study carried out in six institutions in England and Scotland showed that gay men and lesbians holding academic ranks report high perceived levels of discrimination and harassment compared to those faced by ethnic minorities and greater than those faced by heterosexual women.

WHY DIVERSITY?

As we have seen, under-represented groups offer new perspectives to professional practice and research, making a diverse and gender-balanced profession important.

As many professional areas know to their cost, and government ministers are keen to point out, any industry dominated by men uses only half the available talent and creativity (Equalitec, 2002; Hewitt, 2002; Kingsmill, 2003).

> As the economy in the United States and the world grows more and more reliant on a technologically literate work force, the nation cannot afford to overlook the talent and potential contributions of half the population. Women and girls and others under-represented in the sciences offer valuable new perspectives that will affect both the goals and practices of technological work and research. Much work has been done, particularly in the last two decades, to pinpoint the needs of women and girls in science, engineering and technology and to develop programs and interventions to encourage their progress. However, changes need to reach deeply into the culture to permanently alter the institutions where science is taught and practiced (National Council for Research on Women, 2003).

Women have very different approaches to design, something which researchers have only widely recognized in the product design field in the last ten years or so (Moss, 1995). Studies show that women and men bring particular dimensions to the way they work. Belbin (2001), a world expert on teamwork, concludes that 'the case for removing unfair discrimination is self-evident and a cherished value in a liberal society'. Experience, supported by research, has shown that mixed gender teams perform better than single-sex teams. The negative aspects of single-sex groups become ironed out. Belbin finds that all-male groups are prone to macho-competitive tendencies and focus on a single goal to the detriment of all knock-on effects. However, all-female groups, he finds, are prone to lose central focus and become easily sidetracked by personal matters. Clearly the impact of mixed gender teams is just as important in education. Fathers (2003), a product design tutor, who I worked with on the Creative Universities project, quite candidly affirmed that 'female students mother the lads, lower the male testosterone levels and the girls produce really good research proposals'. Research in the UK shows that more women in public sector organizations leads to changes in management practice resulting in greater productivity and less confrontational, conflict-ridden approaches (Walby and Olsen, 2003). It was hoped that a less confrontational and more consensual approach to decision-making would be a side effect of a new gender balance in the devolved parliaments of the UK in Scotland, Wales and Northern Ireland (Meehan, 2002; Chaney and MacKay, 2003; MacKay and Meehan, 2003). Maddock (1999) found that women managers have a strategic approach to change both inside and outside organizations and that women managers have a strong user focus relative to men (Table 6.10).

A number of theories explain women's motivation in the workplace and the positions they strive for. Readers will no doubt find themselves predisposed to one theory or another, although in reality all probably have an input, depending on the

Table 6.10 Cultural codes of gender identified by a study in the healthcare professions

	Masculine	*Feminine*
Development of self	Separation Boundedness Self-esteem Self-love Responsible for self	Relation Connectedness Selflessness Self-sacrifice Responsible for others
Cognitive orientation	Abstract thinking Control Emphasis on skills and expertise	Contextual thinking Emphasis on experience Skills confirmed use
Relational style	Decisive Interrogative Loyal to superiors Agent/instrumental	Loyal to principles Reflective Accommodative Group orientation Expressive/facilitative

Source: Maddock (1999: 95).

context. If you support or advocate the physiological-based theory you will believe that, in defining themselves differently, women are physiologically disposed not to want top jobs. If you take a patriarchal stance, then you will qualify this position by saying that men organize themselves and create establishment structures to further their own interests. Why would women want a top job defined by men? If you take the rational choice approach, then everything comes down to clinical decisions about efficiency so that one half of a domestic partnership specializes in domestic tasks and caring whilst the other specializes in earning money. What could be simpler?

A series of interviews with senior women in the planning profession in the USA and the UK, undertaken by the author in 2000 and 2001 showed that as women gain in seniority they feel they have helped change organizational agendas and make a difference by challenging accepted norms and assumptions which form the basis of decisions. They broaden the agenda and work in a more holistic way, bringing experience from their other lives into the workplace. I found senior women very conscious of their ability to enrich debates and discussions and bring different insights to bear on issues and problems. Certainly this small group of women feel that the male planning profession has encouraged and promoted a very technical approach to the discipline, one which needs to open out, if issues such as sustainability are to be tackled effectively. In terms of working style, women are more likely to work collaboratively, avoiding unnecessary conflict and one of the women interviewed talked about juggling coming naturally. Women encourage women into work, creating training opportunities as well as providing a supportive environment. It is clear that the women interviewed have made an impact as a result of supportive line managers and in one case an explicit strategy of encouraging women into senior management positions – with targets. Networks are important, from lunch clubs to formal groupings. The most important personal qualities are seen as resoluteness, 'wanting to make a difference' and 'challenging the way things are done' (Reeves, 2002b).

BARRIERS

Recent research across the professions in Scotland highlights the following barriers to achieving equality for under-represented groups. These include exclusionary practices, gender stereotyping, lack of flexible working and family-friendly policies, and a failure of professional organizations to actively promote equal opportunities (Kay, 2000). Research in other arenas shows that young women and men talk equality, but few young men will make any personal or professional sacrifices for equality, and young women already sense that. This reflects studies in the health professions which show that young people are moving towards a more androgenous ideal but that, for instance, male registrar doctors are egalitarian until they become consultants when, according to female colleagues, they revert to patronizing gender stereotypes when dealing with women (Wilkinson, 1994).

INSTITUTE RESPONSES FROM MARGINS TO THE MAINSTREAM

Generally, the built-environment institutes have left equality and diversity issues up to specialist panels and divisions which in turn have found it difficult to see issues mainstreamed. Perhaps because planning has a higher proportion of women than other built environment and construction professions, planning institutes, including the RTPI, have shown complacency towards the need to continue to increase women's representation generally and address the needs of women in the profession. A lack of gender balance and ethnoracial diversity has an effect on institutional agendas, priorities and structures. This can result in non-members feeling even less inclined to join. There are parallels to the barriers people experience when deciding whether or not to participate in the planning process. If the substance is not relevant, people decide not to engage.

At the time of the publication of the MacPherson Report (1999) into the police handling of the murder of Stephen Lawrence, the RTPI Council showed no appetite for a review of practices in the profession. Potential discrimination was seen as an issue for local government and employers. The RICS found it much easier and less contentious to campaign to raise the ratio of women in the profession than address issues of racial imbalance (RICS, 2003). The architecture profession has been much the same. Approximately 12 per cent of architecture students and only 2 per cent of all architects are from ethnic minority groups. Since 2000, the UK Commission for

Architecture in the Built Environment (CABE) has committed itself to campaign for equal opportunities (CABE, 2003). It convened a seminar run jointly by The Society of Black Architects (SOBA) on equal opportunities only to find that some high-profile practitioners 'refused to attend'. John Rouse, then Director of CABE, confessed to being 'a bit guilty' that the issue of equal opportunities had 'become a priority only very recently' (Littlefield, 2001).

Where women and black and ethnic minority groups are under-represented, net-works have developed to provide support, which include: Women in Property, Women in Planning, the Black Planners Network, Association of Black Architects, Architects for Change (Sinha, 2003). International networks have also been emerging, one of the most recent being the Women in Transport (WIT) (UITP, 2003). The WIT group is not exclusively dedicated to women, either in its members or scope of work, but it has identified a need to encourage more women to take active roles. It aims to increase awareness of the benefits of a diverse workforce in terms of gender and new competen-cies. Throughout the world public transport is becoming more customer-focused. As agencies realize that the decision-making process should reflect passenger require-ments, providers increasingly recognize the value of a diverse workforce (Howatt, 2003; UITP, 2003). The importance of networks cannot be underestimated. They often develop into effective lobby machines and in her recent work on women's groups, Lovenduski (2003) has shown that without the activity of women's groups at the national and European level, pressure for change would be much less effective.

Prior to 1999, many issues of gender and race were marginalized within the professions. The RTPI Equal Opportunities (women) Panel and the Race Panel had published extensively since the 1980s and lobbied for change within the wider institute. The Race Panel published its first national report in the early 1980s (RTPI, 1983). The RTPI published its first national report on women and planning entitled 'Choice and Opportunity' in the late 1980s (RTPI, 1989). Many in the working group felt that the wider institute ignored the report. But reports in themselves do not change things. The problem was that the report became an end in itself rather than the launch of an actual campaign of action to effect change. The Practice Advice Note on women and planning (RTPI, 1995) and the Gender Audit Toolkit (RTPI, 2003c) have had more practical impacts.

Following the 1997 membership survey, both the women and the race panels of the RTPI found they had to request 'special' analyses to establish gendered and racialized issues. In the USA, the women's division have had to carry out their own survey of women members (Petrie, 2003a). Different sectoral groups in effect compete against each other for resources; something which the race and women's panel have become increasingly aware of. Women and ethnoracial groups want to see equality, including disability issues, mainstreamed across the activities of professional institutes.

Applying mainstreaming to a profession means integrating equality into all aspects of an institute's activities and overcoming the barriers discussed in Chapter 3. When the idea of an equal opportunities committee was put forward in the late 1990s by past President Hazel McKay, it was rejected by the current panels who wanted to see equality issues taken seriously by all committees following the adoption of the mainstreaming approach by the RTPI Council in 1999. To date, mainstreaming has resulted in the New Vision highlighting the importance of social equity, inclusiveness, social and spatial equality. The current Charter revised in 2003 states that the Institute will 'promote equity and equality in the practice of planning and education in planning and in all aspects of the governance of the Chartered Institute' (RTPI, 2003b). The Corporate Plan 2003–2005 identifies a number of key themes along with the two cross-cutting themes of sustainability and equality (RTPI, 2003d). Not only is the corporate plan for the whole institute and impacts on all members, but it also signals to potential members that the RTPI is the kind of forward thinking, progressive, inclusive and supportive body which it is important to belong to.

Since 1994, members of the RTPI have been obliged to comply with their Code of Professional Conduct which states that:

> In all their professional activities, members shall not discriminate on the grounds of race, sex, creed, religion, disability or age and shall seek to eliminate such discrimination by others and to promote equality of opportunity (RTPI, 1994a).

Despite the fact that the code obliges members to promote equality, the RTPI does not collect any information to show how members are achieving this and what support they might need. Should members not be required to demonstrate this as part of their continual professional development? The Research Guidelines also define the obligations of members who undertake research but the level of awareness of this guideline is low and it has very little status.

> Members have a professional obligation to ask themselves how their conduct of the research and presentation of their findings help eliminate discrimination and promote equal opportunity (RTPI, 1994b).

Planning Education Guidelines specify the need for planning learning outcomes to 'appreciate and respect diversity of cultures, views and ideologies and understand how that respect can be applied in planning systems through the pursuit of equal opportunity, social inclusion and non-discrimination (on the grounds of wealth, gender, age, race, disability, religion and culture)' (RTPI, 2003f: section 6.7.8). Planning schools are expected to show how they are attempting to increase the proportion of under-represented groups on their undergraduate and postgraduate programmes year on year.

The 1999 report to RTPI Council on equality in the planning profession identified ways in which the profession could achieve a better gender balance (RTPI, 1999). The equal opportunities panel saw 50/50 profession as a target. Borrowed from the campaign for equal representation of women and men in the new Scottish Parliament co-ordinated by the Scottish Trade Union Council (STUC), 50/50 was popular amongst some. However, most women on Council did not support the notion of 50/50, relating it to the quota system which has become so contentious in the political arena (White, 2003). A common response: 'I want to be chosen as the best candidate not as a women.' The 2001 general members survey also rated the 50/50 profession as the least important. Again, it was perceived as a quota, which in the words of some women members, 'smack of positive discrimination' (illegal in the UK). Some may have felt that the 50/50 profession did not address the wider issue of diversity. However, it does signal a commitment to achieving an equitable profession and it introduces the notion of proportionality which then needs extending to other under-represented groups. The 50/50 profession acknowledged that representation often does not change unless targets are introduced to force a deep change in institutional culture (Reeves, 2001; Reeves and Rozee, 2001). It also recognizes that, similar to improving the gender and ethnic balance of elected councillors in local government, 'more women and ethnic minorities means that equalities are improved or introduced into employment and service areas within local government' (ODPM, 2003b: 75). Equality between women and men means ensuring that both can access and take part in planning education, training, employment opportunities and the activities of the institute on an equal basis. It does not mean treating everyone the same, if this 'same' disadvantages certain individuals.

The report to Council set out a series of recommendations focusing on represent-ation, resourcing and outcomes. It highlighted the need for a renewed commitment to implement the 25 per cent target of female/male membership of panels and committees. It highlighted the need for equality proofing of all material produced and commissioned by the RTPI including committee reports, the website and publicity material. It also highlighted the need for equality proofing of subscriptions plus an equality proofing of the budget, to establish who benefits. It suggested the inclusion of specific equality criteria in the national planning award and stressed the need for a commitment to be made to ensuring that consultation responses include an equality perspective.

PREREQUISITES

Equality and diversity can be built into organizations. A 2002 study looking at the promotion of gender equality in the public sector identified the following prerequisites and they apply to all under-represented groups in a range of sectors (Centre for

Public Services, 2002). First, there is a need for commitment and support from the heart of the organization, in the RTPI's case the Trustees, General Assembly, Secretariat and Branches. Second, there is a need for clear institutional arrangements for the responsibility, promotion, monitoring and reporting of equality supported by sufficient resources (Riley, 2004). Third, there is a need for a clear reporting strategy; such as regular reports to the Board of Trustees and an annual report to the General Assembly to be published. Finally a need for the routine use of equality and diversity tools such as audits, impact assessments and proofing.

Impact assessments could address a practical set of questions:

1.   What different experiences of under-represented groups would affect the way in which the institute operates, delivers services or communicates?
2.   What are the implications of these differences for the promotion of planning, planning policy, education and CPD?
3.   How are specific activities and initiatives going to increase equality between women and men in the profession and in the community?
4.   Who will assume responsibility for implementation?
5.   How will success be measured and reported?

SPECIFIC INITIATIVES IN KEY PLANNING AGENCIES

In 2002 there were at least 50 diversity and equality initiatives in the construction industry (Dainty et al., 2002). Stone (2004) has reflected on the work of the equality task group in the UK Construction Industry Council. The RTPI has supported initiatives to increase the proportion of women in the UK planning inspectorate (PINS) and increase the number of black and ethnic minority groups in planning. In 2000, Leonora Rozee a senior inspector in the UK PINS led a group tasked to advise on how to improve the gender balance. At the turn of the millennium, only about 12 per cent of inspectors were women. Under the modernizing government agenda, the civil service is committed to delivering a dramatic improvement in diversity and has been involved in projects to increase the proportion of women inspectors and increase the number of black and ethnic minority planners. As an executive agency in the Department of the Environment, Transport and the Regions (DETR) and the National Assembly for Wales, PINS deals with planning and allied casework in England and Wales. The agency's main areas of work fall under the Town and Country Planning Act 1990 and include determining planning and enforcement appeals, holding inquiries into objections to development plans and hearing objections into Compulsory Purchase Orders and Rights of Way Orders. It is also responsible for a range of other casework including the holding of inquiries under the housing acts, the environmental protection acts and the transport and works legislation as well as dealing with listed building appeals. The process of decision-making on appeals is governed by Common Law, Acts of Parliament and Statutory Instruments, interpreted by the court and developed by practice and convention. At the time of the 1999 project, PINS employed about 600 staff of whom about 350 were professionally qualified inspectors, working remotely from the headquarters, and about 80 per cent were professional planners. As part of the diversity action plan, PINS set a target of 18 per cent women inspectors by 2005, just a 6 per cent increase from the 1995 figure.

As part of this, an equality project group, involving a self-selected group of staff from across the organization, was launched in 1999 to develop a strategy for addressing the issue of diversity to improve the gender balance in PINS. A survey of women inspectors was carried out in 1999. This provided information about women inspectors' career patterns, why they had joined PINS, what they perceived as the advantages and disadvantages of the job (with a special question devoted to the needs of parents and carers) and whether they would recommend the job to other women. A similar survey of male inspectors was carried out in 2000. This enabled PINS to identify those aspects of an inspector's job likely to appeal to women such as working from home, flexible working patterns, independence and challenging and varied work. One of the key findings was that the recruitment material did not adequately reflect the commitment of the organization to equal opportunities. Second, that promotional work was needed to get the message across to women in person. As a result, presentations were made to the RTPI National Symposium on Gender Equality and the Role of Planning in 1999, and the Town and Country Planning Summer School (Rozee, 2000). In addition, articles appeared in the professional journal *Planning*. All of these measures appear to have assisted PINS in increasing the proportion of women recruited as inspectors. In the last recruitment exercise (in mid-2000) 50 per cent of those recruited (8 in total) were women. So by 2003, 20 per cent of inspectors were women compared with 12 per cent in 1995 and the

Table 6.11 Number of female inspectors since 1995

Year	Total	Number of female inspectors	Women as a percentage of the total
1995	148	17	12
1996	185	23	12
1997	198	28	14
1998	199	28	14
1999	213	31	15
2000	231	36	16
2001	220	35	16
2002	230	38	17
2003	257	50	20

Source: Planning Inspectorate (2003).

PINS target of 18 per cent by 2005 was met three years early as a result of the proactive approach (Table 6.11).

RACE FOR PLANNING

In 2000, Sally Keeble, former parliamentary Under Secretary at the then Department of Transport, Local Government and the Regions (DTLR), set an objective for the planning inspectorate to devise a positive action programme to improve the representation of black and ethnic minorities working in planning in the immediate and longer term. In a dramatic understatement, the report stated that in the UK people from black and ethnic minority groups are considerably under-represented in the planning profession and the numbers currently coming through the education system are insufficient to correct this imbalance.

The scoping report outlined the positive action needed:

- promoting leaders and role models through the media and positive action programmes;
- raising the kudos of planning as a profession;
- working with career counsellors and services to promote planning;
- influencing and linking with school curricula;
- highlighting the relevance of planning for communities and publicize the influence they may have over the process;
- mainstreaming access to planning.

It was also recognized that in order to increase the representation in the longer term, the profession and PINS need to understand the attractiveness of planning as a profession for people from black and ethnic minorities. It is recognized that recruitment should not be tackled in isolation from the larger issue of how planning relates or is perceived to relate to the interests of ethnic minorities. In the short term, a positive action scheme, based on experience in the housing profession, was developed to enable 'black and ethnic minorities' to gain professional planning qualifications using part-time study courses whilst working in a planning department (Shepley, 2003a). This involved a partnership between employers, including PINS and planning schools. It involves a programme of bursaries for university fellowships to fund members of ethnic minorities in the planning profession, to take time out to carry out research that develops skills and credentials and prepares them for higher-level positions. A programme of funding for university student outreach projects that brings planning education into contact with ethnic minority communities, exploring how planning policies and decisions relate to their needs. In 2003, 18 students enrolled; 8 female and 10 male (Shepley, 2003b). The target is to achieve 500 trainees over the next ten years (Winkley, 2004). Will it take the 30 per cent level to be reached before real cultural change occurs (Figures 6.1 and 6.2) (Kanter, 1977)?

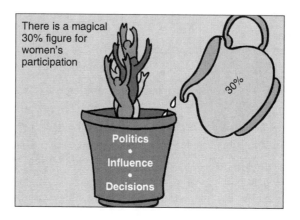

Figure 6.1 The magical 30 per cent

Figure 6.2 When will immigrant women reach 30 per cent?

CONCLUSION

A diverse and gender-balanced profession can only be achieved with a strategy, which systematically tackles the underlying reasons for the inequalities which exist. There is little point in the RTPI or any other planning agency launching a Public Relations campaign to attract under-represented groups into planning without even tackling those aspects of the profession which are problematic. Over the next few years there is likely to be an increasing emphasis on disability with the new guidelines directing professions to ensure that their educational requirements do not discriminate against disabled people. Some of the working practices and cultural norms of many planning departments and consultancies are not only inefficient but a definite deterrent to those who want to combine work and home. Professional bodies have an important role in establishing standards and acting as a shop-window for professions. The danger is that they will continue to become increasingly unrepresentative of those working in planning.

CHAPTER 7

CULTURAL COMPETENCE

Rebecca Gilman's highly acclaimed fictional play, 'Spinning the Butter', is based on personal experience. In a small liberal arts college in New England, USA, one of the very few black students starts to receive racially motivated threats. At one point in the play, a tutor admits her true feelings about black people.

> All I learned was to appreciate black people. The way you might appreciate a painting or a good bottle of Bordeaux. I studied them to figure them out, like Sanskrit. But that's no different from hating them. It is called objectification. And it relies on keeping the object of your investigation at bay. It relies on knowing one or two really well educated black people (Gilman, 2001).

INTRODUCTION

Gilman was not trying to solve racism with a play. What she did was highlight the need for individuals to effect deep changes to attitudes. Critics have warned that 'contemporary visions of cultural difference seek to learn about other cultural forms, not to create a richer and more universal culture but to imprison us more effectively in a human zoo of differences' (Malik, 1996: 150). If multi-cultural education or diversity studies simply preserve differences as they present themselves in society, as professionals and as community members, we must look again at the way we define problems and policy responses.

In Chapter 1, I acknowledged that as well as having a lot of learning to do we all need to start somewhere. How do we develop as professionals with the skills and knowledge of cultural competence? How do we develop the ability to self-reflect? How do we teach professionals to consider difference and diversity? How do we adopt non-sexist, anti-racist and accessible teaching and learning strategies? How can we ensure that those making decisions approach the task with cultural sensitivity?

What has been lacking is a set of tools to help planners and those teaching planning to systematically reflect on what they do and how their beliefs and behaviour impact on their work (Majors, 2003). Drawing on experience from Europe and the USA, this chapter outlines specific approaches to building difference, diversity and equality into our work and daily lives. The approaches, which form part of the mainstreaming toolkit, are often collectively termed cultural competence or cultural sensitivity, where culture means ethnicity, race, gender, nationality, age, economic status, language, sexual orientation, physical characteristics, marital status, role in family, order of birth, immigration status, religion, accent and skin colour. 'Culture gives us our values, attitudes and norms of behaviour. We are constantly attaching culturally-based meaning to what we see and hear, often without being aware we are doing so' (Bryant, 2001: 40). This chapter introduces particular approaches which can help individuals and organizations. The 'Five Habits' approach focuses on how an individual or a professional can assess their approach to planning, and the EDI framework looks at how organizations can reflect on their need to change and build equality and diversity considerations into their work. The chapter concludes with a framework for evaluating the approaches adopted. Critically reflective and active learning, which adopts questioning and self-awareness, lies at the heart of what is advocated. This learning relies on collecting information, doing something with it as well as a third order of learning which means questioning assumptions, seeing things in new ways and experiencing deep change (Senge *et al.*, 1994).

In the USA, the importance of diversity, equality and cross-cultural skills has been recognized since the 1970s. Pioneering work was carried out in management in the 1970s and 1980s with the X–O training schemes (Kanter, 1977; Kanter, Cohen and Cox, 1980, 1994). In the aftermath of the murder of the black leader Martin Luther King in 1963, teachers struggled to provide forums for discussions and one teacher designed the 'blue eye–brown eye' exercises to enable white school-aged children and adults to experience discrimination (Elliot, 2002: 1). The American Medical Association has developed a broad-based initiative to establish cultural competence as the Fifth Physician Competence and the medical legal field has recognized the importance of cultural competence (Bryant, 2001). Studies in medicine show that a person's race and gender influence medical diagnoses (Blacks, 2000: 29; Rathmore, 2000, cited by Bryant, 2001: 54). The UK has seen many instances of insensitive medical practice. In the summer of 2003, the British press and media reported the case of a black woman who was offered a white prosthetic foot and told that if she wanted a black foot it would be more expensive (BBC News, 2003). The case for approaching professional work with sensitivity to difference, diversity and equality, however, is not as widely accepted in the built-environment professions. Wallace and Milroy (1999) have written extensively about Canada, and Thompson (2003) continues to develop her research on planning in Australia. Studies in the UK have shown that a person's race may influence the recommendations made by planners on planning applications (Local Government Association, 1998). When Harvey (1996: 291) reviewed the press coverage of the murder of two retired doctors in Guilford, Baltimore in August 1994, he wanted to highlight the extent of professional stereotyping amongst the media and planners. The immediate assumption was that a black person from the nearby ghettos committed the murder. Oscar Newman, a planner, was asked for his comment on the murders and whether gated communities were needed to protect communities. The press article reported that Newman agreed that a gated community might have prevented the crime. He had apparently not questioned the underlying assumptions he was making and later, police found that the doctor's grandson had in fact carried out the murder.

Until the introduction of equality legislation (such as the Treaty Obligations in New Zealand, Equal Status Act in Ireland [2000] and Race Equality Amendment Act [2000] and the Disability Discrimination Act [1995] in the UK), race issues were not addressed explicitly in institutional plans and strategies and there was little or no attempt to mainstream issues. Professional institutes still have relatively weak requirements when it comes to developing cultural competence. Educational guidelines tend to refer to the need for awareness and understanding of equality and diversity rather than an actual demonstration of competence (RTPI, 1996a, 2003). Take the planner, responsible for the public participation of the local development plan who is preparing to study the incoming comments and, scanning down the list of respondents, says to a colleague 'it's the same old suspects'. In doing this, the professional is in danger of stereotyping; undermining the integrity of the process and providing an inappropriate role model for colleagues. Or take the government official responsible for new planning guidelines who does not question why the department has not increased the length of time needed for consultation even though the same government has introduced legislation giving disabled people equal rights. Take two admission tutors discussing an application from a blind student and the implications of the new code on disability for professional bodies (DRC, 2003) when one says 'how can you have a blind planner?'

Learning how to plan with a sensitivity to diversity and equality involves new ways of thinking. We all live with bias and stereotyping and need to find ways to work in a non-judgmental way. Along with the legislation, disability groups know only too well that 'we need changes in individual attitudes and expectations' (RADAR, 2003b: website).

We need to start with an understanding of the relationship between the planner and their client(s) or customer. Planners work across a range of sectors in paid as well as voluntary capacities. Most operate in the public sector for local, regional or central government and others work with private sector consultancies and a large number of these are sole practitioners. As a consultant, a planner may work for a company or individual seeking permission to develop a piece of land or a building. As a local government employee, a planner is likely to decide planning applications on behalf of a local government agency or lead projects to implement area-based initiatives. For teachers, students are the primary customers with employers and parents the important chequebook carrying stakeholders. When dealing with one client, a planner may be more conscious of where that person lives. When dealing with another client, they may be more conscious of gender, age, disability or ethnicity.

THE 'FIVE HABITS'

The 'Five Habits' approach to working with diversity and equality was developed in the medical legal field in the USA over the last 15 years. The pioneers were Susan Bryant and Jean Koh Peters (Bryant, 2001). I first read about the 'Five Habits' in February 2003, when researching this book, looking for useful, tried and tested frameworks which could be adapted for the planning context. Theoretically robust, the five habits appeal at an intuitive, intellectual and experiential levels. Bryant (2003a) confirmed that she developed the tool with Jean Koh because they could find nothing else in the field of legal education. The key principles of the five habits are that all professional work involves 'cross-cultural thinking' and professionals need to develop a conscious and non-judgmental approach to their work (Dark, 1996). Implicit is the recognition that stereotyping and discrimination are learned responses, something which Jane Elliot could see from her work using the 'blue eye–brown eye' exercises (Elliot, 1970, 2002). Also implicit is the recognition that it is crucial to effect changes in attitudes as well as behaviours. The experience of NLP shows us that behavioural change will not necessarily effect a change in attitude but a change in attitude towards people who are different is more likely to lead to a change in behaviour.

With Susan Bryant's permission, I have taken their approach and adapted it for planning. This has involved taking on board the context and frameworks within which planners operate and putting together planning related case study material based on my own observations and published case studies.

THE STEPS TO THE 'FIVE HABITS'

The first step to using the five habits involves acknowledging that stereotyped thinking, power, privilege as well as racism, ageism, sexism may influence the planner's interactions with clients, customers, communities and colleagues and the need to address this (Bryant, 2001: 55). It may be necessary to suspend judgement completely, particularly where planners believe that the service they deliver is neutral. For a long time, planners and related professionals considered planning as objective and technical and therefore equality neutral. Today we are more acutely aware of the importance of qualitative information. Planners and other related professionals can best learn how to use the 'Five Habits', as they would other aspects of planning through workshops, scenarios, case studies and role-play exercises (Petrie, 2003b). Planners can apply the habits to all aspects of people's lives. The first three habits focus on how we think about and perceive people. Habits 4 and 5 are more holistic and require a much deeper level of reflection and a commitment to change. Habit 1 considers the perceived similarities and differences between the professional and the client or customer. Habit 2 identifies and analyses the possible effects of these

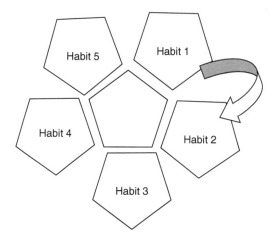

Figure 7.1 The 'Five Habits'

similarities and differences on the interaction between the professional and the client or customer. Habit 3 explores alternative explanations for particular behaviours which might affect the way the professional deals with a client or customer. Habit 4 involves being conscious about all facets of communication. Habit 5 explores the self as a cultural being, with the goal of eliminating bias and promoting the necessary change of perspectives.

When learning about and developing cultural competence, it is helpful to use the habits in a systematic way so that they become second nature (Figure 7.1).

To become automatic, psychology teaches us that we need to repeat a habit about 20 times. In practice, when they become second nature, all five habits need not be used every time and the planner may find themselves using the one most appropriate to the situation.

The next section goes on to consider the habits one by one and then use a series of case studies to show how the habits can be applied in practice.

HABIT 1 – DIFFERENCES AND SIMILARITIES

Using Habit 1, the professional considers the similarities and differences between himself or herself and the client or customer and then goes on to explore their significance. This tool provides a systematic way to identify and name the similarities and differences. It is made up of two stages. Stage 1 involves the planner seeing their client as an individual and brainstorming lists of similarities and differences honestly and non-judgmentally, depicting them as lists or mind maps (Buzan, 2001). Stage 2 involves drawing a simple Venn diagram to show the extent to which the 'perceived worlds' of the professional and client overlap. (A Venn diagram is a set of overlapping circles used to represent the way in which categorical statements overlap.) The professional planner might produce a short list of similarities and yet depict, in the diagram, a high degree of overlap showing the significance of the shared similarities. If a long list of differences is identified, Habit 1 encourages the professional to look for similarities. If the planner produces a long list of similarities, there may be a danger of over-identification with the client, to the extent that the planner sees themselves as the client and as a result makes inaccurate assumptions about their situation and their real needs and wants. Habit 1 asks the professional planner to consider how the similarities and differences affect the way they relate to their client. Significantly, Bryant found that lawyers tend to probe and ask questions when clients make choices they would not make. Similarly, they tend not to ask questions about choices or decisions they would make themselves. The consequences of this may be a mismatch in the information collected and recorded in relation to specific cases (Bryant, 2001: 66). The planners may find themselves in a situation with insufficient information about the nature of a proposed development, having made assumptions about the applicant.

HABIT 2 — THE THREE RINGS

Having established a sense of how the client is perceived, the next step is for the professional to analyze the possible effects of the similarities and differences, on the interaction between the client, the planning system and the planner. In doing this, the planner identifies the cultural differences that could lead them to judge an applicant, or an objector or a community initiative in a negative way. Bryant (2001) found that negative judgements are more likely to occur when a client or professional sees the other as an 'outsider' and this is confirmed in the psychology literature referred to in Chapter 1. If the professional identifies similarities, they are less likely to judge the client negatively. If on first meeting, the planner can see no similarities, this is when it is worth persisting to see what there is in common. Then by focusing on the professional–legal dyad, the planner can consider their interpretation of the planning system and the extent to which they share its values and norms. What similarities and differences exist between the client, the planner and the planning system? The following kinds of questions can help in the analysis:

- Do I think the case for approving or dismissing this application is weak or strong? Do I think the case for supporting this community initiative is weak or strong? Does the applicant or objector have a strong case? In what ways does the planning culture have sympathy with the values and assumptions of the applicant or objector's case?
- When representing an applicant, can I interpret the planning system to encompass and be sympathetic to more of the client's case? What additional facts or information would strengthen the case?
- When considering objections, which terms of reference am I focusing on: the planning system, my framework or the clients?

- How large is the overlap between the planning system and my values as a professional? Are there specific points on which I strongly agree or disagree with current planning law and policy?
- How large is the overlap between myself, the planning system and the client? Am I probing for clarity by using three frames of reference – the client's, the planning system's and mine – or am I focused mostly on my own frame?

Of all the points identified, which remains the most significant for the professional planner, the client or the law? For example, a planner considering an application by a disabled person to refurbish a listed building needs to consider how they interpret the law relating to listed buildings and how to interpret planning guidelines for the benefit of the client.

HABIT 3 – BEHAVIOUR

Habit 3 involves exploring alternative explanations for particular *behaviours* which could affect the way you deal with a client's case. It provides a framework for analysing the judgements you make. By engaging in, what Bryant neatly terms, parallel universe thinking, you can teach yourself not to assume that you understand a client's behaviour (Bryant, 2001: 72). If someone does not turn up at an agreed time, what is your reaction? If your client talks in a very loud voice, how do you react? The tool of 'shifting' allows you to assign a different cultural trait, and then to think through whether and how you would view the situation differently (Gunning, 1995) and cited by Bryant (2001: 50).

HABIT 4 – COMMUNICATION

Habit 4 involves you, the professional, giving attention to all facets of your communication with the client. This includes the protocols planners use for meetings with clients, the introductory rituals and the format of the meetings, conclusions and follow-ups. It also includes the way planners test whether a client understands what the professional is saying. A client may decide not to ask for clarification because they do not want to look foolish, or because, to ask a question looks rude in their culture. For example, a client who wants to object to a planning application may not know to ask whether they should also be objecting to the local plan or government guidance. You can use active listening to gauge what understanding exists and what further information is needed. This approach clearly assigns a responsibility on the professional to ensure that the client understands the situation. Bryant recommends using structured conversations to gather culture-specific information (Bryant, 2001: 86).

What is the issue?
What are the chief problems?

What are your main concerns?
What is the most important result for you?
Why is this important?
What would you like to see happen?

HABIT 5 – REFLECTION

Finally, Habit 5 involves planners standing back and exploring themselves as a cultural being and asking how to become more sensitive to the effects of difference and diversity. The practitioner is in reflective mode aiming to acknowledge every thought including the ugly ones. By looking at a series of case studies, it is possible to see how an application of all or some of the habits can help the professional in their dealings with the client.

ILLUSTRATION 1 – UNDERSTANDING DIFFERENCE

The first case study takes us to the USA, Sandercock (2000). The Navajo Indians claimed that a proposed road and logging development would violate their rights of religious freedom, established in the American Indian Religious Freedom Act (USA, 1978). The case ended up in the Supreme Court where Justice Sandra Day O'Connor ruled in favour of the Forest Service who had submitted the plans for development. As she interpreted the law, the definition of 'religious use' became the fundamental issue. Because the Navajo did not use the land actively for ritual purposes and it did not contain a specific religious building or icon, the judge did not deem the site to exist (Meyer and Reaves, 2000: 94). In this example, Habit 2 would have enabled planners and lawyers to at least consider the highly culturally specific way in which religious sites were being defined in the Judeo-Christian tradition and to consider whether and how the planning system could be interpreted to encompass more of the Navajo Indians case.

ILLUSTRATION 2 – IDENTIFYING WITH THE CLIENT

When a hotel owner on the Channel Islands originally approached the local Council about the need for planning permission to run a hotel as a hostel for homeless men, the local planner advised him that he would not need planning permission. After opening and operating for some months the Council received a number of letters from local residents and the planner consequently issued an enforcement notice requiring the owner to submit an application – which was then refused. The owner appealed on the grounds that there was no evidence the development was genuinely and negatively affecting the amenity of the neighbourhood. Although receiving a number of objections, the planner is likely to have had a number of options other than issuing an enforcement notice right away. In this example, Habit 2 may have helped the planner identify more with the client and to recognize all the options.

The habits may also have been useful in helping decision-makers understand their perceptions of the development.

ILLUSTRATION 3 — CHALLENGING ASSUMPTIONS

In large cities, many women raise concerns about the growth in the number of sex shops opening in local neighbourhoods. Women are frequently solicited walking to and from their own home and made to feel uncomfortable. The corporate department of equality in Glasgow, UK, was approached by a group of local women to help resolve the problem. They had already objected to previous applications and assumed that the local council knew their position. So when yet another planning application was submitted, they did not think they needed to respond. In this example, the five habits might have prompted planners to consider the assumptions they were making about people's knowledge of the planning system and the extent to which the planning system operates to the disbenefit of particular groups.

ILLUSTRATION 4 — COMMUNICATION

The case of the Buddhist Temple in Melbourne shows how the community and the professional planners could have interacted differently to appreciate more fully the implications of particular decisions. When the Buddhist community approached the planning department in search of a site for a temple, they were directed to industrially zoned land on the periphery of the city where the Buddhist monks built the temple. Because of its remoteness, the community could not use it on a day-to-day basis for community activities and so the Monks found they had to purchase suburban houses for use as community centres and local temples. Local residents complained of the smell of incense and the planners, discovering what was 'a non-conforming use', ordered the monks to cease using the house for community and religious purposes (Sandercock and Kliger, 1998a,b). In this case, planners did not seem to appreciate that a Buddhist temple functions both as a community centre and a religious place. It seems that they may have superimposed their own religious cultural understanding of a church, which tends to be used on one or two days each week. The five habits would have helped the planners check their understanding of what a temple means in an everyday sense and the kinds of facilities needed in terms of access and nearness to where the community lives.

ILLUSTRATION 5 — RESPECTING DIFFERENT KINDS OF KNOWLEDGE

The following example from South Sydney (Australia) shows how the application of the habits and respect for different kinds of knowledge can lead to a better understanding between professional and client and between client groups. The example focuses on a factory site immediately adjacent to the residential area known as the

Block in the neighbourhood of Redfern. The council hired a social planning consultant to conduct a consultation process that would result in recommendations for a master plan for a 2,000-metre site for which three local groups had very different ideas. A 'conservative white group of residents' wanted the site to become a park with a prominent police station in the centre. The Redfern Aboriginal Corporation wanted the buildings and site used for Aboriginal economic and community purposes, including a training facility. A third group, the Redfern Residents for Reconciliation supported the Aboriginal group and the larger issue of ongoing Aboriginal presence in the area. For the first three months, the consultant worked separately with groups until she felt the time was right to have a session with all the groups together in what she called a 'speak out'. After this, the groups moved on to forge a set of principles for deciding the future use of the site. Sandercock interpreted the consultant's role as creating a space in one place at one point in time, where perceptions might shift, public learning might occur and some larger transformation takes place.

DISCUSSION

The implications of the habits for planning practice as well as initial planning education, lifelong learning and continual professional development are far-reaching. Planners, developing a vision for a city, may for instance be predisposed to integration as a principle and weave together a set of policies and proposals which, they think, would create more integration between two different ethnic groups. Using the five habits, the planners could usefully establish the differences and similarities between themselves and the client groups and the extent to which they may be over-identifying with one group or failing to understand the concerns of all the groups in an area.

When students are undertaking professional training, it is crucial that their teaching and learning experience mirrors the ethos which is expected of them in practice. The 'Five Habits' approach acknowledges the importance of symmetry between the teacher–student relationship and the future professional–client relationship (Bryant, 2001: 58). The 'Five Habits' approach takes account of the need to learn on three levels; cognitive, behavioural and emotional. This form of learning recognizes the importance of sequencing, starting with cognitive development through didactic sessions where information is imparted, following this with discussions and experiential learning and then group problem-solving, critical incidents and case studies (Bryant, 2001: 61). The approach also recognizes that learners may move from unconscious incompetence to unconscious competence.

In the first stage of unconscious incompetence, the learners lack awareness of what they do not know. Planners are insufficiently aware of the impact of difference, diversity and equality and consequently fail to recognize difference and often overlook blunders when they happen and so do not try to prevent or rectify them. In the second stage of conscious incompetence, the learner becomes aware that difference and equality affects the way they attribute meaning to planning although they may not know how to use theory and skills to develop competent interaction with others. In this stage, they are able to recognize the blunders although not avoid them. The student planners are aware that they may not be connecting with clients, however they may not have the range of skills necessary to build a trusting relationship. In the third stage of conscious competence, student planners function competently in the range of skills necessary for planning which is sensitive to difference, diversity and equality but only after adopting a mindful approach to using the skills. The habits create explicit steps professionals can follow to address issues of similarities or difference. By practicing the habits, all professionals learn skills which can then be consciously applied to interactions with clients and colleagues. During the final stage of development, the professional can unconsciously incorporate the new skills and perspectives in all interaction with clients (Bryant, 2001: 63).

There will be times when a more strategic approach is also required to enable organizations to function sensitively to diversity and equality. The EDI Framework helps deliver this strategic approach.

THE EQUITY, DIVERSITY AND INTERDEPENDENCE (EDI) FRAMEWORK

Developed over the last ten years within the context of Northern Ireland, a region with a 'deep understanding of the difficulties of balancing diversity and equity' EDI draws on the experiences, insights and models of those at the forefront of organizational learning and change in North America and Europe (Eyben et al., 2002: 38). It is this context which helps make it such a robust framework, with relevance and applicability to many organizational settings. It is particularly useful in situations where the legislative framework is disjointed and inconsistent because it lifts people beyond the possibilities of the existing legislation. It is particularly useful in helping people recognize multiple identities.

The EDI Framework is designed to support the mainstreaming of fairness, diversity and interdependence in organizations and workplaces. It is a quality model – with a difference. Equity is understood as the commitment to ensure fair access to resources, structures and decision-making. Diversity involves acknowledging differences and interdependence, and the way in which people live together. The five habits can help individuals within a professional context re-evaluate how they approach their work, whereas the EDI framework is designed to help organizations work through the process of cultural change. EDI challenges organizations to get to grips with diversity and equity by understanding the diversity within the organization and the interrelationships between those working within an organization and those outside with whom staff relate. The process challenges organizations to define how the concepts of equity, diversity and interdependence can improve the effectiveness of an organization. It stimulates the creation of strategies to enable organizations to become more diverse and fair (Eyben *et al.*, 2002: 36). In a sense EDI builds on earlier models designed to tackle culture in business companies, such as the ABCD approach (Simons, Baudoin and Guurt, 1996). The ABCD approach focused on assuring access, breaking bias barriers, cultural competence and delivering diversity's added value. This conceptual model depicts the steps to equality as a pyramid at the base of which a company has already addressed the challenge of assuring and affirming access. This means the company has policies and procedures in place to ensure that all members contribute and participate fully. The company supports and constructively responds to support groups and is seen as a good place to work. The second layer in the pyramid represents breaking the bias barrier and recognizing and dealing with the prejudices which individuals and groups might have. Cultural competence is achieved when individuals within the company are aware of their own cultural blind spots and develop their cultural skills in dealing with customers. Delivering diversity's added value is achieved when individuals learn how to habitually and creatively look at differences as social or organizational strengths. At this level, diversity becomes part of the company's competitive edge.

The principles of EDI are set out in full in Morrow, Eyben and Wilson (2002) (Figure 7.2). The building blocks of the EDI framework include:

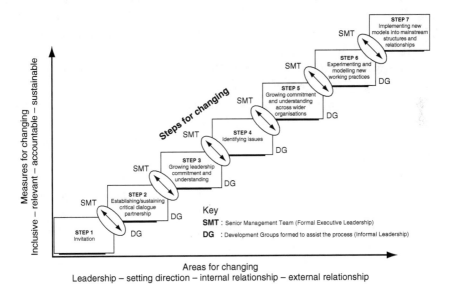

Figure 7.2 The equity, diversity and interdependence framework

- Measures for changing: inclusiveness, relevance, accountability and commitment.
- Areas for changing which relate to three areas of competence: leadership, setting directions, internal and external relationships.
- Steps for changing:

  - invitation,
  - establishing/sustaining the critical dialogue process,
  - growing leadership commitment and understanding of equity, diversity and interdependence,
  - identifying issues,
  - growing wider commitment,
  - experimenting and modelling new working practices,
  - implementing new models of practice into mainstream structures and relationships.

When an organization commits to EDI, this means everyone from senior management outwards. The process can take a long time. The process needs to be facilitated to work effectively; dialogue and communication are the key.

According to Wilson (2003) there are as yet no examples of planning agencies using the EDI framework although local councils and the rural voluntary sector have used it. Murray and Murtagh (2003) have written about the experience of the Rural Community Network (RCN) in Northern Ireland. With core funding from the Department of Agriculture and Rural Development, 'RCN gives a voice to rural communities on issues relating to poverty, disadvantage and inequality' (Murray and Murtagh, 2003: 291). Although RCN has had a long-standing commitment to EDI and this has been expressed through its aims, values and activities over the last 12 years, many in the community perceive that mostly Catholic community groups have been participants and that RCN is a Catholic and male organization. By using the framework, RCN has embarked on the EDI process to gather accurate information on the perceptions of staff and clients, through surveys of members and non-members. These findings ensured that informed dialogues took place within the organization in a series of workshops with different groups of staff, using external facilitators.

The process highlighted that EDI can be a slow process and needs to move at the pace of those within the organization. It is about 'trying to encourage people to act in a relational way to others who are different' (Murray and Murtagh, 2003: 295). Users need to adapt the EDI framework to each set of circumstances. Since confidentiality is paramount, there are few detailed case studies of any one organization documented in the public domain although the case study of RCN does illustrate its potential.

USING EDI IN THE PLANNING PROFESSION

The EDI framework could help professional institutes tackle some very long-standing equality and diversity issues. In the UK-based RTPI, women, black and ethnic minorities and disabled people are under-represented. The rate of increase of women members in the profession lags behind the rate of increase in the numbers of women undergraduate students. The profession is still perceived as male dominated. So, what is going on? What needs to change? EDI could provide a framework for exploring the issues, understanding perceptions and discovering commonly understood solutions.

DEVELOPING SYMMETRY BETWEEN EDUCATION AND PRACTICE

In order to develop professionals sensitive to diversity, difference and inequality, who can work in a non-judgmental way we need to ensure that the teaching and learning situations mirror these goals and aspirations. As well as developing cultural competence in professionals through tools such as the 'Five Habits', it is also important that teaching and learning goals and strategies become equally sensitive to cultural diversity. A symmetry between what is taught and how subjects are taught is crucial. This involves institutions undertaking fundamental reviews of the way they work, the educational paradigms used as well as reflecting on what is taught, the content of courses, how material is taught and the teaching and learning environment.

In response to legislative responsibilities, educational institutions and umbrella bodies have developed a number of generic and subject-specific tools to help tutors reflect on, and where necessary, adapt and change their teaching and learning or pedagogic strategies. The 'Five Habits' is a good example of a tool for cultural competence, developed by those teaching in the medical legal field which can be applied elsewhere. The University of Auckland in New Zealand has developed training material to increase awareness and understanding of Maori culture amongst teaching staff. The UK Teachability Guide (Simpson, 2002, 2003) provides tutors across disciplines with practical tools to reflect on all aspects of their teaching and learning for disabled students, following the new responsibilities set out in the Disability Discrimination Legislation (UK, 1995). Discipline networks such as the centre for education and built-environment special interest group on equality and diversity have become established to provide support for those specializing in this area (CEBE, 2003). Other studies have been set up to collate examples of good practice across disciplines (Ross, 2003, 2004).

The Higher Education Quality Assurance Agency guidelines are designed to ensure that all academic and technical staff (QAA, 1999: 15):

- Plan and employ teaching and learning strategies which make the delivery of the programme as inclusive as is reasonably possible.
- Know and understand the learning implications of any disabilities of the students whom they teach and are responsive to student feedback.
- Make individual adaptations to delivery which are appropriate for particular students, which might include providing handouts in advance and or in different formats (Braille or disk) short breaks for interpreters to rest, or using radio microphone systems, or flexible/interrupted study for students with mental health difficulties.

At the UK level, government funded colleges and higher education institutions are required by law to produce race equality schemes based on the guidance produced by the CRE (2002a) to ensure that teaching and the curriculum takes account of students' cultural backgrounds, language needs and different learning styles by pursuing the development of a model of good practice in race equality on a sectoral basis.

- Encourage students to understand and value cultural and ethnic diversity.
- Ensure that teaching staff create an environment free of prejudice, discrimination and harassment, where students can contribute fully and freely and feel valued.
- Ensure that teaching and the curriculum takes account of students' cultural backgrounds, language needs and different learning styles.
- Ensure that the curriculum deals with questions of racism and diversity where appropriate.
- Ensure that the needs of students from different racial groups are taken into account when planning the curriculum.
- Ensure that race equality aims are built into all programmes.
- Ensure that resources are made available to meet any specific needs that students from particular racial groups might have.
- Ensure that extra-curricular activities and events cater for the interests or needs of all students and take account of any concerns about religion or culture (Aberdeen University, 2003).

However, there is nothing in the guidelines asking institutions to consider or take account of the gendered needs of black and ethnic and disabled students. There is a tendency in Britain to see racism as something to do with the presence of black people. Both black and white people experience their gender, class and sexuality through race. Experiences of racism and discrimination are not homogenous (CER, 2003: section 2.3). The Race Relations Amendment Act 2000 (RRAA) places a positive duty on Higher Education Institutions (HEIs) in England, Wales and Scotland, to promote race equality, through all their relevant functions.

Institutions have a statutory general duty to 'have due regard to the need to eliminate unlawful racial discrimination and promote equality of opportunity and good relations between persons of different racial groups'. They also have a number of enforceable specific duties, placed on them by the Home Secretary and Scottish Ministers, to help them fulfill the requirements of the general duty. In Scotland the key funding bodies recognize that neither Scotland nor Scottish education is free from racism (SHEFC, 2002). The education-working group of the Scottish Executive's Race Equality Advisory Forum (REAF) concluded that Scottish education needs to embed race equality in two ways by institutionalizing race equality within education and promoting education for race equality (Scottish Executive, 2000).

Many of the most immediate needs in education – as in other services – are for better information and analysis. 'The lack of attention to race and racism issues in higher education indicates a need for the development of conceptual and methodological tools and resources to assess, review and reconstruct educational policy and practice' (CER, 2003: section 1.1; Law, 2003; Law, Phillips and Turney, 2004). Early reviews have identified the need for a guide which institutions and departments within institutions can use to assess how race equality issues could be better mainstreamed. The UK recognizes the need for guidance for tutors and all those involved in the delivery of the teaching and learning experience. A project commissioned by the CRE aims to help institutions develop a full understanding of what they need to do to fulfill the statutory requirements of the general duty in order to promote race equality. It also aims to provide practical advice and support to institutions as they find their way through the problems and opportunities of implementation. This developmental, exploratory and supportive approach is designed to produce outcomes which will be beneficial to the sector as a whole. During the first year of the project, targeted support will be offered to the collaborating institutions, focusing on their internal implementation policies, action plans, processes, procedures, mechanisms and initiatives. In the second year, the participating institutions will be encouraged to work collaboratively with other higher education institutions and share their knowledge and practice. The intention is that good racial equality practice will be developed and disseminated across the sector.

BARRIERS AND CHALLENGES

New ways of working generate different responses, some positive and constructive and others negative, obstructive or even destructive. Often change is resisted due to fear of the unknown (Figure 7.3).

Professional cultures can generate their own barriers, especially where traditional training has emphasized technical and managerial expertise (CCETSW, 1998: 26–29). According to Argyris (1999) the ability to self-question, reflect and reconsider the

Figure 7.3 Monster under the bed

wider context can therefore become limited. The process takes time, considerable commitment and outside facilitation.

Resistance is a common response, although this can reflect total intransigence at one extreme to healthy scepticism and apathy. We know that apathy is rife. Research in the UK has shown that although 77 per cent agree that different cultures co-exist but do not connect, 52 per cent feel it is easier to live in a cultural ghetto, isolated from those who seem different and only 13 per cent say they want increased contact with other cultures (VSO, 2003; Waite, 2003).

In a seminar to the Gender Research Forum in London, Paul Chaney (2003) used the metaphor of the letters running through a stick of rock to describe the nature and depth of resistance, which can take many forms, and like the letters which impregnate the rock and are integral to it, the learner does not want their values challenged. Instead they prefer first-order learning where information is simply imparted. Some believe that the focus on difference and diversity detracts from and denies equality for all people. This all too common response results from the premise that equality means treating everyone the same rather than thinking about equal outcomes such as appropriate housing, community facilities or amenities. Equality is not inconsistent with difference. Failure to address difference may result in more inequality or at the very least misunderstanding (Bryant, 2001: 79). The model of diversity advocated in this book embraces equality.

One tool which can help planners and related professional get to grips with barriers to change is the 'forcefield' analysis, originally developed by social psychologist Lewin (1951) and still used extensively today. It is possible to look at where an organization needs to be and identify the things which either help or restrain. If nothing is happening, it is because the opposing forces, both the helpful and restraining forces, are equal. The following sequence takes you through the forcefield stages:

- first of all, note all the driving forces you can think of;
- having listed the driving forces, give them each an appropriate weight;
- then look at the forces which might be preventing you moving towards your goal;
- weight the restraining forces;
- consider why the restraining forces exist, whether or not they are valid and how they could be reduced.

EVALUATING PRACTICE

Professionals only know an approach is working if they evaluate the results. Evaluation is essential in determining the effectiveness of learning. The tools presented here are geared towards critical reflection to establish whether and to what extent learners have genuinely moved as a result of experiences (Table 7.1) (Clements and Jones, 2002).

Table 7.1 Summary of the methods commonly used to achieve and evaluate learning intentions

Learning intention	Definition	Approaches	Evaluation process
Increased knowledge	Observation and recall of information	Reading Lectures Videos/CDs	Self report Multiple choice Verbal question and answer Line manager review Group discussion Appraisal Essay
Behaviour change	Overt, observable reflex action	Demonstration Role model Training Feedback	Role play Assessment centre Group discussion Workplace assessment Self report
Attitudinal change	A disposition to react to certain things, people or events in particular ways	Power/coercive approach Empirical/rational Normative/re-educative	Self report Questionnaire Workplace assessment Group discussion

Source: Compiled from Clements and Jones (2002).

The 'Five Habits' approach focuses on how an individual professional can assess their approach to planning, and the EDI framework looks at how organizations can reflect on their need to change and build equality and diversity considerations into their work. Together, the five habits and the EDI framework are both useful tools. The five habits can be used to help individuals reassess how they approach clients whether commercial, community or political. In addition, the five habits can be used by groups of people to assess how a team or an organization perceives and deals with their clients. An external facilitator is recommended to aid this process of internal review. The EDI framework is designed to help organizations large and small to review how they deal with different groups. The approach brings together equality and diversity. Equality means a commitment to fair access to resources, structures and decision-making. Diversity involves an acknowledgement of differences.

CHAPTER 8

AGENDA FOR CHANGE

> Picture the scene. It is 2015 in a planning agency. Members of the spatial planning team convene to discuss the review of their spatial plan and one asks how things have changed over the last ten years.

> 'The most significant thing is that we now routinely consider diversity and equality issues. We just didn't see the need for this 10 years ago. And what a difference it's made. We have plans that people feel they have a stake in. People feel their plan means something to them as individuals and as members of their community.'

This book sets out, for the first time, to show how diversity and equality issues can be built into spatial planning through the use of mainstreaming. What are the key issues for diversity and equality over the coming years and where will change need to happen? Although living and working in a diverse world is not a new phenomenon, more countries are becoming increasingly diverse as the international, national, legal and social contexts within which we all live and work are changing. Countries are dealing with new sets of differences as global migration and European integration has extended the boundaries of the mobile labour market. Diversity and equality are not mutually exclusive and one does not replace the other. Equality in diverse communities is increasingly seen as a right and not an expectation. Diversity in itself will not deliver equality, although a consideration of diversity and difference may well highlight areas of discrimination not recognized to date. Historically some differences give rise to discrimination and disadvantage and some do not. Gender, race, religion, disability, age and sexuality are at the root of most discrimination in society. Power is at the heart of the distinction between diversity and equality (Davies and Ohri, undated). Equality addresses power; diversity addresses difference. An integrated approach to diversity and equality is essential. A full consideration of equality and diversity should lead to an increase in the effectiveness of planning for sustainable communities.

Spatial planning has a key role to play in creating sustainable communities through its influence on the quality of places, the location and interrelationship of activities and the ways in which they are interconnected. The diversity and equality perspective makes planning more relevant to the way people and communities want to live their lives. Mainstreaming is a key strategy for building diversity and equality into all aspects of planning. It is at the same time systematic, proactive, integrative, holistic and transformational and has applications right across the diversity spectrum.

Mainstreaming equality and diversity does not require another approach to planning. Some countries like the UK take a more economic-orientated approach to planning whilst others such as Germany take a more physical approach. New Zealand and the Netherlands have, over time, developed an environmental approach. Whilst some countries interpret sustainable development as an environmental goal, many countries see it as a more holistic concept which recognizes the interrelationships between the environmental, economic and social aspects. Integrating diversity and equality into all these approaches should ensure that they do not reinforce inequalities between women and men and between different sectoral groups.

A problem for planning and related professional areas of activity is that in many countries both planning and equality legislation are highly circumscribed in the sense that planning may be mentioned explicitly in race and disability legislation but not in sex discrimination legislation. In the UK, many planning practitioners and lawyers think equality legislation does not apply to planning! There is no doubt that the strength of legislation determines people's access to equality and within Europe this has become evermore marked. Where there is a positive duty to promote equality through race legislation and a much weaker duty not to discriminate in disability and sex discrimination legislation, there will continue to be problems. In the UK, the Race Equality Amendment Act (REAA) should provide the best benchmark for planners' day-to-day approach to equality and diversity. Many would argue that legislation ensures only minimum standards of practice and behaviour in equality matters and 'that minimum standards tend to prevent best results from being achieved' (Murray and Murtagh, 2003: 288). Any primary and secondary planning legislation, whether in the UK, New Zealand, the USA, South Africa or elsewhere, should create opportunities for agencies to build in considerations of equality at all levels and stages of spatial planning, from the national spatial framework level, the regional strategies and local development documents.

Since government ministers in the UK have said it will be some years before there is one single piece of equality legislation (Hewitt, 2003), and this is likely to be 2008 at the earliest, planners and built-environment professionals will continue to work within the current statutory framework for equality which is limited, confusing and inconsistent. Planners need and want to focus on what makes better planning than comply with a set of statutory minimums. Planning for diversity and equality means:

- planning which takes into account the needs of different groups of people;
- planning which takes a rights-based and a duty-to-promote approach;
- planning which engages people in a participatory way as equals rather than passive target groups simply to be consulted;
- planning which takes the social dimension of sustainable development as seriously as the environmental and economic dimensions.

A plan must play its part in ensuring that all sections of the community have equal opportunity to access and participate in the environment as well as the economic, political and social life of a community. A plan must acknowledge and value differences within and between communities. Planning for diversity and equality is about inter-dependence as well as fairness and respect for difference. The interdependence aspect of the 'equality, diversity and interdependence framework' ensures that those who live and work in an area have a place in relation to others. 'We could use policies to break up concentrations of people from similar cultural and ethnic backgrounds but that simply ignores how people live – we need to develop bridges between communities' (Phillips [2003], Chair of the Commission for Racial Equality). Planners can help create opportunities through the development of community, leisure, educational facilities and work opportunities and by the way they factor in a sense of what makes places and communities work.

Recognition of the interdependence of groups will help professionals work through the legal inconsistencies to achieve fairer and more equitable planning. The combined diversity and equality approach should encourage professionals to look at issues through a series of lenses. In this way it should be possible to identify the gendered issues for disabled people as well as black and ethnic groups. Historically, the construction of equality legislation has led to a focus on one group and then another and the development of separate equality bodies has led to the syndrome of 'we have done gender and it's race this year, disability next year'. The move towards single equality bodies in the UK should help the recognition and handling of multiple identities. The public policy emphasis on race has had two effects. It has meant that some groups such as disabled people have remained relatively invisible. It has also meant that sex discrimination has received much less public attention and compara-tively less funding.

The case studies outlined in the book illustrate examples of what various agencies have done to date. The developments, although cutting edge, have been *ad hoc*, reliant on political backing and poorly publicized by the professional bodies and government as examples of better practice. There seems no reason why main-streaming could not be applied to all sectoral groups and types of discrimination. The types of information sought and the way it is gathered may vary. What is needed is better baseline data to inform policy development and implementation, better representation of under-represented groups in the professions, in policy making and decision-making arenas and better monitoring of the allocation of resources.

ARENAS OF CHANGE

The achievement of sustainable communities involves operating in the economic, social, environmental and institutional dimensions. It involves organizations in the

Figure 8.1 Let's get to people's hearts and minds

public and private sectors as well as professional bodies, legislative and political arenas. Spatial planning which is more sensitive to diversity and equality has a crucial role to play and this will involve changes in a number of arenas. They involve planning practice and academe, both teaching and research. Some themes are common to each arena and others are specific. In terms of planning, the arenas for change relate to different spatial scales: international and national levels, community and personal (Figure 8.1).

INTERNATIONAL AND NATIONAL ARENAS

The United Nation's charters provide important global standards which should impact on the nation states which sign up. The problem is that governments often appear to pay lip service to standards, creating cosmetic responses for the periodic reports which member countries have agreed to provide. Advocacy groups have been able to hold governments to account as Elson (2004) explained to the PAN Islands Seminar. The Fawcett Society has been able to request formal and regular meetings with government on the basis of claims made in responses to the Organisation for Economic Co-operation and Development (OECD). The UK government claimed that it undertook 'routine mainstreaming of budget options against gender' and 'the UK Women's Budget Group (WBG) is a key feature of the consultation process with respect to gender issues' (Elson, 2004: 6). Advocacy groups need increasing levels of support, and changing contexts will create new demands for alliances of organizations, which in the past have campaigned for particular sectoral groups. The European Union's Structural Fund Programme's emphasis on gender mainstreaming provided a huge boost to equality and diversity work during the 1990s. It is crucial that the post-2006 programmes have a clear goal of diversity and equality. Kjellstrom (2004) affirmed that the EU has 'the capacity and commitment' for gender equality.

One of the issues for the application of diversity and equality is how to decide which cases merit attention. As I discussed in Chapter 3, Fredman (2002) suggested that any new legislation should be based on a set of four principles to enable targeted implementation and help achieve equality for particular groups. Targeting disadvantaged groups and persons who have been subject to historical disadvantage, prejudice or stereotyping is key to breaking the cycle of disadvantage. A redistribution of resources and benefits is key to this (Fredman, 2002: 11). Respect for the equal dignity and worth of the individual should redress the stereotyping, humiliation and violence towards out-groups. Dignity is central to the concerns of many groups subject to discrimination and harassment, particularly older people. Affirming community identities, the third of the principles, recognizes that individuals are partly constituted by their group membership while the fourth principle of facilitating full participation in society acknowledges that equality law must compensate for the absence of the political power of minority groups. Discrimination could undermine any one of these principles. For instance, where someone is being discriminated against as a result of their religious identity, they would be protected by the principle of community identity (Fredman, 2002: 18).

As the benefits of building in diversity and equality become more widely understood, national governments should see the need to continue to widen support. Government guidance and good practice notes should automatically address how new approaches will deliver equality. Recent reports on the skills needed to create sustainable communities, however, have failed to recognize the importance of cross-cultural skills (Egan, 2004). Further work will be needed to address the cross-cultural skills required of all participants. In sustainable communities, gender is a cross-cutting identifier and the challenge for the future will be to create equality-proofing techniques, sensitive to different sectoral groups, which can highlight where disparities and inequalities exist.

ORGANIZATIONAL ARENA

Organizations in the public, private and voluntary sectors have much to gain from addressing equality as part of sound modern management and value for money. Quality management tools and frameworks have increasingly embraced diversity and equality dimensions. Delivering diversity's added value is achieved when individuals learn how to habitually look at differences as social and organizational strengths. Diversity then becomes part of a company's competitive edge and part of the benchmark for public sector service delivery (Simons, Baudoin and Guurt, 1996).

Equality standards, such as the equality standard for local government in the UK provides equality targets and other quality management frameworks such as Best Value. With relatively weak sanctions and insufficient incentives, public sector watchdogs have tended to find a relatively low take-up of new standards and practices (Audit Commission, 2002).

Organizations need to measure themselves against the following indicators:

1.   Is planning closing the equality gaps in access to employment, quality of environment, quality of the environmental experience, access to open space, ability to get around?
2.   Is there parity in the confidence that different sectors of the public have in the way planning applications, complaints or objections are considered; in the relevance of development plans to people's lives; and in the way development plans are formulated?
3.   Is there parity in the satisfaction levels of different groups of people to the development plan process and the outcomes?
4.   Is there a measurable improvement in community relations between different racial, cultural, religious groups or between groups of different ages, neighbourhoods and adjacent communities?
5.   Is there a measurable improvement in workforce representation within government planning agencies and consultancies?
6.   Is there parity in employment satisfaction levels between different groups of people?
7.   Is there parity in employee experiences? Surveys have shown that disabled people are far less likely to register as disabled and far less likely to complain (CRE, 2003).

PROFESSIONAL ARENA

At best, professional institutes provide important leadership in terms of the content and direction of education and lifelong learning, policy and practice. Industry-wide umbrella bodies such as the UK Construction Industry Council also provide industry-wide leadership and direction in terms of constructing diversity (CIC, 2003). Increasingly, professional bodies provide comprehensive services to the community, and the UK-based RTPI now runs one of the largest planning aid services in the world. In 1999, RTPI Council endorsed the approach of mainstreaming and building equality into all aspects of the profession's work. In 2004, the new charter established that the Institute would: 'promote equity and equality in the practice of planning and education in planning and in all aspects of the governance of the Chartered Institute' (RTPI, 2003a).

There have been other developments. The education guidelines now specify the need for planning learning outcomes 'to appreciate and respect diversity of cultures, views and ideologies and understand how that respect can be applied in planning systems through the pursuit of equal opportunity, social inclusion and non-discrimination (on the grounds of wealth, gender, age, race, disability, religion and culture)' (RTPI, 2003b: Section 6.7.8). The partnership arrangements between planning schools and the RTPI stipulates that schools are expected to show how they are attempting to increase the proportion of under-represented groups on their undergraduate and postgraduate programmes year on year and how they are tackling a lack of diversity amongst their staff. The race into planning initiative represents a positive action approach to increasing the representation of a gender balance of black and ethnic groups in planning. The gender audit toolkit provides guidance on how to build in a gender consideration into local planning. The institute is ensuring that the new guidelines for planning education fully comply with the new codes of practice by the Disability Rights Commission, which means that the profession should become open to many more disabled people. However, equality and diversity are too often not yet seen as issues for which everyone has responsibility. To maintain their credibility, institutes need to ensure that, in all the tasks they undertake, equality and diversity issues are built in.

ACADEMY

The academy communicates knowledge through teaching and learning and helps create new knowledge and understanding through research. Tertiary education in the UK has been given more time than other service providers to gear up to equality legislation such as the Disability Discrimination Act (UK, 1995). Where institutions rely on public money, funding agencies can exert a significant influence on the way they operate. Funding could be made conditional on the production and implementation of equality and diversity action plans. Research bodies can exert considerable influence through their agendas and codes of practice, requiring the use of guidelines on mainstreaming equality and diversity into research. They should ensure that research teams are diverse and gender-balanced and that all proposals comply with equality and diversity guidelines (EOC, undated). Many academics assert their academic freedom to intellectualize rather than comply with equality legislation. This often means that equality and diversity issues are marginalized rather than embedded in curricula. Within classes and modules in which diversity and equality issues are taught there needs to be a symmetry between what material is taught, and how the learning experience is designed and delivered. Diversity and equality lends itself to interactive and thought-provoking teaching which enables students to become aware of their prejudices. Some guidelines are available such as the Oxfam sponsored material (Leach, 2003).

Futurists are a very important and influential group of professionals who, in sketching the future, may unwittingly superimpose their own values and beliefs in their trend analysis and scenarios, perhaps helping create self-fulfilling prophecies. The invisibility of disabled people in the pre-millennium crop of futurist texts is notable and yet not something which has excited a great deal of comment or debate. The next set of futurist texts, no doubt being produced for 2010, need to consider equality and diversity issues in depth.

COMMUNITY ARENA

When we use the term 'community' we normally mean groups of people who live in or who use the same space (real or virtual). Many communities have campaigned for more say in the decisions which affect their lives and many hoped the advent of community planning would provide the opportunity for such an input. Unfortunately in many areas, community groups have not been able to participate and community-planning partnerships fail to deliver diversity and equality standards in relation to representation, resourcing and policy outcomes. Gender budgeting techniques should be used to show which groups of people benefit from particular programmes and projects. When the EC first advocated mainstreaming, bureaucrats were the initial priority for training. Since 2000, many countries have widened training to include community groups as well as professionals.

INDIVIDUAL ARENA

Individual professionals want to do their best and want to have the necessary resources and support to do their job effectively. In Chapter 3, I quoted the advice given by Wendy Davies and it merits repeating here. When working within an organization Davies believes individuals need to take responsibility for:

- Establishing clear terms of reference which ensure that diversity is understood as a means of achieving equality.
- Ensuring that there is commitment from the top of the organization and the commitment is public and vociferous.
- Ensuring that it is clear who is accountable for diversity and equality.
- Working on achieving ownership of the issue and recognize that this may necessitate bringing in an outside consultant to facilitate change.
- Talking the issue through with colleagues to address any concerns they may have.

- Providing effective training as well as information. Encourage people to look at the value base of their practice and to see things differently.
- Helping people think through what they can do at a team level in terms of how their work contributes to the promotion of equality through the diversity approach.
- Making diversity and equality visible in the mainstreaming agenda.
- Identifying how policy is contributing to the promotion of equality (Davies in Reeves, 2003b).

PROFESSIONAL AND PERSONAL DEVELOPMENT

Professionals have responsibilities, set down by their institutes, to maintain their competence to practice in whatever particular field they operate. In any one year, there will be over one thousand students on planning courses in the UK (RTPI, 2003). Initial education needs to be much more effective in introducing students to the notion of planning for a diverse community. Many planners complete their initial planning education with little knowledge of how equality legislation is likely to affect their work. Many do not undertake any kind of cultural competence training which develops the skill of looking at issues from different perspectives and challenging one's own beliefs and attitudes towards people. The RTPI, for instance, has 15,000 corporate members, over 80 per cent of whom have qualified over five years ago. New ideas and techniques, as well as the results of research need to be communicated to professionals. When the initial professional education has ended, the continuous development of the professional sets in. Continual professional development (CPD) has been the traditional means of establishing a professional's responsibility to maintain their competence. This outdated approach is being superceded by more comprehensive notions of lifelong learning in which the professional demonstrates development of core technical skills and other competencies which will make them more effective. The EC definition of lifelong learning is: 'All learning activity undertaken throughout life with the aim of improving knowledge, skills and competence within a personal, civic, social or employment related perspective' (EC, 2001a).

Institutes could usefully specify diversity and equality as one area which all members are expected to cover in their lifelong learning given that it cuts across all areas and sectors of planning. The concepts of difference, diversity and equality are dynamic and context-specific. Through continuous learning and development, professionals and those engaged in planning must continue to develop their knowledge and expertise. Bryant's 'Five Habits', which I have adapted for planning, provides a useful teaching and professional learning tool, which can be developed as case study material is shared. Unless officials and politicians explicitly set out equality issues in the policy documents which form the basis of future decisions, we will not make progress towards an equal society. Experience shows that without systematic audits, plans may unintentionally reinforce inequalities which exist and miss opportunities to do more to promote equality and respect for difference through diversity.

Forcefield analysis

A forcefield analysis presented below reflects my assessment of developments in diversity and equality to date – albeit from a primarily European perspective. It shows that the main driving force will continue to be legislative requirements.

Table 8.1 highlights where energies need to focus: consistent and clear legislative framework; education and lifelong learning resources for professionals and communities; positive action to encourage the development of an increasingly diverse and gender-balanced profession to deliver sustainable communities. The

Table 8.1 Forcefield analysis – What forces are affecting the development of planning for diversity and equality?

Driving forces		Restraining forces
Legislation exists and needs to be used to best effect		Legislation at the national and international level is relatively weak and inconsistent
Initiatives by the profession and government have started to move the diversity and equality agenda forward		Professionals are not yet equipped to work with diversity and equality issues and to see its relevance to planning
Professional bodies are recognizing the need to diversify		The rate of diversification is very slow and more will need to be done to make the profession more attractive to a wider range of people
The requirements for planning education include equality		These requirements do require a professional to demonstrate a competence in equality and diversity
Under-represented groups are increasing their influence through networking		Under-represented groups are often marginalized within professions
Practical guidelines are available		There is a limited number of better practice examples
There is a commitment to increasing public involvement by governments		Under-represented groups often lack the resources to participate fully

Figure 8.2 Weave of Diversity by Helen Averley

aim must be to ensure that publics can participate in planning and that diverse voices are heard. Along with this, a fair allocation of resources is needed to ensure that everyone benefits from policy outcomes which reflect the needs and concerns of diverse communities (Figure 8.2).

APPENDIX 1: SUMMARY OF THE FIVE HABITS

HABIT 1 – DIFFERENCES AND SIMILARITIES

In what way are you as a planner different from the client(s)?	In what way are you as a planner similar to the client?

When you have completed this first stage, draw a Venn diagram which shows the extent to which you feel there is a cultural overlap between yourself and the client.

HABIT 2 – THE THREE RINGS

In what way are you as a planner different from the client(s)?	What effect might these differences have on the interaction between you and the client?

In what way are you as a planner similar to the client?	What effect might the similarities have on the interaction between you and the client?

HABIT 3 – BEHAVIOURS

What behaviours of the client are annoying me?	What behaviours of the client are pleasing me?

HABIT 4

What aspects of the client's communication annoy me?	What aspects of the client's communication am I pleased with?

HABIT 5

| Taking everything into account, how do I need to change my view of the client? | Taking everything into account, what can remain the same? |

APPENDIX 2: PRINCIPAL EQUALITY WEBSITES IN AUSTRALIA, CANADA, EU, SOUTH AFRICA, UK AND US

AUSTRALIA

FEDERAL LAWS
Australian Constitution
http://www.austlii.edu.au/au/legis/cth/consol_act/c167/

Disability Discrimination Act 1992
http://www.austlii.edu.au/au/legis/cth/consol_act/dda1992264/index.html

Equal Opportunity for Women in the Workplace Act 1999
(Formerly the Affirmative Action Act)
http://scaletext.law.gov.au/html/pasteact/0/355/top.htm

Racial Discrimination Act 1975
http://www.austlii.edu.au/au/legis/cth/consol_act/rda1975202/index.html

Sex Discrimination Act 1984
http://www.austlii.edu.au/au/legis/cth/consol_act/sda1984209/index.html

Australian Government Office of the Status of Women
http://www.osw.dpmc.gov.au/

Aboriginal Links (Australian and International)
http://www.bloorstreet.com/300block/aborintl.htm

CANADA

Canadian Charter of Rights and Freedoms (1982)
http://laws.justice.gc.ca/en/charter/index.html#egalite

Canadian Human Rights Act

Canadian Multiculturalism Act (1985)
http://laws.justice.gc.ca/en/C-18.7/31859.html

Canadian Race Relations Foundation Act 1991
http://laws.justice.gc.ca/en/C-21.8/32305.html

Employment Equity Act (1995)

Official Languages Act (1985)

EU

The website of the EU accession monitoring programme
http://www.eumap.org

A comparison of national anti-discrimination legislation on the grounds of racial or ethnic origin, religion or belief, with the Council Directives.
http://www.eumap.org/library/datab/Documents/1024479238.33/1Sweden.pdf

NEW ZEALAND

Human Rights Amendment Act 2001
http://www.hrc.co.nz/index.php?p=307
http://www.govt.nz/

The New Zealand Bill of Rights Act 1990

The New Zealand Bill of Rights Act 1990 safeguards the civil and political rights of New Zealanders.

SOUTH AFRICA

South Africa Government. Online. Available HTTP: http://www.gov.za/search97cgi/s97_cgi

Promotion of Equality and Prevention of Unfair Discrimination Act [No. 4 of 2000] 4 of 2000: Promotion of Equality and Prevention of Unfair & Discrimination Act. To give effect to section 9 read with item 23(1) of Schedule 6 to the Constitution of the Republic of South Africa, 1996, so as to prevent and prohibit unfair discrimination.
http://www.gov.za/gazette/acts/2000/a4-00.pdf

UK

UK (1975) *Sex Discrimination Act.* Online. Available HTTP: <http://www.pfc.org.uk/legal/sda.htm> (accessed 31 October 2003).

UK (1975 as amended in 2001) *Sex Discrimination Act.* Online. Available HTTP: <http://www.eoc-law.org.uk/cseng/legislation/sda.pdf> (accessed 31 October 2003).

UK (1976) *Race Relations Act*. Online. Available HTTP: <http://www.homeoffice.gov.uk/docs/racerel1.html> (accessed 31 October 2003).

UK (1995) *Disability Discrimination Act*. Online. Available HTTP: <http://www.disability.gov.uk/dda/> (accessed 14 October 2003).

UK (1998) *Human Rights Act*. Online. Available HTTP: <http://www.hmso.gov.uk/acts/acts1998/19980042.htm> (accessed 14 October 2003).

UK (2001) *Race Relations Amendment Act*. Online. Available HTTP: <http://www.hmso.gov.uk/acts/acts2000/20000034.htm> (accessed 14 October 2003).

UK Equal Opportunity Commission
http://www.eoc.org.uk/

UK Commission for Racial Equality
http://www.cre.gov.uk/

UK Disability Rights Commission
http://www.drc-gb.org/

US

United States Equal Employment Opportunity Commission
http://www.eeoc.gov

The Federal laws prohibiting job discrimination are:
   Title VII of the Civil Rights Act of 1964 (Title VII) which prohibits employment discrimination based on race, color, religion, sex or national origin;
   The Equal Pay Act of 1963 (EPA) which protects men and women who perform substantially equal work in the same establishment from sex-based wage discrimination;
   The Age Discrimination in Employment Act of 1967 (ADEA) which protects individuals who are 40 years of age or older;
   Title I and Title V of the Americans with Disabilities Act of 1990 (ADA) which prohibit employment discrimination against qualified individuals with disabilities in the private sector, and in state and local governments;
   Sections 501 and 505 of the Rehabilitation Act of 1973 which prohibit discrimination against qualified individuals with disabilities who work in the federal government; and
   The Civil Rights Act of 1991 which, among other things, provides monetary damages in cases of intentional employment discrimination.

APPENDIX 3: RESOURCES

FIVE BOOKS

There are no books which combine sustainable development, diversity and equality and mainstreaming with practical tools to assess your own levels of sensitivity. However, there are books which are useful references.

Age as an Equality Issue is a new book by Sandra Fredman and Sue Spencer (Oxford: Hart Publishing). Written by academic lawyers, this book looks at the implications of the new European Directive on Age which comes into effect in 2006 and should provide useful background material for planners.

Exploring Social Psychology by David Myers published in 2000 by McGraw-Hill is a useful book for those involved in the built environment, providing the language with which built-environment professionals can engage with psychology.

Managing Diversity by Gill Kirton and Anne-Marie Greene first published in 2000 by Butterworth-Heinemann and reprinted in 2003. Although focusing on employment, this book is useful for those working in the built environment since it shows the importance of seeing diversity and equality as mutually reinforcing rather than competing forces. The integrative model of diversity and equality is advocated in this book.

Cosmopolis II promises to be an important sequel to Leonie Sandercock's book *Towards Cosmopolis*, published in 1998 by Wiley, in which she revisits the cities featured in the first book and interprets the changes as she has seen them over the last half decade.

The Diversity Training Handbook by Phil Clements and John Jones published in 2002 by Kogan Page does what it says on the pack: provides clear guidelines on dealing with diversity. This is a useful book for those new to the area.

FIVE RESOURCES

These resources include very specific material to help policy planners in their day-to-day work as well as the development of an all-round understanding and competence through lifelong learning.

'Gender Relevance Sheets for Measures under Ireland's National Development Plan 2000–2006' was published in 2004 by the Irish Department of Justice Equality and Law Reform and launched at the Gender Mainstreaming Conference in May 2004. These condensed fact sheets set out to assist those implementing Ireland's

National Development Plan and they illustrate what it means to build gender into all aspects of the plan.

You can keep an eye on developments in UK Universities through the database set up by Karen Ross at Coventry. This provides examples of some of the best practice in UK Universities in terms of diversity and equality.

Jane Elliot in association with Neish Training has produced training videos on diversity and equality issues which are filmed in the UK. For example, 'The eye in the storm' is an award-winning video of the blue-eyed–brown-eyed exercise during which Jane Elliot deliberately introduced discrimination by dividing her primary class into two groups, the superior and inferior, based not on skin colour but eye colour. One of her other videos, 'Perception is everything', discusses height, skin colour, gender and age and exposes the rarely acknowledged advantages and disadvantages of being perceived as part of a particular group. Details are available online. <http://www.neishtraining.com/pdf/NeishVideosFlyer.pdf>

Jane Elliot has produced a range of other videos filmed in the US and the video 'Angry eye' is specifically about college students.

Practising Gender Analysis in Education by Fiona Leach, published by Oxfam in 2004, takes the tools which have been used in the development context and looks at how they can be modified for an educational setting. Gender is the primary lens and the integrative model of diversity and equality runs through the book. This text is very useful for those developing curricula and running programmes.

Government websites such as the Office of the Deputy Prime Minister in the UK provide full texts of the recently sponsored work on diversity.

The Convention on the Elimination of all Forms of Discrimination Against Women (CEDAW) Online. Available HTTP: <http://www.un.org/womenwatch/daw/cedaw>.

OXFAM (2003) Online. Available HTTP: <http://www.oxfamgb.org/UKPP/poverty/thefacts.htm> (accessed 26 October 2003).

BIBLIOGRAPHY

Abacus (2003) *University of Strathclyde in Glasgow.* Online. Available HTTP: <http://iris.abacus.strath.ac.uk/new/projects.htm> (accessed 11 November 2003).

Aberdeen University (2003) *Race Equality Action Plan.* Online. Available HTTP: <http://www.abdn.ac.uk/personnel/racplan2.doc> (accessed 7 April 2004).

Age Concern (2003) *Written Submission for the Examination in Public of the Draft London Plan.* Online. Available HTTP: <http://www.london.gov.uk/london-plan-eip/submissions/subs-2a.jsp> (accessed 3 March 2003).

Ahmed, A., Couch, C. and Wright, L. (1998) *Feasibility Study into the Recruitment of Black and Ethnic Minorities into the Planning Profession*, London: RTPI.

Ahmed, K. (2003) 'And on the Seventh Day Tony Blair created', *The Observer*, 3 August: 3. Online. Available HTTP: <http://observer.guardian.co.uk/politics/story/0,6903,1011460,00.html> (accessed 16 August 2003).

Alderson, S. (2003) 'From minority to mainstream, 20 years of women and planning in Scotland', *Scottish Planner*, June: 9.

Alty, R. and Darke, R. (1987) 'A city centre for people: Involving the community in planning for Sheffield's central area', *Planning Practice and Research*, September: 7–12.

American Planning Association (APA) (2003) Online. Available HTTP: <http://www.planning.org> (accessed 11 November 2003).

Amos, G. (1998) 'A people's regeneration?', *Town and Country Planning*, 67(3): 132–133.

Anderson, W. (2003) *Engineers and Planners*, Conversation with Prof. of Engineering, University of Sheffield (14 November 2003).

Anthony, K. (2001) *Designing for Diversity, Gender, Race and Ethnicity in the Architectural Profession*, UIUC School of Architecture: Illinois.

Appleton, S. (1999) 'The Participation of Women in Urban Regeneration: A Longitudinal Study in Sheffield', PhD thesis, Sheffield Hallam University and University of Sheffield.

Argyris, C. (1999) *On Organisational Learning*, Oxford: Blackwell.

Astrom, G. (2003) 'Short Introduction to Gender Equality Issues in Sweden'. E-mail (8 July 2003).

Atkinson, R. (1997) 'Countering Urban Social Inclusion: The Role of Community Participation in Urban Regeneration', paper presented at Regional Frontiers Conference, European Universitat Viadrina Frankfurt (oder) September: 20–23.

Audit Commission (1999) *Listen Up! Effective Community Consultation*, London: Audit Commission.

Audit Commission (2002) *Equality and Diversity*, London: Audit Commission. Online. Available HTTP: <http://www.audit-commission.gov.uk/reports/NATIONAL-REPORT.

asp?CategoryID = &ProdID = 13A7DCD0-8339-11d6-AC3D-00010303D196>
(accessed 28 October).

Audit Commission (2003) *Best Value*. Online. Available HTTP: <http://www.bvpps.
audit-commission.gov.uk/> (accessed 14 October 2003).

AUT (2002) *Equal Opportunities in Employment in Higher Education: A Framework
for Partnership*. Online. Available HTTP: <http://www.aut.org.uk/media/pdf/
equaloppsframework.pdf> (accessed 17 November 2003).

AUT and Proud (2001) *Lesbian, Gay and Bisexual Participation in UK Universities*,
London: AUT.

Axelrod, R. (1997) *The Complexity of Cooperation: Agent-Based Models of Competition
and Collaboration*, Princeton, NJ: Princeton University Press. <http://www-personal.
umich.edu/~axe/> (accessed 2 April 2004).

Axelrod, R., Riolo, R. and Cohen, M. (2002) 'Beyond Geography: Cooperation with per-
sistent links in the absence of clustered neighborhoods', *Personality and Social
Psychology Review*, 6(4): 341–346. Online. Available HTTP: <http://www-personal.
umich.edu/~axe/> (accessed 2 April 2004).

Baker, L. (2001) 'The revolution's here', *Planning*, 26 January: 13.

Baker, S., Kousis, M., Richardson, D. and Young, S. (eds) (1997) *The Politics of Sustainable Development*, London: Routledge.

Banbury, K. (2000) *Rethinking Professional Institutions in Construction: A Preliminary
Study into How Some Professional Institutions in Construction See Themselves and
How They are Seen by Others as We Enter the 21st Century*, London: Institution
of Civil Engineers.

Barabasi, L. (2001) 'The physics of the Web', *Physics World*, 14: 33. Online. Available
HTTP: <http://www.nd.edu/~alb/public.html> (accessed 2 April 2004).

Barrow, C. (2001) *Social Impact Assessment: An Introduction*, London: Arnold.

Battles, J. (2003) '80% of homosexuals have been victims of hate crime', *The Sunday
Times*, 27 July: 2.

Batty, D. (2003) 'The voice of experience, a women with learning difficulties helps get to
the truth', *The Guardian Society*, Wednesday 16 April: 95.

BBC (2003) *Restoration*. Online. Available HTTP: <http://www.bbc.co.uk/history/
programmes/restoration> (accessed 24 October 2003).

BBC News (2003) *Policy Change after Limb Mix-up*. Online. Available HTTP:
<http://news.bbc.co.uk/1/hi/england/berkshire/3370869.stm> (accessed 15
April 2004).

Beck, U. (1992) *Risk Society: Towards a New Modernity*, London: Sage.

Beck, U. (1998) *Democracy Without Enemies*, Cambridge: Polity Press.

Belbin, M. (2001) 'Does gender balance matter', *Belbin Newsletter*, Autumn: 1.

Belgium (1989) *Initial Report of Belgium to CEDAW*, 23 February and 1 March,
CEDAW/C/SR143 and 146. Online. Available HTTP: <http://66.36.242.93/pdf/
belgium_t4_cedaw.pdf> (accessed 14 October 2003).

Bennett, C. (2000) 'Mainstreaming in Organisations: Strategies for Delivering Women's Equality in UK Local Government', unpublished PhD thesis, Sheffield Hallam University.

Bennett, C., Booth, C., Yeandle, S. and Reeves, D. (2002) *Mainstreaming Equality in the Committees of the Scottish Parliament Final Report*, CRESR, Sheffield Hallam University in collaboration with Dory Reeves, University of Strathclyde (unpublished).

Berlin City Council (2003) *Planwerk Innenstadt*. Online. Available HTTP: <http://www.stadtentwicklung.berlin.de/planen/metropolis/Index_en.shtml> (accessed 24 October 2003).

Bett, M. (1999) *Independent Review of Higher Education Pay and Conditions*. Online. Available HTTP: <http://www.archive.official-documents.co.uk/irhec/irhec.htm> (accessed 16 November 2003).

Beveridge, R. and Nott, S. (2000) 'Gender mainstreaming – a means to an end?', *Journal of European Public Policy*, 7(4).

Bibby, A. (undated) *Coin Street Case Study*. Online. Available HTTP: <http://www.andrewbibby.com/socialenterprise/coin-street.html> (accessed 10 November 2003).

Black Londoner's Forum (2003) *Written Submission for the Examination in Public of the Draft London Plan*. Online. Available HTTP: <http://www.london.gov.uk/london-plan-eip/submissions/subs-2a.jsp> (accessed 3 March 2003).

Blacks, J. (2000) 'Medical school students produce different diagnoses of white and black patients', *Higher Education*, 38, cited in S. Bryant (2001), 'The five habits for cross-cultural lawyering', *Clinical Law Review*, 8(1): 29.

Blowers, A. (1997) 'Society and sustainability, the context of change for planning', in M. Blowers and B. Evans (eds), *Town Planning in the 20th Century*, London: Routledge.

Bondi, L. and Peake, L. (1988) 'Gender and the city: Urban politics revisited', in J. Little, L. Peake and P. Richardson (eds), *Women in Cities, Gender and the Urban Environment*, Hampshire: Macmillan Education Ltd.

Booth, C. and Gilroy, R. (1996) 'Dreaming the possibility of change', *Built Environment*, 22(1): 72–82.

Bourne, L. (2000) *People and Places: A Portrait of the Evolving Character of the Toronto Area*, Toronto: Neptis Foundation.

Bowlby, S. (1984) 'Planning for women to shop in post-war Britain', *Environment and Planning D: Society and Space*, 2: 179–190.

Bowlby, S. (1985) 'Shoppers' needs', *Town and Country Planning*, 54: 219–222.

Boyack, S. (2000) 'Debate on Sustainable Development', Scottish Parliament debate 3/2/2000.

Braithwaite, M. (1998) *Integrating Gender Equality into Local and Regional Development*, Brussels, EC.

Braithwaite, M. (2000) *Manual for Integrating Equality into Local and Regional Development*, Brussels: Engender.

Breugal, C. and Kean, H. (1995) 'The moment of municipal feminism: Gender and class in 1980s local governance and democratic theory', *Local Governance*, 24(1): 43–55.

Brierley, D. (2003) *Joined Up: An Introduction to Youthwork and Ministry*, Carlisle: Authentic Media.

Bronstein, A. (1999) 'Challenging Assumptions: Gender Issues', paper presented to the Symposium Gender Equality and the Role of Planning; Royal Town Planning Institute Conference, 1 July.

Brown, R. and Wootton-Millward, L. (1993) *Perceptions of Group Homogeneity During Group Formation and Change*, New York: W.W. Norton.

Brownhill, S. and Darke, J. (1998) *Rich Mix Inclusive Strategies for Urban Regeneration*, Bristol: University of Bristol Policy Press.

Brundtland, G. (1987a) *Our Common Future*, New York: United Nations.

Brundtland, G. (ed.) (1987b) *Our Common Future: The World Commission on Environment and Development*, Oxford: Oxford University Press.

Brundtland, G. (2000) 'Health and population', *Reith Lecture*, May, BBC. Online. Available HTTP: <http://news.bbc.co.uk/hi/english/static/events/reith-2000/lecture4.stm> (accessed 16 October 2003).

Bryant, S. (2001) 'The five habits for cross-cultural lawyering', *Clinical Law Review*, 8(1): 33–107.

Bryant, S. (2003a) 'Five Habits'. E-mail (27 February 2003).

Bryant, S. (2003b) 'Professional Bodies'. E-mail (23 March 2003).

Bryant, S. and Peters, J. K. (undated) *Five Habits for Cross Cultural Lawyering* (Work in progress). Online. Available HTTP: <http://www.law.cuny.edu/clea/multiculture/index.html> (accessed 25 April 2004).

Buckingham, S., Batchelor, A. and Reeves, D. (2004) *Mainstreaming Gender into Waste Management Planning*, London: Brunel.

Budlender, D. and Sharp, R. (1998) *How to Do a Gender Sensitive Gender Analysis: Contemporary Research and Practice*, Commonwealth Secretariat and Australian Agency for International Development: Canberra.

Budlender, D., Elson, D., Hewitt, G. and Mukhopadhyay, T. (2002) *Make Cents: Understanding Gender Responsive Budgets*, Commonwealth Secretariat: London.

Bullard, R. (1990) *Dumping in Dixie*, Boulder: Westview.

Bunker, P. (2001) in T. Heller *et al.* (eds) *Working for Health*, London: Open University, Sage.

Burbage, D. (2003) 'Responding to Change, London Borough of Newham', paper presented to the Diversity in Britain Conference, 3 October, The Guardian and TMP Worldwide.

Burden, A. (2003) 'Statement by the Chair of the City Planning Commission and Director of the Department of City Planning', New York City. Online. Available HTTP: <http://www.nyc.gov/html/dcp/html/about/greeting.html> (accessed 19 May 2003).

Burley, H. (2000) 'Mentoring Scheme in the West Midlands', Presentation to the women in planning group at Summer School, St. Andrews, 7 September.

Buzan, T. (2001) *Mind-Map Definition*. Online. Available HTTP: <http://www.mind-map.com/mindmaps_definition.htm> (accessed 25 April 2004).

Cabinet Office (2002) *Equality and Diversity, Making it Happen*, Consultation Document, October, London: Cabinet Office. Online. Available HTTP: <http://www.womenandequalityunit.gov.uk/research/pubn_2002.htm#making_it_happen> (accessed 31 October 2003).

Campbell, J. and Oliver, M. (1996) *Disability Politics – Understanding Our Past, Changing Our Future*, London: Routledge.

Canadian Institute of Planners (CIP) (2003) Online. Available HTTP: <http://www.cip-icu.ca> (accessed 29 August 2003).

Caplan, P. (1995) *Lifting a Ton of Feathers, Women's Guide to Surviving in the Academic World*, Toronto: Council of Ontario Universities.

Carley, M. and Christie, I. (2000) *Social Impact Assessment*, London: Earthscan.

Carli, L., Columbo, J., Dowling, S., Kulis, M. and Minalga, C. (1990) 'Victim Derogation as a Function of Hindsight and Cognitive Bolstering', paper presented at the meeting of the American Psychological Association.

Carney, G. (2002) 'Feminism, the women's movement and the internationalization of gender equality policy: The case of gender mainstreaming', *Irish Political Studies*, 17(2): 17–34.

Carney, G. (forthcoming) 'Gender Mainstreaming in Ireland', PhD thesis, Trinity College, Dublin.

Carson, R. (1962) *Silent Spring*, Boston: Houghton Mifflin Company. Online. Available HTTP: <http://www.rachelcarson.org/index.cfm?/useaction=homepage> (accessed 16 October 2003).

Carson, R. (2002) *Silent Spring*, 40th anniversary edition, Boston: Houghton Mifflin Company. Online. Available HTTP: <http://www.rachelcarson.org/index.cfm?/useaction=homepage> (accessed 16 October 2003).

Carver, S. (2001) 'Public participation, GIS and cyber-democracy: Evaluating on-line spatial decision support systems', *Environment and Planning B: Planning and Design*, 28: 907–921.

Castells, M. (1996) 'An interview with Manuel Castells', *Cities*, 13: 8.

CCETSW (1998) *Getting off the Fence, Challenging Sectarianism in the Personal Social Services*, Belfast: CCETSW.

CEDAW (2003) *The Convention on the Elimination of all Forms of Discrimination Against Women*. Online. Available HTTP: <www.un.org/womenwatch/daw/cedaw> (accessed 16 October 2003).

Centre for the Environment and the Built Environment (2003) *Special Interest Group Equality and Diversity in Built Environment Education*. Online. Available HTTP: <http://cebe.cf.ac.uk/learning/sig/equality/index.html> (accessed 23 November 2003).

Center for Environment and Planning (CEP) (2000) *A Comparison of Environmental Planning Systems Legislation in Selected Countries*, Final Report for the Royal Commission on Environmental Pollution. Online. Available HTTP: <http://rcep.org.uk> (accessed 24 October 2003).

Centre for Ethnicity and Racism Studies (2003) *Racism Studies*. Online. Available HTTP: <http://www.leeds.ac.uk/cers/toolkit/toolkit.htm> (accessed 12 June 2003).

Center for Local Economic Strategies (2004) *Disability and Regeneration Agenda*, Manchester: CLES.

Centre for Public Services (2002) *Promoting Gender Equality in the Public Sector*, Manchester: EOC.

Centre for Race Equality (2003) *The Anti-Racist Toolkit*. Online. Available HTTP: <http:www.leeds.ac.uk/cers/toolkit/Section%2Otwo.htm> (accessed 10 June 2003).

Chan, W. (2003) 'Chinese Identities: Official Representations and New Ethnicities', PhD thesis, University of Birmingham, Department of Geography.

Chan, W. (forthcoming) 'Planning at the limit: Immigration and post-war Birmingham', *Journal of Historical Geography*.

Chaney, P. (2003) 'Mainstreaming in UK Public Policy', paper presented to the Gender Research Forum, London and to the Gender and Governance: Mainstreaming in UK public policy? Workshop, 10th May, University of Bristol. Online. Available HTTP: <http://www.cardiff.ac.uk/socsi/inclusive-governance/gender%20mainstreaming%20%20the%20case%20of%20the%20welsh%20assembly,%20paul%20chaney.pdf>.

Chaney, P. and MacKay, F. (2003) 'Mainstreaming Equality – A Comparative Analysis of Contemporary Developments in Scotland and Wales', presentation to the Gender Research Forum, 3 November 2003, London: Women and Equality Unit.

Chant, S. and Gutmann, M. (2000) *Mainstreaming Men into Gender and Development*, London: Oxfam.

Cherry, G. (1994) 'Birmingham: A study in Geography', *History and Planning*, Chichester, Sussex: John Wiley & Sons.

Chouinard, V. (1999) 'Life at the margins: Disabled women's explorations of ableist spaces', in E. Kenworthy Teather (ed.), *Embodied Geographies: Spaces, Bodies and Rites of Passage*, 142–156, London: Routledge.

Christie, J. (1997) 'A forgotten resource: An overview of women and regeneration', *Women's Design Service Broadsheet*, 26.

City of Birmingham (1960) *City of Brimingham Development Plan*, Birmingham: Birmingham City Council.

City of Liberty (2003) *Blueprint for Liberty, Future Land Use Plan*, Missouri: City of Liberty.

City of Seattle (2002) *Our Local Stories of Urban Sustainability*. Online. HTTP: <www2.cityofseattle.net/urbansustainability/sustainability.asp> (accessed 3 July 2002).

Clarke, G. (2003) 'Pike Place Market'. E-mail (10 November 2003).

Claydon, J. and Daniels, I. (2001) *Report on Questionnaire Survey of RTPI New Members for the Professional Qualifications Committee*, June, London: RTPI.

Clements, P. and Jones, J. (2002) *The Diversity Training Handbook: A Practical Guide to Understanding and Changing Attitudes*, London: Kogan Page.

Cogan, E. (2000) *Successful Public Meetings*, Chicago: American Planners Association.

Cohen, A., Cox, M. and Moss-Kanter, R. (1980) *A Tale of O on Being Different: A Training Tool for Managing Diversity*, New York: Goodmeasure Inc.

Coin Street Action Group (2003) Online. Available HTTP: <http://westworld.dmu.ac.uk/cetd/coheren3e/newcoin/7705-com.htm> (accessed 21 August 2003).

Commission for Architecture and the Built Environment (2003) *Enablers*. Online. Available HTTP: <http://www.cabe.org.uk> (accessed 17 November 2003).

Commission for the European Communities (1992) *5th Environmental Action Programme*, Brussels: CEC.

Commission for the European Communities (1996a) *Communication from the Commission: Incorporating Equal Opportunities for Women and Men into All Community Policies and Activities*, COM (96)67 final, 21/02/1996.

Commission for the European Communities (1996b) *Guide to Gender Impact Assessment*, Brussels, CEC. Online. Available HTTP: <http://europa.eu.int/comm/employment_social/equ_opp/gender/gender_en.pdf> (accessed 28 October 2003); <http://europa.eu.int/comm/dg05/key-en.htm> (accessed 29 October 2003).

Commission for Racial Equality (2002a) *A Guide for Institutions of Further and Higher Education*, London: CRE.

Commission for Racial Equality (2002b) *Code of Practice and Guidance: The Duty to Promote Equality*, London: CRE. Online. Available HTTP: <http://www.cre.gov.uk/publs/cat_duty.html> (accessed 28 October 2003).

Commission for Racial Equality (2003) Online. Available HTTP: <http://www.cre.gov.uk> (accessed 4 December 2003).

Commission for Racial Equality (2003) 'Diversity in Performance and Service Delivery', paper presented to Diversity in Britain Conference, London: The Guardian and TMP Worldwide.

The Commission on Social Justice (1994) *Social Justice, Strategies for National Renewal*, London: Vintage.

Common, M. (1995) *Sustainability and Policy*, Cambridge: Cambridge University Press.

Commonwealth Association of Planners (2003) Online. Available HTTP: <http://www.commonwealth-planners.org> (accessed 16 November 2003).

Community Development Foundation (1996) *Regeneration and the Community*, London: CDF.

The Community Relations Council (1999) *A Young Person's Guide to Cultural Diversity in Northern Ireland*, Belfast: Community Relations Council.

Connor, D. (2001) *Constructive Citizen Participation – A Resource Book*, 8th edition, Victoria: Development Press.

Connor, D. (2002) 'Constructive Participation'. E-mail (2002).

Construction Industry Council (2003) *Constructing Diversity Video*, London: CIC.

Corn, J. and Horrigan, B. (1984) *Yesterday's Tomorrows, Past Visions of the American Future*, London: John Hopkins University Press.

COSLA (2003) Online. Available HTTP: <http://www.cosla.gov.uk> (accessed 23 November 2003).

Cott, N. (1989) 'What's in a name? The limits of social feminism or expanding the vocabulary of women's history', *Journal of American History*, 76: 809–829.

Council of Europe (1998) *Gender Mainstreaming, Conceptual Framework, Methodology and Presentation of Good Practices*, Strasbourg: Council of Europe. Online. Available HTTP: <http://book.coe.int/gb/cat/liv/htm/l1324.htm> (accessed 31 October 2003).

Council of Sustainable Development (1994/1999) *Towards a Sustainable America*. Online. Available HTTP: <http:clinton2.nara.gov/pcsd/publications/tsa.pdf> (accessed 7 July 2003).

County Administrative Board of West Gotaland (undated) *Reflex – A Decision Makers Guide to Gender Proofing Policy and Practice*, Goteborg: County Administrative Board of West Gotaland.

Croft, S. and Beresford, B. (1992) 'A third approach to participation', *Critical Social Policy*, 35(12): 20–44.

Crookson, V. (2003) 'Legislative Approaches to Disability'. E-mail (10 January 2003).

Cross, M., Brar, H. and McLeod, M. (1991) *Racial Equality and the Local State: An Evaluation of Policy Implementation in the London Borough of Brent*, Monographs in Ethnic Relations, no. 1, ESRC and Centre for Research in Ethnic Relations: Coventry.

Crowley, W. (1999) *Pike Place Market*, Seattle. Online. Available HTTP: <http://www.historylink.org/_output.CFM?file_ID=1602> (accessed 10 November 2003).

Cullingworth, B. and Nadin, V. (2001) *Town and Country Planning in the UK*, 13th edition, London: Routledge.

Dainty, A., Bagilhole, B., Gibb, A. and Pepper, C. (2002) *An Evaluation and Development of the 'Diversity in the Workplace' Toolkit and Key Performance Indicator as Mechanisms for Improving Business Performance in the UK Construction Sector*, Loughborough: Loughborough University.

Dame, T. and Grant, A. (2002) *Women and Community Safety: A Resource Book on Planning for Safer Communities*, Cowichan: Women Against Violence Society.

Dark, C. O. (1996) 'Incorporating issues of race, gender, class, sexual orientation and disability into law school teaching', *Willamette Law Review*, 32(541): 59.

Darke, J., Ledwith, S. and Woods, R. (eds) (2000) *Women and the City: Visibility and Voice in Urban Space*, Basingstoke: Palgrave.

Darke, R. (1998) 'Public participation, perceptions and equal opportunities', in P. Allendinger, A. Prior and J. Raemakers (eds), *An Introduction to Planning Practice*, Chichester: Wiley.

Davidson, M. and Burke, R. (1994) *Women in Management: Current Research Issues*, London: Paul Chapman Publishing.

Davies, J. (2002) *Male Dominance of Videogame, Production and Consumption*. Online. Available HTTP: <http://www.gamasutra.com/education/theses/20020708/davies_01.htm> (accessed 27 March 2004).

Davies, W. and Ohri, A. (undated, unpublished) *The Nature of Oppression*, Edinburgh: OSDC.

Davoudi, S. (2002) 'Sustainability: A new vision for the British planning system', *Planning Perspectives*, 15: 123–137.

Daws, P. (2003) 'Membership Records'. E-mail (4 September 2003).

Dean, J. (1997) 'The long march', *Planning*, 14 November: 18.

Dekker, L. (2001) 'The Netherland 5th Report, Public Participation'. Email (May 2001).

Department for Education and Employment (DFEE) (1996) *Policy Appraisal for Equal Treatment*, London: DFEE.

Department of the Environment (1992) *Planning Policy Guidance Note 4 on Industrial and Commerical Development*, London: DoE.

Department of the Environment (1994a) *Circular 5/94 Planning and Crime*, London: DoE.

Department of the Environment (1994b) *Community Involvement in Planning and Development Processes*, London: HMSO. Online. Available HTTP: <http://www.archive.official-documents.co.uk/document/cm43/4310/4310.htm> (accessed 18 April 2004).

Department of the Environment (1994c) *Planning Policy Guidance 4 Industrial and Commercial Development*, London: ODPM.

Department of the Environment (1996) *Planning Policy Guidance Note 6, Major Retail Development and Planning Policy*, London: DoE. Online. Available HTTP: <http://www.odpm.gov.uk/stellent/groups/odpm_planning/documents/page/odpm_plan_606915.pdf> (accessed 16 March 2004).

Department of the Environment (1997) *Planning Policy Guidance Note 1 on General Policies and Principles*, London: DoE.

Department of the Environment (1998) *Design Bulletin 32 Residential Roads and Footpaths*, London: DoE.

Department of the Environment (2001) *Planning Policy Guidance Note 13 on Highways Considerations*, London: DoE.

Department of Environment, Transport and the Regions (1997) *Involving Communities in Urban and Rural Regeneration*, London: HMSO.

Department of Environment, Transport and the Regions (1999a) *Proposals for a Good Practice Guide on Sustainability Appraisal of Regional Planning Guidance*, London: DETR.

Department of Environment, Transport and the Regions (1999b) *Modernising Government*, White Paper Cm 4310, London: Stationary Office. Online. Available HTTP: <http://www.archive.official-documents.co.uk/document/cm43/4310/4310.htm> (accessed 18 November 2004).

Department of Environment, Transport and the Regions (2000) National Travel Survey 1996–1998 Update SB(99)21, *Women and Transport Checklist*, London: DETR.

Department of Justice Equality and Law Reform (2001) *The Draft National Plan for Women*, Dublin: Department of Justice Equality and Law Reform.

Department of Trade and Industry (2004) *Employers Grant 8 Out of 10, Flexible Working Requests*, Press Release. Online. Available HTTP: <http://213.38.88.221/gnn/national.nsf/TI/4FCE941147EDD49880256E6D0036C386?opendocument> (accessed 5 April 2004).

Department of Transport (1997) *Women and Transport Checklist*, London: DOT. Online. Available HTTP: <http://www.dft.gov.uk/stellent/groups/dft_mobility/documents/page/dft_mobility_506789-06.hcsp> (accessed 28 October 2003).

Devon County Council (1997) *New Earnings Survey*. Online. Available HTTP: <http://www.devon.gov.uk/dris/economic/dv_earn.html> (accessed 9 April 2004).

Dewar, D. (2001) 'Consultancy Survey', *Planning*, 26 October.

Dewar, D. (2003) 'Consultancy Survey', *Planning*, 14 November.

Disability Rights Commission (1999) *Disability Discrimination Act 1995: A Code of Practice – Duties of Trade Organisations to Their Disabled Members and Applicants*, London: DRC. Online. Available HTTP: <http://www.drc-gb.org/law/codes.asp> (accessed 21 November 2003).

Disability Rights Commission (2003) *Draft Code of Practice, Trade Organisations and Qualifications Bodies*, London: DRC. Online. Available HTTP: <http://www.drcgb.org/searchresults.asp?search=trade+organisations> (accessed 21 November 2003).

Disabled Persons Transport Advisory Committee (2003) *Inclusive Projects: A Guide to Best Practice on Preparing and Delivering Project Briefs to Secure Access*, June, London: DPTAC.

Dodge, M. and Kitchen, R. (2001) *Mapping Cyberspace*, London: Routledge.

Down and Ards Council (2002) *Plan in Preparation*. Online. Available HTTP: <http://www.doeni.gov.uk/planning/Area_Plans/down.htm> (accessed 24 October 2003).

Drake, R. (1999) *Understanding Disability Policies*, London: Macmillan Press.

Driskell, D. (2002) *Creating Better Cities with Children and Youth: A Manual for Participation*, London: Earthscan Publications.

Duhl, L. and Sanchez, A. (eds) (1999) *Healthy Cities and the City Planning Process – A Background Document on Links between Health and Urban Planning*, Copenhagen: WHO Regional Office in Europe.

Duncan, S. (1994) 'Theorising differences in patriarchy', *Environment and Planning A*, 26: 1177–1194.

Earthscan (2000) *The Community Planning Handbook*, London: Earthscan Ltd.

The Ecologist (1972) *Blueprint for Survival*, Harmondsworth: Penguin.

Eden, M., Falkheden, L. and Malberet, B. (2000) 'The built environment and sustainable development: Research meets practice in a Scandanavian context', *Planning Theory and Practice*, 1(2): 260–284.

Egan, J. (2004) *Skills for Sustainable Communities*. Online. Available HTTP: <http://www.odpm.gov.uk/stellent/groups/odpm_urbanpolicy/documents/page/odpm_urbpol_028300.pdf> (accessed 25 April 2004).

Elliot, J. (1970) *Blue Eye, Brown Eye*, New York: Elliot and Elliot Inc.

Elliot, J. (2002) *The Stolen Eye*, New York: Elliot and Elliot Inc.

Elliot, J. (2004) *Perception is Everything* (video), Neish Training. Online. Available HTTP: <http://www.neishtraining.com/pdf/NeishVideosFlyer.pdf> (accessed 8 May 2004).

Ellis, G. (2003) *Good Practice Guide to Promote Racial Equality in Planning for Travellers*, Belfast: Equality Commission, Northern Ireland.

Ellison, L. (1999) *Surveying the Glass Ceiling*, London: RICS.

Elson, D. (1993) 'Gender relations and economic issues', *Women and Economic Policy*, Oxfam Focus on Gender 3, Oxford: Oxfam.

Elson, D. (1998) 'Integrating gender issues into national budgetary policies and procedures: Some policy options', *Journal of International Development*, 10: 929–941.

Elson, D. (2003) 'Gender Mainstreaming and Gender Budgeting', paper presented to the Conference on Gender Equality and Europe's Future, Brussels, 4 March, European Commission, DG Education and Culture and Jean Monnet Project.

Elson, D. (2004) 'Gender Budgeting in an International Context: Supports and Barriers', paper presented to the PAN Island Gender Budgets Seminar, 24 March.

Employers Organisation for Local Government (2001) *Equality Standard for Local Government*. Online. Available HTTP: <http://www.lg-employers.gov.uk/diversity/equality/index.html> (accessed 14 October).

Employers Organisation for Local Government (2003) *No Quality Without Equality*. Online. Available HTTP: <http://www.lg-employers.gov.uk/publications/fullpublications/nqwe.html> (accessed 14 October 2003).

Enfield, S. and Harris, A. (2003) *Disability, Equality and Human Rights: A Training Manual for Development and Humanitarian Organisations*, Oxford: Oxfam.

ENTEC (2002) *Sustainability Appraisal of the Draft London Plan*, London: GLA. Online. Available: HTTP: <http://www.london.gov.uk/mayor/strategies/sds/sustainability.jsp> (accessed 23 November 2003).

Equal Opportunities Commission (1997) *Mainstreaming Gender Equality in Local Government*, Manchester: Equal Opportunities Commission, UK.

Equal Opportunities Commission (2000) *Mainstreaming Gender in Structural Fund Programmes*, Edinburgh: EOC.

Equal Opportunities Commission (2002) *15% off Campaign Pack*, Manchester: EOC.

Equal Opportunities Commission (undated) *A Checklist for Gender Proofing Research*, Manchester: EOC. Online. Available HTTP: <http://www.eoc.org.uk/cseng/ research/a_checklist_for_gender_proofing_research.asp> (accessed 27 September 2004).

Equal Opportunities Commission Scotland (1999) *Toolkit for Mainstreaming Equal Opportunities in the European Union for Structural Fund Programmes in Scotland*, Glasgow: EOC.

Equalitec (2002) *Mentoring*. Online. Available HTTP: <http://www.equalitec.com/ forwomen/whatcanmentoringdoforyou.php> (accessed 17 November 2003).

Equality Authority (2003) *Request for Tender to Model an Integrated Approach to Proofing that Covers Poverty, Gender and the Wider Equality Agenda*, Dublin: Equality Authority.

Equality Commission for Northern Ireland (2003) Online. Available HTTP: <http:// www.equalityni.org> (accessed 28 October 2003).

Equality Direct (2002) *Advice*. Online. Available HTTP: <http://www.equalitydirect.org.uk> (accessed 21 September 2002).

Escott, K. and Dexter, W. (2002) *Mainstreaming Gender Equality in the Public Sector*, Manchester: EOC.

Ethington, P. (2001) *Diversity Index and Location of Multiracial Persons: Los Angeles County*. Online. Available HTTP: <http://www.usc.edu/schools/sppd/research/ census2000/race_census/racecontours/ethington/ethington_maps3.htm> (accessed 4 December 2003).

European Commission (1994) 'The E-Quality award', in G. Simons and D. Min (eds) (2002), *EuroDiversity*, 235, London: Butterworth-Heinemann.

European Commission (1999) *Environment and Sustainable Development*, Series: Evaluation and Documents No. 6, 3.

European Commission (1999a) *Environment and Sustainable Development: A Guide for the Ex-ante Evaluation of the Environmental Impact of Regional Development Programmes*, Series: Evaluation and Documents No. 6, Brussels: DG XVI Regional Policy and Cohesion.

European Commission (1999b) *Equality is the Future*, Symposium, Brussels: EC.

European Commission (2000a) *The Framework Regulation for the Structural Funds (2000–2006)*, Brussels: EU.

European Commission (2000b) *Community Framework Strategy on Gender Equality (2001–2005)*, Brussels: EU. Online. Available HTTP: <http://europa.eu.int/comm/ employment_social/equ_opp/strategy_en.html> (accessed 13 November 2003).

European Commission (2000c) *Mainstreaming Equal Opportunities for Women and Men in Structural Fund Programmes and Projects*, The New Programming Period 2000–2006: Technical Papers by Theme, Brussels: EC.

European Commission (2001a) *Communication on Making a European Area of Lifelong Learning a Reality*, 21 November. Online. Available HTTP: <http://europa.eu.int/comm/education/policies/lll/life/what_islll_en.html> (accessed 25 April 2004).

European Commission (2001b) *Strategic Environmental Assessment Directive 2001/21/EC*. Online. Available HTTP: <http://europa.eu.int/comm/environment/eia/sea-legalcontext.htm#legal> (accessed 21 September 2004).

European Convention of Human Rights (1950) Online. Available HTTP: <http://www.echr.coe.int/Convention/Convention%20countries%20link.htm> (accessed 14 October 2003).

European Foundation of Quality Management (2003) Online. Available HTTP: <http://www.efqm.org/search/search.asp> (accessed 14 October 2003).

European Spatial Development Perspective (2003) Online. Available HTTP: <http://www.kepemepcree.org/European_Policies/eu_policies_1_en.ht> (accessed 16 October 2003).

European Union (1957) *Treaty of Rome*. Online. Available HTTP: <http://www.hri.org/docs/Rome57/Part3Title08.html> (accessed 14 October 2003).

European Union (1987) *Single European Act*. Online. Available HTTP: <http://europa.eu.int/abc/obj/treaties/en/entr14a.htm> (accessed 31 October 2003).

European Union (1992) *Maastricht Treaty*. Online. Available HTTP: <http://europa.eu.int/en/record/mt/final.html> (accessed 31 October 2003).

European Union (1997) *Amsterdam Treaty*. Online. Available HTTP: <http://europa.eu.int/eurlex/en/search/treaties_founding.html> (accessed 14 October 2003).

European Union (2000a) *General Framework for Equal Treatment*. Online. Available HTTP: <http://europa.eu.int/smartapi/cgi/sga_doc> (accessed 26 October 2003).

European Union (2000b) *Race Directive*. Online. Available HTTP: <http://europa.eu.int/smartapi/cgi/sga_doc> (accessed 26 October 2003).

European Women's Lobby (2003) *Equality in Europe: Urgent Lobbying Action Before 10.09.2003*, Email from European Parliament Women's Rights Committee. Online. Available HTTP: <http://www.womenlobby.org/Document.asp?DocID=623&tod=192628> (accessed 14 October 2003).

Eurostat Statistical Office of the European Communities (1998) *Social Portrait of Europe*, Office for the Official Publications of the European Communities.

Evening, L. (2003) 'Equal Educational Opportunities at Auckland University'. E-mail (17 June 2003).

Eversley, J. (2003) 'International Comparisons'. E-mail (12 September 2003).

Eyben, K., Morrow, D., Wilson, D. and Robinson, B. (2002) *The Equity, Diversity and Interdependence Framework*, Coleraine: University of Ulster.

Fairhurst, G. and Sarr, R. (1996) *The Art of Framing*, San Francisco: Jossey-Bass Publishers.

Faithworks (2003) Online. Available HTTP: <http://www.faithworks.info> (accessed 23 August 2003).

Fathers, J. (2003) 'Women students', conversation with Product Design Lecturer (14 March 2003).

Fawcett, B. (2000) *Feminist Perspectives on Disability*, London: Pearson Education.

Fenster, T. (1999) *Gender, Planning and Human Rights*, London: Routledge.

Financial Times (2003) 'Spending Review', 28 November 2003: 1.

Finland (1995) *The Finnish Local Government Act*, Helsinki, 17 March. Online. Available HTTP: <http://www.kunnat.net/k_perussivu.asp?path=1;161;279;280;37560;44307> (accessed 12 November 2003).

Finnish Ministry of the Environment (2000) *Land Use and Building Act*, Stockholm: Ministry of the Environment. Online. Available HTTP: <http://www.vyh.fi/eng/environ/legis/landuse.htm> (accessed 13 November 2003).

Fitzgerald, R. (2002) *Making Mainstreaming Work*, Glasgow: European Policies Research Centre.

Forbes, J. (2001) *Planning Newcastle for 2020*, contribution to the Planning Service as a contribution to the Down and Ards Area Plan.

Forbes, J. (2003) 'Newcastle 2020 Plan'. E-mails (14 and 24 February 2003).

Ford, J. and Lewis, J. (1984) 'New towns and new gender relations in old industrial regions: Women's employment in Peterlee and East Kilbride', *Built Environment*, 10: 42–52.

Forrester, J. (1989) *Planning in the Face of Power*, Berkley: University of California Press.

Fortuin, G. (2001) *History of the Legislation Race Relations Conciliator*. Online. Available HTTP: <http://www.hrc.co.nz/index.php?p=13819> (accessed 14 October 2003).

Fredman, S. (2002) *The Future of Equality in Britain*, Oxford: University of Oxford. Online. Available HTTP: <http://www.eoc.org.uk/EOCeng/EOCcs/Research/a_future_of_equality_in_britain.pdf> (accessed 31 October 2003).

Fredman, S. (2003a) 'Hierarchies of Legislation'. E-mail (8 August; 8 September 2003).

Fredman, S. (2003b) 'Opening Plenary', *Gender Research Forum*, 3 November, London: Women and Equality Unit.

Fredman, S. and Spencer, S. (forthcoming) *Age as an Equality Issue*, Oxford: Hart Publishing.

French Gilson, S. and Deploy, E. (2000) 'Multiculturalism and disability: A critical perspective', *Disability and Society*, 15(2): 207–218.

Friberg, T. (1996) 'New Regional Policies Favourable to Women: A Result of Mobilising Women's Power', Report on the Swedish Example, Best practice for Habitat II Istanbul.

Friberg, T. and Larsson, A. (1998) *Gender Perspective in Swedish Comprehensive Planning*, Lund: Lund University.

Friedman, J. and Douglass, M. (eds) (1998) *Cities for Citizens: Planning and the Rise of the Civil Society in a Global Age*, Chichester: John Wiley.

Fuss, D. (1989) *Essentially Speaking: Feminism, Nature and Difference*, New York: Routledge.

Galt, J. (1985) *Guelph and the Early Canadian Town Planning*. Online. Available HTTP: <http://www.uoguelph.ca/history/urban/article2.html> (accessed 20 October 2003).

Gates, H. L. Junior (2003) *America Beyond the Colour Line*, BBC2, Sunday 10 July. Online. Available HTTP: <http://www.walltowall.co.uk/projects/project.asp?ProjectID=171> (accessed 16 August 2003).

Gaventa, J. (1993) 'The powerful, the powerless and the experts: Knowledge struggles in an information age', in P. Park, M. Brydon-Miller, B. Hall and T. Jackson (eds), *Voices of Change: Participatory Research in the United States and Canada*, Westport, CT: Bergin & Garvey.

Gebler, C. (1991) *The Glass Curtain*, London: Abacus.

Gehl, J. (1996) *Life Between Buildings: Using Public Space*, Copenhagen: Arkitektens Forlag.

Giddens, A. (2000) *The ESRC 10th Annual Lecture, Social Change in Britain*. Online. Available HTTP: <http://www.esrc.ac.uk/esrccontent/PublicationsList/esrclecture10/full.html> (accessed 16 October 2003).

Giddens, A. (2001) *Sociology*, Oxford: Blackwell Publishers.

Gilman, R. (2001) 'Spinning into butter', in L. Gardner (ed.), 'Racists like us', *The Guardian Review*, 3 January: 14.

Girardet, H. (2001) *Creating Sustainable Cities*, Dartington: Green Books.

Glasgow City Council (2003) *City Development Plan*. Online. Available HTTP: <http://www.glasgow.gov.uk/cityplan/pdf/part_1/PAR_0003.PDF> (accessed 24 October 2003).

Goodstadt, V. (2003) 'Final Plenary', President of the RTPI to the RTPI Scottish Annual Planning Conference, *Making a Difference*, Glasgow, 14 November.

Government Office for London (2000) *Strategic Planning in London, The Secretary of State for the Environment, Transport and the Regions, Guidance on the Arrangements for Strategic Planning in London, GOL Circular 1/2000*, London: GOL.

Gramsci, A. (1971) *Selections from the Prison Notebooks*, Q. Hoare and G. Nowell Smith (eds), London: Lawrence & Wishart.

Grant, M. (1998) 'Planning as a Learned Profession', Report to the Professional Qualifications Committee, September, London: RTPI.

Grant, M. (1999) 'Planning as a learned profession', *Plans and Planners*, Summer: 21–26.

Greater London Authority Act (1999) Online. Available HTTP: <http://www.hmso.gov.uk/acts/acts1999/19990029.htm> (accessed 1 July 2003).

Greater London Authority (2000) 'Town and country planning', *London Spatial Development Strategy Regulations*, London: GLA.

Greater London Authority (2001) *Scoping Report Towards the London Plan*, London: GLA.

Greater London Authority (2002a) *Towards the London Plan*. Online. Available HTTP: <http://www.london.gov.uk/mayor/strategies/sds/towards_lon_plan.jsp> (accessed 20 May 2003).

Greater London Authority (2002b) *Sustainable Appraisal of the Draft London Plan*. Online. Available HTTP: <http://www.london.gov.uk/mayor/strategies/sds/sustainability. jsp> (accessed 28 June 2003).

Greater London Authority (2003a) *Gender Equality Scheme*, London: GLA. Online. Available HTTP: <http://www.london.gov.uk/gla/publications/women/gender-equal03.pdf> (accessed 1 July 2003).

Greater London Authority (2003b) *Celebrating Diversity, Safeguarding Equalities*. Online. Available HTTP: <http://www.london.gov.uk/londonissues/equalityanddiversity.jsp> (accessed 1 July 2003).

Greater London Authority (2003c) *Equality Impact Assessments, How to Do Them*, London: GLA.

Greater London Authority (2004a) *Final London Plan*, London: GLA. Online. Available HTTP: <http://www.london.gov.uk/mayor/strategies/sds/index.jsp> (accessed 27 March 2004).

Greater London Authority (2004b) *Meeting the Spatial Needs of London's Diverse Community*, Supplementary Planning Guidance, London: GLA.

Greater London Council (1986) *Changing Places*, London: Greater London Council.

Greed, C. (1994) *Women and Planning, Creating Gendered Realities*, London: Routledge.

Greed, C. (1996a) 'Urban spatial policy. A European gender perspective', *European Spatial Research and Policy*, 3(1): 47–60.

Greed, C. (1996b) *Women and Planning*, London: Routledge: 12.

Greed, C. (1997) *Social Town Planning*, London: Routledge.

Greed, C. (1999a) *Social Town Planning*, London: Routledge.

Greed, C. (1999b) 'Social Exclusion or Inclusion, The Continuing Story of Women and Planning', paper to the Symposium on Gender Equality and the Role of Planning, London.

Greed, C. (2000) 'Women in the construction professions: Achieving critical mass', *Gender Work and Organisation*, 7(3) July: 181–196.

Greed, C. (2003) *Inclusive Urban Design – Public Toilets*, London: Architectural Press.

Greed, C. (unpublished) *Mainstreaming Gender into Planning Practice: Enablers and Barriers*.

Greenpeace (2003) Online. Available HTTP: <http://www.greenpeace.org/international_en/> (accessed 27 October 2003).

Greenwood, M., Wallis, G., Connolly, M. and Hawkins, H. (2003) *The Rough Guide to Ireland*, London: Penguin.

Greer, G. (2000) *The Whole Woman*, London: Transworld Publishers.

Gunning, I. (1995) 'Diversity issues in mediation: Controlling negative cultural myths', *Journal of Dispute Resolution*, 55.

Haggett, P. and Chorley, R. (1969) *Network Analysis in Geography*, Edward Arnold: London.

Hain, S. (2003) 'Struggle for the inner city – a plan becomes a declaration of war', in W. Neill and H. Schwedler (eds), *Urban Planning and Cultural Inclusion*, Basingstoke: Palgrave.

Hajer, M. (1997) *The Politics of Environmental Discourse*, Oxford: Oxford University Press.

Hakim, C. (1996) *Key Issues in Women's Work: Female Heterogeneity and the Polarisation of Women's Employment*, London: Athlone.

Hall, P. (2002a) *Cities of Tomorrow*, London: Wiley.

Hall, P. (2002b) *Urban and Regional Planning*, London: Wiley.

Halvorsen, E. (2002) 'Sexuality in academics', *AUT Outlook*, January: 20–21.

Hamilton, K. and Jenkins, L. (2000) 'A gender audit for public transport: A new policy tool in the tackling of social exclusion', *Urban Studies*, 37(10): 1793–1800.

Hargreaves, I., Lewis, J. and Speers, T. (2003) *Science in the Media, Towards a Better Map: Science, the Public and Media*. Online. Available HTTP: <http://www.esrc.ac.uk/esrccontent/DownloadDocs/Mapdocfinal.pdf> (accessed 5 March 2004).

Harridge, C. (2002) 'Sustainability appraisal', *London Planning and Development Forum*, Issue 43, October–December: 51–53.

Harris, N. (2002) 'Collaborative planning', in P. Allmendinger and M. Tewdwr-Jones (eds), *Planning Futures, New Directions in Planning Theory*, London: Routledge.

Harvey, D. (1996) *Justice, Nature and the Geography of Difference*, Cambridge: Blackwell.

Hastings, A., McArthur, A. and McGregor, A. (1996) *Less than Equal?* Bristol: University of Bristol Policy Press.

Hastings, J. (2001) 'Levelling the Land? – Disability, Identity and Access to the Scottish Parliament and the National Assembly for Wales', Thesis submitted for MSc in City and Regional Planning, Cardiff: University of Wales.

Hayden, D. (1980) 'What would a non-sexist city be like? Speculations on housing, urban design, and human work', *Signs*, 5(3) (supplement): 170–187.

Healy, A. (2003) (ECOTEC) 'Mainstreaming Environment'. E-mail (28 April 2003).

Healey, P. (1994) 'Bringing Women into Urban and Regional Planning: Slow Progress to Big Gains', paper to the Council of Europe Colloquy: The Challenges facing European Society with the approach of the year 2000: role and representation of women: urban and regional planning for sustainable development, Ornskolvick, Sweden, March: 24–46.

Healey, P. (1997) *Collaborative Planning, Shaping Places in a Fragmented Society*, London: Macmillan Press Ltd.

Heikkila, E. (2001) 'Identity and inequality: Race and space in planning', *Planning Theory and Practice*, 2(3): 261–275.

Henderson, H. (1995) *The UN: Policy and Financing Alternatives*, Amsterdam: Elsevier Science.

Henderson, H. (1996) *Creating Alternative Futures: The End of Economics*, Bloomfield, C.T.: Kumarian Press.

Hester, R. (1996) 'Wanted: Local participation with a view', in J. Nasar and N. Brown (eds), *Public and Private Places*, Salt Lake City: Environmental Design Research Association.

Hewitt, P. (2002) *Launching Equalitec*. Online. Available HTTP: <http://www.equalitec. co.uk> (accessed 20 November 2003).

Hewitt, P. (2003) 'Key Note Speech', paper presented to Diversity in Britain Conference, Secretary of State for Trade and Industry and Minister of State of Women Conference, 9 October, London: Guardian.

Hewitt, P. (2004) *Speech on the Launch of the White Paper on the Commission for Equality and Human Rights*. Online. Available HTTP: <http://www.dti.gov.uk/ access/equalitywhitepaper.pdf> (accessed 15 May 2004).

Hewstone, M., Hantzi, A. and Johnston, L. (1991) 'Social categorisation and person memory: The pervasiveness of race as an organising principle', *European Journal of Social Psychology*, 21: 517–528.

Higgins and Davies (1996) 'Planning for women how much has been achieved?', *Built Environment*, 22(1): 32–46.

Hinds, K. and Jarvis, L. (2000) *The Gender Gap in National Centre for Social Research British Social Attitudes Survey 17th Report*, Focusing on Diversity, London: Sage Publications.

Hirdman, Y. (1990) *The Gender System: Theorethical Reflections on the Social Subordination of Women, A Study of Power and Democracy in Sweden*. English Series, Report No. 40, Uppsda: Maktutredningen.

Hiss, T. (1990) *The Experience of Place*, New York: Vintage Books.

History Link (2003) *Pike Place Market*. Online. Available HTTP: <http://www. historylink.org/_output.CFM?file_ID=1602> (accessed 11 November 2003).

Hogg, M. (1996) 'Intragroup processes, group structure and social identity', in W. P. Robinson (ed.), *Social Group and Identities: Developing the Legacy of Henri Tajfel*, Oxford: Butterworth-Heinemann.

Horelli, L. (1996) 'Engendering Evaluation of the Structural Funds Intervention – Methodological Reflections', a paper presented at the European Conference on Evaluation Methods for Structural Funds Intervention, Berlin, 2–3 December.

Horelli, L. (2003a) 'Planning and Young People'. E-mail (September 2003).

Horelli, L. (2003b) *Integration and Participation of Children and Young People in Urban Planning – A Network Approach*, Helsinki University of Technology, Centre for Urban and Regional Studies.

Horelli, L. (2005) 'A learning-based network approach to urban planning with young people', in M. Blades and C. Spencer (eds), *Children and their Environments: Learning, Using and Desiging Spaces*. Cambridge: Cambridge University Press.

Horelli, L., Booth, C. and Gilroy, R. (1997) *Infrastructure for Everyday Life: Evaluation of EuroFEM Projects, Action-Research Project* FN1/47/96 funded under 4th Action Programme of Equal Opportunities for Women and Men, 1996–1999.

Horrocks, M., Rea, J., Darke, J. and Darke, R. (1972) *Social Planning*, Sheffield: Sheffield Centre for Environmental Research.

Howard, M. and Tibballs, S. (2003) *Talking Equality: What Men and Women Think about Equality in Britain Today*, London: Future Foundation. Online. Available HTTP: <http://www.eoc.org.uk/EOCeng/EOCcs/Research/talking%20equality%20report.pdf> (accessed 14 October 2003).

Howatt, H. (2003) 'From minority to mainstream', *Scottish Planner*, 9 June.

Hugh, J. and Carmichael, P. (1998) 'Building partnerships in urban regeneration: A case study from Belfast', *Community Development Journal*, 33(3): 204–225.

Humphries, J. (2003) 'Interview', 22 May, BBC Radio 4 Today.

Hutton (2004) *Investigation into the Circumstances Surrounding the Death of Dr. David Kelly*. Online. Available HTTP: <http://www.the-hutton-inquiry.org.uka> (accessed 1 May 2004).

Ihimaera, W. (2003) *The Whale Rider*, London: Auckland.

Illsley, B. (2002) *Planning with Communities*, London: Royal Town Planning Institute.

Imrie, R. (1996) *Disability and the City: International Perspectives*, London: Paul Chapman.

Institute of Town Planners India (2003) *Origins*. Online. Available HTTP: <http://www.itpindia.org> (accessed 16 November 2003).

International Association of Public Participation (2003) *Principles of Participation*. Online. Available HTTP: <http://www.co-intelligence.org/CIPol_publicparticiaption.html> (accessed 10 November 2003).

International Association of Public Particiaption (2004) 'The Wisdom of Voices', 2004 Conference. Online. Available HTTP: <http://www.co-intelligence.org/CIPol_publicparticipation.html> (accessed 10 November 2003).

Inter-Organisational Committee on Guidelines and Principles (1994) *Guidelines for Social Impact Assessment*, NOAA, Washington. Online. Available HTTP: <http://www.nzaia.org.nz/iaia/siaguidelines.htm> (accessed 31 October 2003).

Inwood, J. (2003) *Membership Figures and Gender Split*, Executive Director New Zealand Planning Institute. E-mail (9 August 2003).

Ireland (2000) *Equal Status Act*. Online. Available HTTP: <http://www.justice.ie/80256976002CB7A4/vWeb/fsWMAK4Q7JKY> (accessed 14 October 2003).

Ireland (2001) *Waste Management Amendment Act*, Dublin: Stationary Office.

Jackson, G. (1999) 'Meeting Women's Transport Needs through the Integrated Transport Strategy', speech by the Minister for Transport, RTPI National Symposium: Equality and Role of Planning, London: RTPI.

Jackson, J. (2003) 'Radio interview', *BBC World Service*, 5a.m., 23 August.

Jacobs, J. (1961) *The Life and Death of American Cities*, New York: Random House.

Jahan, R. (1995) *The Elusive Agenda: Mainstreaming Women in Development*, Atlantic Highlands: Zed Books.

Jarman, N. (2003) *An Acceptable Prejudice? Homophobic Violence and Harassment in Northern Ireland*, Belfast: Institute for Conflict Research.

Johnson, T. (ed.) (2001) *Gender Budgets Make Cents*, London: Commonwealth Secretariat.

Johnston, A., Davies, L. and Greed, C. (2003) *Why Women Leave Architecture*, London: RIBA.

Johnston, B. (1999) 'Seeking a fair share', *Planning*, 8 October: 24.

Johnston, B. (2000) 'Consultants survey', *Planning*, 8 December: 19.

Justice Initiative (2003) *Discrimination Litigation in the UK and Strasbourg*. Online. Available HTTP: <http://www.justiceinitiative.org/publications> (accessed 26 October 2003).

Kanter, R. (1977) *Men and Women of the Corporation*, New York: Basic Books.

Kanter, R., Cohen, A. and Cox, M. (1980) *The Tale of "O", on Being Different: A Training Tool for Managing Diversity*, Massachucetts: Goodmeasure.

Kanter, R., Cohen, A. and Cox, M. (1994) *The Tale of "O", on Being Different: A Training Tool for Managing Diversity*, Massachucetts: Goodmeasure.

Kay, H. (2000) *Women and Men in the Professions in Scotland*, Women's Issues Research Findings No. 3, Scottish Executive Central Research Unit.

Kennedy, J. (2002) 'Bridging the gap', *AUT Look*, September: 23.

Kerr, A. (2002) 'Representing Users in the Design of Digital Games', presented at Computer Games and Digital Cultures, Tampere, Finland, 6–8 June.

King, M. L. (Martin Luther King) (1963) *I Have a Dream Speech*. Online. Available HTTP: <http://news.bbc.co.uk/onthisday/hi/dates/stories/august/28/newsid_2656000/2656805.stm> (accessed 1 November 2003).

Kingsmill, D. (2003) 'Competition Commission', breakfast session, The Guardian and TMP Worldwide, Diversity in Britain Conference, Responding to Change, DTI. 9 October.

Kintrea, K. (1996) 'Whose Partnership? Community Interests in the Regeneration of a Scottish Housing Scheme', *Housing Studies*, 11(2): 287–306.

Kirton, G. and Greene, A.-M. (2000) *The Dynamics of Managing Diversity*, London: Butterworth-Heinemann.

Kjellstrom, S. (2004) 'Gender Mainstreaming Partnership and Practice', Closing Speech, Irish Presidency Conference, Brussels: European Commission.

Lach, D. and Hixson, P. (1996) 'Developing indicators to measure values and costs of public involvement activities, interact', *The Journal of Public Participation*, 2(1): 51–63.

Law, I. (2003) 'Anti-racist Teaching'. E-mails (10–11 June 2003).

Law, I., Phillips, D. and Turney, L. (ed.) (2004) 'Institutional racism', *Higher Education*, Stoke on Trent: Trentham Press.

Layard, A., Davoudi, S. and Batty, S. (2001) *Planning for a Sustainable Future*, London: Routledge.

Leach, F. (2003) *Practising Gender Analysis in Education*, Oxford: Oxfam.

Ledwith, S. (1999) 'Silk Purses and Sow's Ears: Women Making Good in the Academy', working Paper for workshop gender, Organisation and Management, British Academy of Management Conference, Manchester, 1–3 September.

Leicester City Council (1991) *Safety Guidelines*, Leicester: Planning Department.

Lewin, K. (1951) *Forcefield Theory in Social Science*, New York: Harper & Row.

Lichfield, N. (1996) *Community Impact Assessment*, London: UCL Press.

Lindheim, R. and Syme, L. (1983) in L. Duhl and A. Sanchez (eds) (1999) *Healthy Cities and the City Planning Process – A Background Document on Links between Health and Urban Planning*, Copenhagen: WHO Regional Office in Europe.

Lister, R. (1997) *Citizenship, Feminist Perspectives*, New York: Palgrave Macmillan.

Lister, R. (1998) 'Citizen in action: Citizenship and community development in the Northern Ireland context', *Community Development Journal*, 33(3): 226–235.

Lister, R. (2003) *Citizenship, Feminist Perspectives*, New York: Palgrave Macmillan.

Little, J. (1994a) 'Women's initiatives in town planning in England: A critical review', *Town Planning Review*, 65(3): 261–276.

Little, J. (1994b) *Gender, Planning and the Policy Process*, London: Butterworth-Heinemann.

Littlefield, D. (2001) 'CABE to campaign for equal opportunities', *Building Design*, 26 October: 26.

Livingston, K. (2002) 'My vision for London', *The Draft London Plan*, London: GLA: xi.

Local Government Association (1998) *Race, Equality and Planning*, London: LGA Publications.

Local Government Association (2001) *Room at the Top*. Online. Available HTTP: <http://www.lga.gov.uk/Briefing.asp?lsection = 59&id = SX1018-A7806688&ccat = 238> (accessed 20 November 2003).

Local Government Association (2003) *Equality and Diversity the Way Ahead*, London: LGA. Online. Available HTTP: <http://www.lga.gov.uk/content.asp?l Section = 0&id = SX1013-A7815127> (accessed 28 October 2003).

London Development Agency (2001) *Success Through Diversity, London's Economic Development Strategy*, London: LDA. Online. Available HTTP: <http://www.lda.

gov.uk/workofthelda/strategy/strategy/content/18_50.asp> (accessed 27 October 2003).

London First (2003) Online. Available HTTP: <http://www.london-first.co.uk/improving_london/diversity.asp?L2=84> (accessed 19 May 2003).

London Sustainable Development Commission (2003) *Sustainable Framework for London*. Online. Available HTTP: <http://www.london.gov.uk/mayor/sustainabledevelopment/sustainable_development_commission.jsp> (accessed 28 June 2003).

London Sustainable Development Commission (2004) Online. Available HTTP: <http://www.london.gov.uk/mayor/sustainable-development/sustainable_development_commission.jsp> (accessed 4 March 2004).

London Women and Planning Forum (2003) *Where are Women in the London Plan*, Conference, November, London: St Margaret's University.

Lovenduski, J. (2003) *Assessing the Impact of Women's Policy Agencies (WPA) on the Gendering of Political Representation Debates*, Presentation to the Gender Research Forum, London: Women and Equality Unit.

Lowndes, V., Pratchett, L. and Stoker, G. (2001a) 'Trends in public participation: Part 1 – Local government perspectives', *Public Administration*, 79(1): 205–222.

Lowndes, V., Pratchett, L. and Stoker, G. (2001b) 'Trends in public participation: Part 2 – Citizens' perspectives', *Public Administration*, 79(2): 445–455.

Lung Ha's Theatre Company (2003) Online. Available HTTP: <http://www.lunghas.co.uk> (accessed 3 April 2004).

MacCarthy, H. (2003) *Women's Networks, Diversity and Cultural Change in the Workplace*, Presentation to the Gender Research Forum, 3 November, London: Women and Equality Unit.

MacCormick, N. (1999) 'Nations and nationalism', in R. Beiner (ed.), *Theorising Nationalism*, New York: University of New York Press.

McCurdock, P. and Ramsey, N. (1996) *The Futures of Women*, New York: Addison-Wesley Publishing.

McDowell, L. (1983) 'Towards an understanding of the gender diversity of urban space', *Environment and Planning D: Society and Space*, 1: 59–72.

MacKay, F. and Bilton, B. (2000) *Learning from Experience: Lessons in Mainstreaming Equal Opportunities*, Edinburgh: Edinburgh University.

MacKay, F. and Chaney, P. (2003) *Mainstreaming Equality – A Comparative Analysis of Contemporary Developments in Scotland and Wales*, paper to Gender Research Forum, 3 November 2003, London.

MacKay, F. and Meehan, E. (2003) *Women and Devolution in Northern Ireland, Scotland and Wales*. Online. Available HTTP: <http://www.pol.ed.ac.uk/gcc/pubs.html> (accessed 17 November 2003).

McKittrick, D. (2003) 'New victims of bigotry in Northern Ireland: Belfast's Africans, Muslims and Chinese', *The Independent*, Monday 14 July: 8.

MacPherson, W. (1999) *The Stephen Lawrence Inquiry: Report of an Inquiry by Sir William Macpherson of Cluny*, London: HMSO. Online. Available HTTP: <http://www.archive.official-documents.co.uk/cm42/4262/4262.htm> (accessed 16 October 2003).

McRae, H. (1995) *The World in 2020*, London: HarperCollins.

Maddock, S. (1999) *Challenging Women*, London: Sage Publications.

Major, L. (2000) 'Not just a question of biology', *Guardian Higher*, 15 February: 37.

Majors, R. (2003) 'The lack of cultural competence for teachers', *Politics Show*, BBC Radio 4.

Malik, K. (1996) *The Meaning of Race*, London: Macmillan Press Ltd.

Manley, S. (2003a) 'Comparing Planning and Architecture'. E-mail (18 May 2003).

Manley, S. (2003b) 'Why Women Leave Architecture?' E-mail (29 August 2003).

Mannheim, K. (1950) *Freedom, Power and Democratic Planning*, London: Routledge & Kegan Paul.

Marcus, S. (1969) 'Planners – Who are they?' *Journal of the Town Planning Institute*, 57(2): 54–59.

Margerum, R. (2002) 'Evaluating collaborative planning, implications from an analysis of growth management', *American Planners Association Journal*, Spring, 68(2): 179–193.

Margolis, J. (2001) *A Brief History of Tomorrow*, London: Bloomsbury Publishing.

Martin, S. (1999) *Achieving Best Value Through Public Engagement*, Warwick/DETR Best Value Series. Online. Available HTTP: <http://www.local.dtlr.gov.uk/research/bestva~1/paper8/bv802.htm> (accessed 2 April 2004).

Matathia, I. and Salzman, M. (1999) *Next: A Vision of Our Lives in the Future*, London: HarperCollins.

May, N. (1997) *Challenging Assumptions: Gender Considerations in Urban Regeneration in the United Kingdom*, a report to the Joseph Rowntree Foundation, UK/Ireland: Oxfam.

Mayer, R. (1972) *Social Planning and Social Change*, London: Prentice Hall.

Mazey, S. (1995) 'The development of EU equality policies: Bureaucratic expansion on behalf of women?', *Public Administration*, 73(4): 591–610.

Mazey, S. (2001) *Gender Mainstreaming in the EU: Principles and Practice*, Oxford: Hereford College.

Mazey, S. (2002) 'Gender mainstreaming strategies in the EU: Delivering an agenda', *Feminist Legal Studies*, 10: 227–240.

Meadows, D., Randers, J. and Behrens, W. (1972) *The Limits to Growth: A Report for the Club of Rome's Project on the Predicament of Mankind*, London: Pan.

Meehan, E. (2002) *Gender and Constitutional Change, ESRC Research Programme, Whose Britain is it Anyway*. Online. Available HTTP: <http://www.pol.ed.ac.uk/gcc/pubs/meehanspeech.htm> (accessed 24 October 2003).

Mercer, D. (1998) *Future Revolutions*, London: Orion Business Books.

Meyer, P. and Reaves, C. (2000) 'Objectives and values: Planning for multi-cultural groups rather than multiple constituencies', in M. Burayidi (ed.), *Urban Planning in a Multi-cultural Society*, Westport: CT Praeger.

Milroy, B. (1999) 'Some thoughts about difference and pluralism', in S. Campbell and S. Fainstein (eds), *Readings in Planning Theory*, 461–466, Oxford: Blackwell Publishers Ltd.

Milroy, B. (2003) *What is Planning*. Online. Available HTTP: <http://www.geog.utoronto.ca/programs/planning/planning%20new/planning.htm> (accessed 27 October 2003).

Milroy, B. and Wallace, M. (2002) *Ethnoracial diversity and planning practices in the Greater Toronto Area: Final Report, Working Paper No. 18*, Toronto: Joint Center of Excellence for Research on Immigration and Settlement (CERIS).

Ministry of Housing and Local Government (1972) *Town and Country Planning Act*, London: HMSO.

Minnesota Academy for the Blind (2002) Online. Available HTTP: <http://www.msab.state.mn.us/msabinfo.htm> (accessed 15 June 2002).

Minnesota Academy for the Deaf (2002) Online. Available HTTP: <http://www.msad.state.mn.us/Default2.htm> (accessed 15 June 2002).

Morran, M. (2003) '15% Pay Gap, Careers Advice, University of Strathclyde in Glasgow'. E-mail (March 2003).

Morris, E. (1994) 'Physical Planning for Women in Scotland 1945–2000', paper delivered at the European Congress Driebergen, The Netherlands, 11–14 September.

Morris, E. (1995) 'Physical Planning for Women in Scotland 1945–2000', in L. Ottes, E. Poventud, M. van Schendelen and G. Segond von Banchet (eds), *Gender and the Built Environment*, Netherlands: Assen.

Morris, E. (2003) 'Women in Planning in Scotland'. E-mail (20 November 2003).

Morrow, D., Eyben, K. and Wilson, D. (2002) 'From the margin to the middle: Taking equity, diversity and interdependence seriously', in O'Hargie (ed.), *Researching the Troubles*, Edinburgh: Spectrum.

Moss, G. (1995) 'One man's neat design', *Independent Section Two*, 7 August.

Mourne Observer (2001) 'Planning Newcastle', Wednesday 7: 22–23.

Murray, M. and Murtagh, B. (2003) 'Exploring equity, diversity and interdependence through dialogue and understanding in Northern Ireland', *Community Development Journal*, 38(4), October: 287–297.

Murtagh, B. (1994) *Ethnic Space and the Challenge to Land-Use Planning: Study of Belfast's Peace Lines*, Research Paper 7, Centre for Policy Research: University of Ulster.

Murtagh, B. (1999) 'Urban segregation and community initiatives in Northern Ireland', *Community Development Journal*, 34(3): 219–226.

Muther, C. and Robbins, J. (2000) 'Women's Technology Cluster' (Organisation), *Forbes Supplement ASAP, 05/29/2000*, 165(13): 186.

Myers, D. (2001) *Exploring Social Psychology*, 2nd edition, New York: McGraw-Hill.

National Consumer Council (2003) Online. Available HTTP: <http://www.gencat.es/mediamb/encore/physical.pdf> (accessed 2 April 2004).

National Council for Research on Women (2003) *Balancing the Equation: Where Women and Girls are in Science, Engineering and Technology.* Online. Available HTTP: <http://www.ncrw.org> (accessed 29 August 2003).

National Development Plan Gender Equality Unit (2001a) 'Issues and Challenges in Furthering Equal Opportunities in the National Development Plan', paper presented to the first meeting of the Equal Opportunities and Social Inclusion Coordinating Committee of the National Development Plan 2000–2006, March, Dublin: NDP.

National Development Plan Gender Equality Unit (2001b) Report to the Second Meeting of the Equal Opportunities and Social Inclusion Coordinating Committee of the National Development Plan, 2000–2006, October, Dublin: NDP.

National Trust (2004) Online. Available HTTP: <http://www.nationaltrust.org.uk> (accessed 4 March 2004).

Neill, W. (2000) *Planning and Cultural Pluralism*, Belfast: School of Environmental Planning.

Neill, W. (2004) *Urban Planning and Cultural Identity*, London: Routledge.

Netherlands Government (1983) *Constitution.* Online. Available HTTP: <http://www.oefre.unibe.ch/law/icl/nl00000_.html> (accessed 14 October 2003).

Netherlands Planning Institute (2003) Online. Available HTTP: <http://www.bnsp.nl> (accessed 29 August 2003).

New Zealand (1993) *Human Rights Legislation.* Online. Available HTTP: <http://www.hrc.co.nz/index.php?p=307> (accessed 14 October 2003).

New Zealand (2003) *Human Rights Timeline.* Online. Available HTTP: <http://www.hrc.co.nz/index.php?p=448> (accessed 14 October 2003).

New Zealand Planning Institute (2003) Online. Available HTTP: <http://www.nzplanning.co.nz> (accessed 29 August 2003).

NFO Social Research (unpublished) *Sectarianism in Glasgow*, Report Prepared for Glasgow City Council in 2003.

Nieuwboer, J. (2003) *Anti-discrimination Legislation in the USA, Canada and the Netherlands.* Online. Available HTTP: <http://www.international.metropolis.net/events/rotterdam/papers/20_Nieuwboer.htm> (accessed 15 August 2003).

Northern Ireland Central Community Relations Unit (1993) *Guidelines for Policy Appraisal and Fair Treatment*, Belfast: CCRU.

Northern Ireland Central Community Relations Unit (1996) *Policy Appraisal and Fair Treatment Annual Report*, Belfast: CCRU.

Northern Ireland Office (1998) *Good Friday Agreement.* Online. Available HTTP: <http://www.nio.gov.uk/issues/agreement.htm> (accessed 15 October 2003).

Northern Ireland Office (2003) *A Shared Future, Consultation Document*, Belfast: NIO.

O'Brien, C. and O'Brien, J. (2000) *Origins of Person-Centered Planning: A Community of Practice Perspective*, Syracuse: Research and Training Center on Community Living.

ODPM (2002a) *Sustainable Communities – Delivering Through Planning*. Online. Available HTTP: <http://www.planning.odpm.gov.uk/consult/greenpap/scdtp/index.htm> (accessed 12 September 2002).

ODPM (2002b) *The Strategic Environmental Assessment Directive* (2001/42/EC), Draft Guidance.

ODPM (2003a) *Planning and Access for Disabled People*, March, London: ODPM. Online. Available HTTP: <http://www.planning.odpm.gov.uk/index.htm> (accessed 29 October 2003).

ODPM (2003b) *Planning and Diversity Literature Review*, London: ODPM.

ODPM (2003c) *Diversity and Planning Research Report on Planning Policies and Practice*, London: ODPM. Online. Available HTTP: <http://www.odpm.gov.uk/stellent/ groups/odpm_planning/documents/page/odpm_plan_028084.hcsp> (accessed 10 April 2004).

ODPM (2003d) *Making Plans Good Practice Guide in Plan Preparation and Management*. Online. Available HTTP: <http://www.odpm.gov.uk/stellent/groups/odpm_control/ documents/contentservertemplate/odpm_index.hcst?n=2344&l=2> (accessed 27 October 2003).

ODPM (2003e) *Sustainable Communities Plan*. Online. Available HTTP: <http:// www.odpm.gov.uk/stellent/groups/odpm_communities/documents/page/odpm_ comm_022184.hcsp> (accessed 17 March 2004).

ODPM (2003f) *Participatory Planning for Sustainable Communities: International Experience in Mediation, Negotiation and Engagement in Making Plans*. Online. Available HTTP: <http://www.odpm.gov.uk/stellent/groups/odpm_planning/ documents/pdf/odpm_plan_pdf_023784.pdf> (accessed 2 April 2004).

ODPM (forthcoming 2005) *Good Practice Examples of Planning for Diversity*, London: ODPM.

Office of Children's Rights Commissioner for London (2003) *Written Submission for the Examination in Public of the Draft London Plan*. Online. Available HTTP: <http:// www.london.gov.uk/london-plan-eip/submissions/subs-2a.jsp> (accessed 3 March 2003).

Office of National Statistics (2003) *Statistics*. Online. Available HTTP: <http://www. statistics.gov.uk/eci/nugget.asp?id=395> (accessed 16 October 2003).

Ojanen, K. (1998) *Using the Walking Tour with Children*, Eurofem Conference, Hameenlina.

Oliver, M. (1995) *Understanding Disability*, Basingstoke: Macmillan Distribution Ltd.

Oliver, M. and Mercer, G. (2002) *Disability*, London: Polity Press.

Olufemi, S. (1997) 'The Homelessness Problem: Planning Phenomenology and Gender Perspectives', an unpublished PhD thesis submitted to the faculty of Architecture, University of the Witwatersrand, Johannesburg, South Africa.

Olufemi, S. (1998) 'Street homelessness in Johannesburg inner city: A preliminary survey', *Environment and Urbanisation*, 10(2): October, 223–234.

Olufemi, O. (2000) 'Feminisation of poverty among the street homeless women in South Africa', *Development Southern Africa*, 17(2): June, 221–234.

Olufemi, S. (2003) 'Commonwealth Association of Planners, Women's Network'. E-mail (May 2003).

Olufemi, S. and Reeves, D. (2004) 'Life world strategies of women who find themselves homeless in South Africa', *Planning Theory and Practice*, 5(1): 69–91.

The Orangeman (2003) Channel 4.

Oxfam (2002) *Gender, Development and Poverty*, ed. C. Sweetman, Oxford: Oxfam.

Oxfam (2003) *How does Poverty Relate to Gender Equality?* Online. Available HTTP: <http://www.oxfam.org.uk/what_we_do/issues/gender/index.htm> (accessed 15 October 2003).

Pain, R. (2001) 'Gender, race, age and fear in the city', *Urban Studies*, 38(5–6): 899–913.

Pearson, A. (2003) *I Don't Know How She Does It*, London: Vintage.

Petrie, P. (2003a) 'Women Who Leave Planning'. E-mail (18 January 2003).

Petrie, P. (2003b) *How Do Practicing Planners Learn and What Do They Learn?* Online. Available HTTP: <http:www.urban.uiuc.edu/apa-pw/> (accessed 22 November 2003).

Philips, A. (1999) *Which Equalities Matter*, Cambridge: Polity.

Phillips, T. (2003) 'Key Note Address', paper presented to Diversity in Britain Conference, 9 October, London: The Guardian and TMP Worldwide.

Planning (2003) *Agenda 2003: Where Next for Sustainable Development*, 28 February: 4.

Planning Inspectorate (2003) *Annual Report 2002–2003*. Online. Available HTTP: <http://www.planning-inspectorate.gov.uk/pins/reports/annreport_2002_2003/annreport_2002_2003.pdf> (accessed 5 April 2004).

Planning Institute of Australia (PIA) (2003a) Online. Available HTTP: <http://www.planning.org.au> (accessed 29 August 2003).

Planning Institute of Australia (PIA) (2003b) 'Membership and Gender Balance'. E-mail (9 August 2003)

Plymouth City Council (1997) *Census of Employment*. Online. Available HTTP: <http://www.plymouth.gov.uk> (accessed 10 June 2003).

Plymouth City Council (2000a) *Plymouth Planning Strategy*, Plymouth: Plymouth City Council.

Plymouth City Council (2000b) *Planning Committee February 3*, Commissioning of Gender Audit from Plymouth University.

Plymouth City Council (2001) *City of Plymouth Local Plan 1995–2011*, first deposit, Plymouth: City Council. Online. Available HTTP: <http://www.plymouth.gov.uk/Local%20Plan%20Pages/frameset.htm> (accessed 27 March 2004).

Plymouth City Council and Devon and Cornwall Constabulary (1999) *Crime Reduction Strategy: Towards a Safer Plymouth*, Plymouth: Plymouth City Council.

Poklewski Koziell, S. (2003) *Homes not Office: The Story of Coin Street is an Urban Fairy-tale. Against all odds, a Local Community Saved Itself from a Faceless Office*. Online. Available HTTP: <http://resurgence.gn.apc.org/186/koziell.htm> (accessed 21 August 2003).

Pollack, M. and Hafner-Burton, E. (2000) 'Mainstreaming gender in the European Union', *Journal of European Public Policy*, 7(3): 432–456.

Polverari, L. and Fitzgerald, R. (2002) *Integrating Gender Equality in the Evaluation of the Irish 2000–2006 National Development Plan*, Glasgow: European Policies Research Centre.

Popcorn, F. (1991) *The Popcorn Report*, New York: HarperCollins.

Popcorn, F. (2003) *Trends*. Online. Available HTTP: <http://www.faithpopcorn.com/trends/trends.htm> (accessed 10 July 2003).

Porter, M. (2003) 'Key Note Speech' to One London, June 2003, reported in *Regeneration*, 27 June: 11.

Prahalad, C. (2003) 'Serving the World's Poor', *In Business* BBC Radio 4, 9 January. Online. Available HTTP: <http://www.bbc.co.uk/radio4/news/Inbusiness/Inbusiness_20030109.5html> (accessed 24 October 2003).

Prentice, C. (2003) 'Through the glass ceiling', *ILTHE Newsletter*, 12, Autumn: 6–7.

Presley, L. (2003) 'Sleeping with the Enemy', BBC Radio 4, Sunday 14 September.

Price, M. (1994) 'City Planner, City of Cape Town' (Correspondence January 1994).

Pride in the Park (2003) Online. Available HTTP: <http://www.prideinthepark.com> (accessed 1 November 2003).

Priestley, M. (2001) *Disability and the Life Course, Global Perspectives*, Cambridge: Cambridge University Press.

Priestley, M. (2003) *A Life Course Approach*, London: Polity Press.

Prospects (2003) *Graduate Pay*. Online. Available HTTP: <http://www.prospects.ac.uk/cms/ShowPage/Home_page/How_much_will_I_earn_/Salary_and_vacanebkp> (accessed 5 April 2004).

Quality Assurance Agency (QAA) (1999) *Code of Practice: Students with Disabilities*. Online. Available HTTP: <http://www.qaa.ac.uk/public/cop/copswd/cop/5Fdisab.pdf> (accessed 5 April 2004).

Radcliffe, L. (2003) 'Working with People with Mental Illness'. Interview and E-mail (May 2003).

Rahder, B. (1998) 'Women and planning: Education for social change', *Planning Practice and Research*, 13(3).

Rake, K. (2000) 'Into the mainstream? Why gender audit is an essential tool for policy makers', *New Economy*, 7(2), June: 107–110.

Randall, S. (1991) 'Local government and equal opportunities in the 1990s', *Critical Social Policy*, 11(1): 38–58.

Rathmore, S. (2000) 'The effects of patient sex and race on medical students ratings of quality of life', *American Journal of Medicine*, 108: 561–566.

Razavi, S. and Miller, C. (1995) *Gender Mainstreaming: A Study of Efforts by the UNDP the World Bank and the ILO to Institutionalize Gender Issues*, United Nations Research Institute for Social Development (UNRISD), Occasional Paper, No. 4.

Rees, T. (1999) 'Managing Diversity and Mainstreaming Equality', paper to the ESRC Seminar Series, The Interface between Gender Equality and Public Policy, Sheffield: Sheffield Hallam University.

Reeves, D. (1995) 'Developing effective public consultation', *Planning Practice and Research*, April, 10(2): 199–213.

Reeves, D. (1996a) 'The ABCD of Planning for Equality', Presentation to the University of Strathclyde in Glasgow Planning Society.

Reeves, D. (1996b) 'Women shopping', in C. Booth, J. Darke and S. Yeandle (eds), *Women and the Built Environment*, London: Paul Chapman.

Reeves, D. (1996c) *Mobility and Accessible Housing – Tokenism to Positivism*, Glasgow: Department of Environmental Planning.

Reeves, D. (1997a) 'Public consultation and development plans: Involving disadvantaged groups', *Community Development Journal*, 32(4): 332–341.

Reeves, D. (1997b) 'Autobiography of a Planner', unpublished transcript of the workshop held as part of the RTPI Conference, Where to Now? Women Planners into the 21st Century.

Reeves, D. (1998) 'Implications of the Futures of Women to Planning', paper presented to The International Eurofem Conference Gender and Human Settlements, June.

Reeves, D. (1999a) *RESIDER Community Initiative S70/002/1*, Report to the Virtual Reality, Centre at the University of Teesside (unpublished).

Reeves, D. (1999b) 'Members Survey – Gender Perspective', paper to the RTPI National Symposium; Gender equality and the role of Planning, Realising the Goal.

Reeves, D. (2000a) *Executive Summary, Gender Audit*, Plymouth: Plymouth University.

Reeves, D. (2000b) *Framework for Mainstreaming Gender in the Structure Plan Process* (unpublished).

Reeves, D. (2000c) *Involving the Public at National Level – The Netherlands 5th Report* (unpublished).

Reeves, D. (2001) *The 50/50 Profession and Mainstreaming – How will this Change the Context of Planning*, APA Conference in New Orleans, 12 March. Online. Available HTTP: <http://www.asu.edu/caed/proceedingssoi/REEVES/reeves.htm> (accessed 17 November 2003).

Reeves, D. (2002a) 'Spatial Issues', report of the workshop of the Making it Happen Conference Gender Mainstreaming in the UK and Ireland Structural Funds,13 May, Cardiff: Welsh European Funding Office.

Reeves, D. (2002b) 'Mainstreaming equality to achieve socially sustainable development – an examination of the gender sensitivity of strategic plans in the UK', *Town Planning Review*, 73(2): 197–214.

Reeves, D. (2002c) *Gender Equality and IT, E-Commerce and Internet Usage*, Fact sheet for the Economic and Social Infrastructure Operational Programme of the National Development Plan 2002–2006, Dublin: Department of Justice, Equality and Law Reform.

Reeves, D. (2003a) *Mainstreaming Gender in Environment and Waste*, NDP Equality Unit. Online. Available HTTP: <http://www.ndpgenderequality.ie/downloads/factsheets/enviro&waste_02.pdf> (accessed 1 July 2003).

Reeves, D. (2003b) 'Equality and diversity', *Planning*, 7 February: 24.

Reeves, D. (2004) 'Mainstreaming Diversity into Planning', Professional and Contemporary Issues Class, University of Strathclyde in Glasgow.

Reeves, D. (unpublished) 'Developing Participation Skills', 3rd year undergraduate project, January–March 2004, University of Strathclyde in Glasgow.

Reeves, D. and Howatt, H. (2004) 'Tackling global gender inequality: Advancing the status of women', *Planning*, 26 March: 24.

Reeves, D. and Littlejohn, A. (1999) 'Using virtual reality for public involvement', *Town and Country Planning Journal*, May, 68(5): 162–163.

Reeves, D. and Rozee, L. (2001) *Women and the Profession of Planning: The 50/50 profession – How this will Change the Context of Planning*. Online. Available HTTP: <http://www.urban.uiuc.edu/APA.PW/R-Paper.htm> (accessed 17 November 2003).

Reid-Howie Associates (1999) *Women and Transport: Moving Forward – A Review of Current Understanding and the Development of Priorities for Further Research*, The Scottish Executive Central Research Unit.

Rein, M. (1970) 'Social planning: Welfare planning', *International Encyclopedia of the Social Sciences*, New York: Macmillan Company & The Free Press.

Ridder, L. and Modderman, E. (1991) *Regional Planning and Women: Taking Stock of Ways in which Women's Interests are Represented*, Proceedings of the seminar held in Athens on 25–27 October 1990, Brussels: Counsel of Europe.

Riley, F. (2004) 'What position does race equality occupy in planning today?', *Planning*, 2 April: 24.

Riseborough, M. (1997) *The Gender Report, Women and Regional Regeneration in the Midlands*, Birmingham: Centre for Urban and Regional Studies (CURS).

Robinson, M. (2000) 'Editorial, Special Issue', *Human Rights*, Spring: 3.

Roche, C. (1999) *Impact Assessment for Development Agencies: Learning to Value Change*, Oxford: Oxfam.

Rogers, E. M. (1995) *Diffusion of Innovations*, New York: Free Press.

Rogers, R. (1998) *Cities for a Small Planet*, London: Faber & Faber.

Rosenberg, M. and Everitt, J. (2001) 'Planning for aging populations: Inside and outside the walls', in D. Diamond and H. Massam (eds), *Progress in Planning*, October, 56(3), London: Pergamon.

Rosof, M. (1998) *Overcoming Traditional Stereotypes of Gender in the European Union*. Online. Available HTTP: <http://www.law.emory.edu/EILR/volumes/fall98/rosof.html> (accessed 22 March 2002).

Ross, D. (2003) 'Cuillin Mountains will go to the people', *Herald*, 10 July.

Ross, K. (2003) 'Meeting the Challenge: Managing Equality and Diversity in Higher Education', paper to the Gender Research Forum, London: Women and Equality Unit. Online. Available HTTP: <http://www.coventry.ac.uk/equal> (accessed 25 November 2003).

Ross, K. (2004) *The Mapping Equality and Diversity Initiatives in Higher Education Project*. Online. Available HTTP: <http://www.edihe.info/> (accessed 3 April 2004).

Royal Association for Disability and Rehabilitation (2003a) *The Seven Year Itch*, London: RADAR. Online. Available HTTP: <http://www.radar.org.uk> (accessed 28 June 2003).

Royal Association for Disability and Rehabilitation (2003b) *The Seven Year Itch, What Next in the Campaign for Full Civil Rights for Disabled People*, London: RADAR. Online. Available HTTP: <http://www.radar.org.uk> (accessed 12 October 2003).

Royal Commission on Environmental Pollution (2003) Online. Available HTTP: <http://rcep.org.uk> (accessed 24 October 2003).

Royal Institute of British Architects (2004) *Architects for Change*. Online. Available HTTP: <http://www.riba.org/go/RIBA/News/Press_52.html?q=equality> (accessed 5 April 2004).

Royal Institute of Chartered Surveyors (2003) *Raising the Ratio*. Online. Available HTTP: <http://www.rics.org/careers/women_in_surveying> (accessed 5 April 2004).

Royal Society for the Protection of Birds (2003) Online. Available HTTP: <http://www.rspb.org.uk> (accessed 4 March 2004).

Rozee, L. (2000) *Mainstreaming Equality in the Planning Inspectorate*, Town and Country Planning Summer School, St. Andrews.

Rozee, L. (2003) 'Diversity in the Inspectorate'. E-mail (18 November 2003).

RTPI (1982) *Final Report on Public Participation*, London: RTPI.

RTPI (1983) *Report of the Race Panel*, London: RTPI.

RTPI (1989) *Planning for Choice and Opportunity*, London: RTPI.

RTPI (1994a) *Code of Professional Conduct*, London: RTPI.

RTPI (1994b) *Research Guidelines*, London: RTPI.

RTPI (1995) *Practice Advice Note PAN 12*, London: RTPI.

RTPI (1996a) *The Education of Planners, Policy Statement and General Guidance for Academic Institutions offering Initial Professional Education*, First approved by the

Council of the Royal Town Planning Institute on 3 July 1991, revised in July 1996, and last revised in March 2001.

RTPI (1996b) *Practice Advice Note 12 Planning for Women*, London: RTPI. Online. Available HTTP: <http://www.rtpi.org.uk/resources/publications/p5.html> (accessed 31 October 2003).

RTPI (1997) *Members Survey*, London: RTPI.

RTPI (1999) *Mainstreaming Gender Equality in Planning, Report to RTPI Council*, 10 November, London: RTPI.

RTPI (2000, 2003) *Supply and Demand Figures*, London: RTPI.

RTPI (2000a) *Membership Records*, London: RTPI.

RTPI (2000b) *Corporate Plan 2000–2003*, London: RTPI.

RTPI (2001a) *Members Survey*, Unpublished results, London: RTPI.

RTPI (2001b) *The Governance Manifesto*, 13 December, London: RTPI.

RTPI (2003a) *Education Commission Report*, London: RTPI.

RTPI (2003b) *Charter and Byelaws*, London: RTPI.

RTPI (2003c) *Gender Audit Toolkit*, London: RTPI. Online. Available HTTP: <http://www.rtpi.org.uk/resources/panels/equal-w/toolkit.html> (accessed 31 October 2003).

RTPI (2003d) *Corporate Plan 2003–2005*, London: RTPI.

RTPI (2003e) *Quarterly Report to Council*, London: RTPI.

RTPI (2003f) *RTPI Policy Statement on Initial Planning Education*, London: RTPI.

Ruddick, S. (1996) 'Constructing difference in urban space: Class, race and gender as interlocking systems', *Urban Geography*, 17: 132–151.

Rutherford, S. and Ollerearnshaw, S. (2002) *The Business of Diversity: How Organisations in the Public and Private Sectors are Integrating Equality and Diversity to Enhance Business Performance*, Andover: Sneider-Ross.

Saltaire (2003) *World Heritage Site*. Online. Available HTTP: <http://www.saltaire.yorks.com> (accessed 24 October 2003).

Salzman, M. (2003) 'A life in the day', *Sunday Times Magazine*, 8 August: 54.

Sandercock, L. (1998) *Towards Cosmopolis*, London: Wiley.

Sandercock, L. (2000) 'When strangers become neighbours: Managing cities of difference', *Planning Theory and Practice*, 1: 13–30.

Sandercock, L. and Forsyth, A. (1992) 'A gender agenda: New directions in planning theory', *Journal of the American Planning Association*, Winter: 49–59.

Sandercock, L. and Kliger, B. (1998a) 'Multiculturalism and the planning system, Part One', *The Australian Planner*, 15(3): 127–132.

Sandercock, L. and Kliger, B. (1998b) 'Multiculturalism and the planning system, Part Two', *The Australian Planner*, 15(4): 223–227.

Sanoff, H. (2000) *Community Participation Methods in Design and Planning*, New York: John Wiley & Sons Inc.

Sanoff, H. (2002) *Minnesota Academies for the Blind and the Deaf (MSAB)*. E-mail (March 2003).

Schon, D. and Rein, M. (1994) *Frame Reflection, Towards the Resolution of Intractable Policy Controversies*, New York: Basic Books.

School of Policy, Planning, and Development, University of Southern California (2001) *Census 2000*. Online. Available HTTP: <http://www.usc.edu/schools/sppd/research/census2000> (accessed 28 June 2003).

Scotland (1998) *The Scotland Act*. Online. Available HTTP: <http://www.hmso.gov.uk/acts/acts1998/19980046.htm> (accessed 14 October 2003).

Scottish Executive (2000) *REAF Report*, Edinburgh: Scottish Executive. Online. Available HTTP: <http://www.Scotland.gov.uk/society/equality/default.asp> (accessed 12 June 2003).

Scottish Executive Development Department (2001) *Getting Involved with Planning*, Edinburgh: Scottish Executive. Online. Available HTTP: <http://www.scotland.gov.uk/planning> (accessed 15 June 2002).

Scottish Higher Education Funding Council (2002) *Race Equality Scheme*. Online. Available HTTP: <http://www.shefc.org.uk> (accessed 23 November 2003).

Scottish Trades Union Council (2003) Online. Available HTTP: <http://www.unison-scotland.org.uk/women/women4.html> (accessed 17 November 2003).

Second Commission on the Status of Women (1993) *Final Report*, Dublin: Stationery Office.

Self, W. (2002) 'Psychogeography: Cities', *High Life*, April 2002: 94–95.

Selman, P. (2001) 'Social capital, sustainability and environmental planning', *Planning Theory and Practice*, 2(1): 13–30.

Selman, P. (2003) 'Social Capital'. E-mail (March 2003).

Senge, P., Kleiner, A., Roberts, C. and Ross, R. (1994) *The Fifth Discipline Fieldbook: Strategies and Tools for Building a Learning Organisation*, New York: Doubleday.

Shakespeare, T. and Corker, M. (eds) (2002) *Disability and Post Modernity*, London: Polity.

Shaw, T., Pendlebury, J. and Mawson, J. (2004) *The Supply and Demand for Qualified Planners*, London: Royal Town Planning Institute.

Shepley, C. (2003a) 'Race for planning', *Planning*, 19 September: 24.

Shepley, C. (2003b) 'Race for Planning Female/Male Balance'. E-mail (24 September 2003).

Simons, G. (2002) *Eurodiversity*, London: Butterworth-Heinemann.

Simons, G., Baudoin, K. and Guurt, K. A. (1996) 'Comprehensive model for addressing diversity and business', in G. Simons and Bob Abramms (eds), *The Cultural Diversity Sourcebook*, Amherst, MA: ODT.

Simpson, A. (2002) *Teachability Guide*, Glasgow: University of Strathclyde.

Simpson, A. (2003) 'Teachability'. E-mails (10–11 June 2003).

Singh, I. (2003) *Thought for the Day*, 15 July, BBC Radio 4. Online. Available HTTP: <http://www.bbc.co.uk/religion/programmes/thought/documents/t20030715.html> (accessed 23 July 2003).

Sinha, Sumita (2002) 'A shameful disparity', *Building Design*, Issue 1529, 19 April: 8.

Sinha, S. (2003) *Architects for Change*. Online. Available HTTP: <http://www.riba.org.uk> (accessed 17 November 2003).

Skeffington (1969) *People and Planning*, London: HMSO.

Smit, T. (2001) *Eden*, London: Bantam Press.

Smith, G. and Kirby, V. (1986) *Report of a Questionnaire Survey of Women in Planning*, The Royal Town Planning Institute, Yorkshire Branch.

Soja, E. (1999) *Postmetropolis: Critical Studies of Cities and Regions*, Oxford: Blackwell.

Solomos, J. and Back, L. (1995) *Race, Politics and Social Change*, London: Routledge.

South African Council for Town and Regional Planners (2003) Online. Available HTTP: <http://www.saplanners.org.za> (accessed 29 August 2003).

South East Queensland (2003) *SEQ Regional Plan*. Online. Available HTTP: <http://www.seq2021.qld.gov.au/home.asp> (accessed 24 October 2003).

South and West Devon Health Authority (1999a) *Draft Regional Planning Guidance for the South West*, Taunton: SWDHA.

South and West Devon Health Authority (1999b) *Improving the Health of Children in South and West Devon*, Taunton: SWDHA, 13.

Spitz, T. (2003) 'Equality in the Netherlands'. E-mail (19 August 2003).

Sport England (1999) *The Participation of Women in Sport*, Sport England: Research Section. Online. Available HTTP: <http://www.sportengland.org.uk> (accessed 27 March 2004).

Squires, J. (1994) 'Beyond the Liberal Conception of Equal Opportunity', paper delivered to the Equity, Labour and Social Division Initiative, Faculty of Social Sciences, University of Bristol.

Staff Development (2003) *Constructive Alignment*. Online. Available HTTP: <http://www.scu.edu.au/servies/tl/sd_online/intro.html> (accessed 23 November 2003).

Stoker, G. (ed.) (2000) *The New Politics of British Local Governance*, Basingstoke: Macmillan.

Stone, G. (2003) 'VR Regen Project, Virtual Reality Centre of Teesside Ltd'. E-mail (11 November 2003).

Stone, G. and Hearne, B. (2004) *Virtual Reality for Consultation, Tenant Participation Advisory Service (TPAS)*. Online. Available HTTP: <http://www.tpas.org.uk/PDF/conferences/annualconf2004.pdf> (accessed 18 April 2004).

Stone, H. (2004) 'Action Towards Diversity in the Construction Industry', paper to the ESRC Transdisciplinary Research Seminar Series, People and the Culture of Construction, 21 April, Loughborough: Loughborough University.

Sustainable Development Commission (2004) Online. Available HTTP: <http://www.sd-commission.gov.uk/> (accessed 17 March 2004).

Swann, S. (2001) *Gender Mainstreaming, Agriculture and Rural Development*, May, Dublin: NDP Gender Equality Unit Seminar.

Swedish REFLEX, see County Administrative Board of West Gotaland (undated).

Tajfel, H. (1981) *Human Groups and Social Categories: Studies in Social Psychology*, London: Cambridge University Press.

Taylor, S. (1981) 'A categorisation approach to stereotyping', in D. L. Hamilton (ed.), *Cognitive Processes in Stereotyping and Intergroup Behaviour*, Hillsdale, NJ: Erlbaum.

Taylor, S. and Fiske, S. (1978) 'Salience, attention and attribution: Top of the head phenomena', in L. Berkowitz (ed.), *Advances in Experimental Social Psychology*, vol. 2, New York: Academic Press.

Taylor, S. and Nelson Consumer (1994) *Omnimas Shopping Survey*, Epsom: Taylor Nelson Consumer.

Tenant Participation Advisory Service (2003) 'The Crystal Ball', Conference Report. Online. Available HTTP: <http://www.tpas.org.uk/PDF/conferences/ac2003report.pdf> (accessed 18 April 2004).

Thomas, D. and Ely, R. (1996) 'Making differences matter: A new paradigm for managing diversity', *Harvard Business Review*, 74(5), September–October: 79–90.

Thomas, H. (1997) 'Explaining marginalisation of social welfare within planning', in G. Greed (ed.), *Social Town Planning*, London: Routledge.

Thomas, H. (2003) *British Planning and the Promotion of Race Equality: The Welsh Experience of Race Equality Schemes* (unpublished).

Thompson, S. (2003) 'Planning and multi-culturalism, a reflection on Australian local practice', *Planning Theory and Practice*, 4(3), September: 275–295.

Tiala, T. (2002) *The Participation Project in Finland*. Online. Available HTTP: <http://www.intermin.fi/intermin/images.nsf/files/AABF90A3CEA6C433C2256BA500386D39/$file/europa.pdf> (accessed 2 April 2004).

Tokyo Bureau of City Planning (2001) *New City Planning Vision for Tokyo*. Online. Available HTTP: <http://www.toshikei.metro.tokyo.jp/plan/pe-020.htm> (accessed 28 June 2003).

Torre, S. (ed.) (1977) *Women in American Architecture: A Historic and Contemporary Perspective*, New York: Whitney Library of Design.

Town and Country Planning Association (1999) *Your Place and Mine*, London: TCPA.

Town and Country Planning Association (2000) *Strategies for Promoting Public Participation*, London: ENTEC and TCPA.

Town and Country Planning Association (2003) Online. Available HTTP: <http://www.tcpa.org.uk> (accessed 16 November 2003).

Tuan, Yi-Fu (1990) *Space and Place*, Minnesota: University of Minnesota Press.

Tuan, Yi-Fu (2001) *Space and Place*, Minnesota: University of Minnesota Press.

Tucker, P. (2001) 'Understanding recycling behaviour', *Warmer Bulletin*, No. 78, May: 5. *Warmer Bulletin*. Online. Available HTTP: <http://www.residua.com/wb/links/index.htm> (accessed 27 March 2004).

Turner, J. (1987) *Rediscovering the Social Group: A Self-Categorisation Theory*, New York: Basil Blackwell.

Turner, J. (1991) *Social Influence*, Milton Keynes: Open University.

UCLA (2003) *Virtual Reality*. Online. Available HTTP: <http://www.ats.ucla.edu/portal/about_p.htm#environ> (accessed 11 November 2003).

UITP (2003) *Women in Transport Network*. Online. Available HTTP: <http://www.uitp.com/forum/gender/steering-group.cfm> (accessed 20 November 2003).

UK (1975 as amended in 2001) *Sex Discrimination Act*. Online. Available HTTP: <http://www.eoc-law.org.uk/cseng/legislation/sda.pdf> (accessed 31 October 2003).

UK (1976) *Race Relations Act*. Online. Available HTTP: <http://www.homeoffice.gov.uk/docs/racerel1.html> (accessed 31 October 2003).

UK (1995) *Disability Discrimination Act*. Online. Available HTTP: <http://www.disability.gov.uk/dda/> (accessed 14 October 2003).

UK (1998) *Human Rights Act*. Online. Available HTTP: <http://www.hmso.gov.uk/acts/acts1998/19980042.htm> (accessed 14 October 2003).

UK (2001) *Race Relations Amendment Act*. Online. Available HTTP: <http://www.hmso.gov.uk/acts/acts2000/20000034.htm> (accessed 14 October 2003).

United Nations (1985) *Third World Conference on Women in Nairobi, Global Platform for Action*, New York: United Nations.

United Nations (1989) *The Convention on the Rights of the Child*, New York: United Nations General Assembly.

United Nations (1992) *Report of the United Nations Conference on Environment and Development*, Rio de Janeiro 3–14 June, Chapter 24, Global action for women towards sustainable and equitable development, Geneva: UNCED.

United Nations (1995) *Fourth World Conference on Women in Beijing, Global Platform for Action*, New York: United Nations.

United Nations Division for the Advancement of Women (2003) *The Value-Added of Gender Equality for Men and Boys – Moderator's Summary*, Online Discussion 30 June to 25 July 2003, The role of men and boys in achieving gender equality, Week Three (14–18 July 2003).

United Nations General Assembly (1985) *Implementation of the Nairobi Forward Looking Strategies for the Advancement of Women*. Online. Available HTTP: <http://www.un.org/documents/ga/res/40/a40r108.htm> (accessed 14 October 2003).

University of Plymouth (2001) *Plymouth Gender Audit*, Plymouth: University of Plymouth.

University of Strathclyde (2001) *Survey of Graduate Destinations*, Glasgow: The Careers Service, University of Strathclyde.

US Annals of Congress (1787) 'Constitution originally adopted', *Transcription of the Introduction and the US Constitution from the First Volume of the Annals of Congress*. Online. Available HTTP: <http://memory.loc.gov/ammem/amlaw/ac001/lawpres.html> (accessed 14 October 2003).

USA (1978) *American Religious Freedom Act*. Online. Available HTTP: <http://nativenet.uthscsa.edu/archive/nl/9407/0016.html> (accessed 23 November 2003).

United States Congress (1969) *The National Environmental Protection Act*. Online. Available HTTP: <http://ceq.eh.doe.gov/nepa/regs/nepa/nepaeqia.htm> (accessed 21 September 2004).

Ustinov, P. (2003) 'Breaking the grip of prejudice', *Durham First*, Spring: 18–19.

Valentin, A. and Spangeberg, J. (1999) 'Indicators for Sustainable Communities', paper presented at the International COST C8 Workshop on Assessment Methodologies for Urban Infrastructure, Stockholm, Sweden, 19–21 September.

Vallely, B. (1996) *What Women Want*, London: Virago Press.

Vallely, B. and Cowe, I. (1996) *Values and Visions: The Report from the What Women Want Survey*, London: Women's Communication Centre.

Vancouver City Council (2002) *City Plan Community Visions Terms of Reference*, City Council. Online. Available HTTP: <http://www.city.vancouver.bc.ca/commsvcs/planning/cityplan/termsre.htm#GR> (accessed 4 April 2004).

Vancouver City Council (undated) *City Plan Toolkit*, Vancouver City Council.

Verloo, M. (1999) 'On the Conceptual and Theoretical Roots of Gender Mainstreaming', paper presented at the ESRC seminar on 12 March, Sheffield: Sheffield Hallam University.

Verloo, M. (2003) 'Inter-Organisational Committee on Guidelines and Principles 1994'. E-mail (20 March 2003).

Verloo, M. and Roogeband, C. (1996) 'Gender and impact assessment: The development of a new instrument for the Netherlands', *Impact Assessment*, 14(1): 3–20.

Virtual Reality Centre of Teesside Ltd (VRC) (2003) *VR Regen projects*. Online. Available HTTP: <http://vr.tees.ac.uk> (accessed 4 April 2004).

Voas, D., Olson, D. V. A. and Crockett, A. (2002) 'Religious pluralism and participation: Why previous research is wrong', *American Sociological Review*, 67: 212–230.

VSO (2003) *Cultural Breakthrough*. Online. Available HTTP: <http://www.vso.org.uk/culturalbreakthrough/cb_report.pdf> (accessed 23 November 2003).

Waite, T. (2003) 'We need to live creatively with difference. VSO cultural breakthrough campaign', *Politics Show*, Sunday 15 June 2003.

Walby, S. (1990) *Theorising Patriarchy*, Oxford: Basil Blackwell.

Walby, S. (1994) 'Methodological and theoretical issues in the comparative analysis of gender relations in western Europe', *Environment and Planning A*, 26: 1339–1354.

Walby, S. and Olsen, W. (2003) *The Impact of Women's Position in the Labour Market on Pay and Implications for UK Productivity*, London: DTI. Online. Available HTTP: <http://www.womenandequalityunit.gov.uk/publications/weu_pay_and_productivity.pdf> (accessed 20 November 2003).

Wallace, M. and Milroy, B. (1999) 'Intersecting claims: Planning in Canada's cities', in T. Fenster (ed.), *Gender, Planning and Human Rights*, London: Routledge.

Walton, P. (1985) 'The New Ways to Work Approach to Job Sharing', paper presented to seminar at the Yorkshire Branch of the RTPI, Sheffield.

Warburton, D. (2000) 'Participation in the future', *Town and Country Planning*, 69(5), May.

Ward, C. (1978) *The Child in the City*, London: Architectural Press Ltd.

Washington State Department of Ecology (2003) *A Field Guide to Sustainability*. Online. Available HTTP: <http://www.ecy.wa.gov/pubs/0304005.pdf> (accessed 6 July 2003).

Webber, S. (1996) 'From Equal Opportunities to Mainstreaming Equality', paper on Mainstreaming in UK national government, given to seminar, SPS University of Bristol.

Weisman, L. (1992) *Discrimination by Design*, Chicago: University of Illinois Press.

Wekerle, G. (1998) *Women Changing Cities, Proceedings of Eurofem: Women in Human Settlements*, Hameenlinna, Finland: 25–35.

Wekerle, G. and Whitzman, C. (1995) *Safe Cities, Guidelines for Planning, Design and Management*, New York: Van Nostrand Reinhold.

West Midland Group (1946) *Conurbation Post War Reconstruction and Planning*.

Wetherell, M. (2003) *Identities and Social Action, ESRC Research Programme*. Online. Available HTTP: <http://www.esrc.ac.uk/esrccontent/researchfunding/social_identities.asp> (accessed 25 October 2003).

White, M. (2003) 'Problem with quotas council female quota angers MPs', *The Guardian*, Friday, 23 May.

Wilkinson, H. (1994) *No Turning Back, Generations and Gender Quake*, London: DEMOS.

Wilkinson, H. (2002) *Dot Bobshell: Women, E-quality and the New Economy*. Online. Available HTTP: <http://www.genderquake.com/register/index.htm> (accessed 27 October 2003).

Williams, C. (1994) *The Oxfam Gender Training Manual*, Oxford: Oxfam.

Williams, S., Seed, J. and Mwau, A. (1994) *The Oxfam Training Manual*, Oxford: Oxfam.

Wilson, D. (2003) 'The EDI Framework and its Use in Planning'. E-mails (18 November and 8 December 2003).

Winkley, R. (2004) 'A positive highway to better services', *Planning*, 20 February: 14.

WISE (2003) *Women into Science and Engineering Campaign*. Online. Available HTTP: <http://www.wisecampaign.org.uk/wise.nsf/?Open> (accessed 5 April 2004).

Women and Equality Unit (1998) *Policy Appraisal for Equal Treatment*. Online. Available HTTP: <http://www.womenandequalityunit.gov.uk/archive/gender_Mainstreaming/equal.htm#FORWARD> (accessed 31 October 2003).

Women and Equality Unit (2003) *Gender Impact Assessment*. Online. Available HTTP: <http://www.womenandequalityunit.gov.uk/equality/gender_impact_assessment.pdf> (accessed 31 October 2003).

Women in Property (2003) *The Association of Women in Property*. Online. Available HTTP: <http://www.wipnet.org> (accessed 21 November 2003).

Women's Budget Group (WBG) (2003) *Balancing Work and Family Life: Enhancing Choice and Support for Parents*. Online. Available HTTP: <http://www.wbg.org.uk> (accessed 24 October 2003).

Women's Environmental Network (1994), *Greenteacher*, No. 29, London: WEN.

Women's Resource Centre (2003) *Written Submission for the Examination in Public of the Draft London Plan*. Online. Available HTTP: <http://www.london.gov.uk/london-plan-eip/submissions/subs-2a.jsp> (accessed 3 March 2003).

Women's Unit of the Cabinet Office (1998) *Voices: Turning Listening into Action*, London: Cabinet Office.

Woodward, V. (2000) 'The Gender Audit of Local Planning in Plymouth – Mainstreaming Empowering Consultation', paper presented at Mainstreaming Conference in Glasgow, November.

World Resources Institute (1998) *World Resources 1998–1999*, New York: Oxford University Press.

Wu, B. Commissioner (2002) *Remarks made at the 13th Annual Equal Opportunity Conference*, 31 July. Online. Available HTTP: <http://home.nyc.gov/html/doe/pdf/eeo_7-31-02.pdf-9.4KB-NYC.GOV Collection> (accessed 19 May 2003).

Yack, B. (1999) 'The myth of the civic nation', in R. Beiner (ed.), *Theorising Nationalism*, 103–118, New York: University of New York Press.

Yeandle, S. (1996) 'Women, work and home', in C. Booth, J. Darke and S. Yeandle (eds), *Changing Places,* London: Paul Chapman Publishing Ltd.

Yeandle, S. *et al.* (1999) *Gender Profile South Yorkshire*, unpublished.

Young, K. (1997) 'Beyond policy and politics: Contingencies of employment equity', *Policy and Politics*, 25(4).

AUTHOR INDEX

SUBJECT INDEX